TIMESOURCE

Paul Rice

🔟 TEN SPEED PRESS
BERKELEY, CALIFORNIA

1☯
TEN SPEED PRESS
Box 7123
Berkeley, CA 94707

Cover design by Fifth Street Design
Text design by Sarah Levin
Typeset by Wilsted & Taylor
Illustrations by Marilyn Hill

Excerpt in Reading Time from *The Harried Leisure Class* by Staffan Linder © 1970 Columbia University Press. Used by permission.

The Social Readjustment Rating Scale originally appeared in the *Journal of Psychosomatic Research*, vol. 2 © 1967 Thomas H. Holmes and Richard H. Rahe. Used by permission.

Library of Congress Cataloging in Publication Data

Rice, Paul, 1926–
    Timesource / by Paul Rice.
    336 p.   cm.
    ISBN 0-89815-311-5 (pbk.)
    1. Time.   I. Title.
QB209.R53   1989
650.1—dc20   89-5034 CIP

Printed in the United States of America

1   2   3   4   5—93   92   91   90   89

CONTENTS

GLOSSARY

As one explores the essence and effects of time, it soon becomes evident that there are different *categories* of time, related to the social, historical, and physical elements of our world and universe. This glossary of terms may be useful for identifying the various temporalities.

Biotic time is that pertaining to life forms and their evolutionary development.

Eonian time relates to the succession of cosmological events that have followed the big bang, and which appear to follow the laws of astrophysics and quantum mechanics.

Noetic time is the time sense created by the human brain, which frequently may differ from other forms of measurement.

Radical time pertains to basic atomic particle structure and behavior.

Social time relates to the collective changes in time concepts in national and international communities that occur as lifestyles and environmental conditions change.

Ultimate time refers to the atemporal state of matter that moves at the speed of light, when the flow of time as normally understood ceases to exist, or becomes zero.

INTRODUCTION

The pulsing universe in which we live dictates the rhythm of our lives. From the outermost reaches of space to the intimacy of our homes, there is an order and measure to our living consciousness that can, if understood, give us a sense of well-being; a feeling that our lives are worth living, and a sense of contentment. If it is ignored, we become mentally and physically stressed, and die before our time. That's the word—*time*. It is a basic component of the entire cosmos, and it deserves much more attention than most of us accord it.

Those who understand time, and learn to use it intelligently and productively, are those whose lives will be full and rewarding.

Bookstores carry many exhortative texts on time management, aimed at teaching us to accomplish tasks in the minimum time possible. But what is the "saved" time to be used for? Most of those born in the last few decades can live to be one hundred years old. Is this century of consciousness to be thrown into a trash can, or can an individual learn to construct his life to gain all that it has to offer? What balance of self-development, work, and leisure will achieve the sense of fulfillment enjoyed by those who have used their time span most effectively?

The basic goal of *Timesource* is to provide, as succinctly as possible, a source for learning about time; how we have come to measure and understand it, how we react to it, and how we may use it to our best advantage.

The text has been organized to provide rapid access to specific aspects of time, to assist in making the reading time as productive as possible. Read it from cover to cover, and discover the multitude of time-related facts that affect our lives. Or, focus on a particular problem, such as getting a better return on the time spent in business meetings. Learn how time relates to any part of your personal or working lifestyle.

For a part of my life, I was involved in the analysis of potential business acquisitions and mergers. I learned that the financial data is the simplest to obtain and understand. The tough bets are those that must be made on the human resources in an operating business. Are they truly effective; is the management style success oriented, and will it integrate smoothly with the rest of the organizational elements? In these areas, there is an abysmal lack of solid information, and there's not much that can be done about it. The president and key operating people in a business that may be acquired are not likely to welcome screening by an industrial psychologist before the deal is made—and probably not afterward, either.

I discovered that those executives who subsequently proved their worth were those who exhibited two factors in their management style. First, they had clearly defined and reasonable business objectives. Second, *their personal time was intelligently linked to those work objectives.* With some probing questions, it is possible to make assessments in both of these areas. When the answers are positive, the business is much more likely to succeed.

Suggestions, methods, and recommendations are provided within *Timesource* for the development of personal, step-by-step plans to improve your pleasure and productivity. Use them to discover how you relate to time; how you can improve and measure the payoff on your time, and how you can have the time of your life.

AUDIT TIME

*Time and style relationships · Self-rating
questionnaire · Management style
diagnosis · Human resource auditing*

Dealing with time is a very personal matter. It's constrained by how one feels about time, one's physiological time cycles, the type of job one has, and the type of person one is. The recently graduated newcomer in a business environment will view time from a different perspective than the veteran approaching retirement. A home manager with children quickly learns that, without time management, he or she is soon likely to become a candidate for the asylum. Retired persons who adopt a passive role in time use, and permit their days to drift aimlessly by, are prone to psychosomatic illnesses, and are likely to reduce their life span.

At first, then, it makes sense to determine one's position in this time-related universe. Once that has been accomplished, it's possible to focus on specific areas in which some change or improvement is desired. The objective is to achieve a sense of harmony with the flow of time—a point somewhere between boredom and anxiety—where one's sense of *wellness* is satisfied, with the comforting knowledge of being in the driver's seat as one's journey through life progresses, rather than being at the back of the bus.

An understanding of the time environment is also necessary for those who would cope with it best. New scientific concepts and data have, over the last few decades, vastly changed our ideas of time. As we have learned to measure and understand it better, the realization has developed that time is a powerful and affective force, linking countless elements in the cosmos, the solar system, our physical structure and our body cycles. What is known of these matters is described in the relevant sections of this book. The import of our rapid transition from water clocks and sundials to a nanosecond culture must not be underestimated; there is even evidence to suggest that we may be stretching our adaptive capability to the limit of safety. Western industrialized society imposes a tightly scheduled activity pattern that forces us to synchronize our lives with alarm

clocks, appointments, television programming, and transit schedules. Split second timing is used to measure new speed records in everything from sports to pie-eating contests. The income producing value of time is pressed upon us as we are exhorted to increase our consumption of goods and services. Yet our bodies are still geared to the simple rising and setting of the sun.

So what sort of a person are you, and how do you fit into this time-structured world? If you will answer these few simple questions, a personal profile will develop.

1. In what year do you think the following events occurred?

    a. The first domestic jet airline passenger service.   _____

    b. The Cuban "Bay of Pigs" invasion attempt.   _____

    c. The first American Earth orbit in a space capsule.   _____

    d. The Supreme Court ruling in favor of voluntary   _____
       abortion.

    e. The Three Mile Island nuclear reactor accident.   _____

    f. The Mt. St. Helens volcano eruption.   _____

2. Are you often depressed during the winter months?
               YES _____   NO _____

3. Check your watch against the correct time.
   Is it slow or fast?   _____

4. Indicate your feeling about time in general by placing a mark on the bar below:

1	2	3	4	5	6	7	8	9	10	9	8	7	6	5	4	3	2	1

I'm stressed by not   Things flow smoothly   I'm bored because I don't
having enough time.   for me.   have enough to do.

Pick *one* answer from the following question groups:

5. When there's a tight deadline, you like:
    a. to finish the job on overtime.
    b. to see if there's a way to delay it.
    c. to pretend it doesn't exist.
    d. to make it clear that it must be met.
    e. to get everybody into the act.
    f. to avoid pushing people too hard.

6. As far as meetings are concerned, you believe:
    a. that you should be there early.

b. that you should hear others' opinions before voicing your own.
c. that your subordinates should not argue with you in front of others.
d. that they should be delayed to a more convenient time if people are unprepared.
e. that written minutes are essential.
f. in avoiding them whenever possible.

7. When people visit you in your office, you:
    a. act bored, so they will go away quickly.
    b. insure that they have an appointment.
    c. give them help, whenever it's requested.
    d. make it clear that your time is valuable.
    e. avoid direct commitments.
    f. listen to whatever they have to say.

8. The key to getting results from others is:
    a. checking on them frequently.
    b. letting them know you care about them.
    c. insuring that their reports are on time.
    d. leaving it to them.
    e. making sure they know what's expected.
    f. being ready to compromise.

9. When there's a serious mistake made, you should:
    a. try and prevent its disclosure.
    b. be ready to accept an excuse.
    c. be prepared to work harder to make up for it.
    d. punish the offender.
    e. separate yourself from it.
    f. pinpoint its cause.

10. One of the best ways to control telephone calls is to:
    a. not answer the phone.
    b. set up a screening procedure.
    c. keep a record of all calls.
    d. be polite to everyone.
    e. tell people off who call unnecessarily.
    f. find out who's calling before you give your identity.

11. The best way to get ahead is to:
    a. be prepared to work long hours.
    b. make sure they know who's the boss.
    c. always take the middle ground.
    d. adjust time to objectives.
    e. look after others first.
    f. stay out of trouble.

The manner in which time is used usually reflects the dominant operating style of individuals. It may be conveniently categorized in two ways:

A *task-oriented* style is used by individuals who are primarily concerned with the nuts-and-bolts factual elements of life: control systems, plans, reports, schedules, and organization.

A *people-oriented* style is used by individuals who are primarily concerned with relationships: developing others, motivating, training, trusting, and a lot of interactive communication.

It is the skill with which these styles are balanced that often distinguishes between more effective and less effective individuals. The ability to adopt differing styles, appropriate to a range of situations, is not easy, and there is a human tendency to fall into a narrow style-range and use it in *all* situations, reducing overall effectiveness. I have found it helpful to define six types of operating styles, each with its own attitude toward time:

> *Ace* An individual with high time awareness, disciplined, ambitious and goal-oriented, yet able to act as a team player and motivate others. A *Time Balancer.*

> *Politician* One who has average time awareness, task- and people-orientation, but who avoids taking a stand; prefers compromise, apple-polishing and popularity. A *Time Manipulator.*

> *Czar* An individual with high time awareness and low sensitivity to people. Self-oriented, likely to use power inappropriately; dictatorial and judgmental. A *Time Imposer.*

> *Shepherd* Usually described as "caring," with low time awareness; service- and people-oriented, emotional, and always ready to help others and excuse their errors and faults for the sake of harmony. A *Time Forgetter.*

> *Bureaucrat* A system-oriented individual, with high time concern and low people-orientation, who prefers a highly structured, rule-driven environment in which they may appear hardworking and conscientious. A *Time Obsessed* person.

> *Abdicator* One who has little concern for time, and who usually takes a passive and critical, yet uninvolved role, with low people-orientation and ill-defined personal goals. A *Time Waster.*

We all play one or more of these roles from time to time. One, however, is usually dominant, and will be indicated by the Scoring Key at the end of this chapter. Secondary roles, of which there may be more than one, will also be evident.

Tomorrow, and
 tomorrow, and
 tomorrow,
Creeps in this petty
 place from day to day,
To the last syllable of
 recorded time.
   William Shakespeare,
   Macbeth, Act V

Understanding one's operating style is valuable, for it permits an assessment of its appropriateness, and the possible need for change. For example, one playing the Czar role will not enjoy two-way communication in meetings. *MEETING TIME* may help in correcting this situation. On the other hand, the Czar role may be preferable to that of the Abdicator in a crisis situation.

The Scoring Key will also provide the correct dates of the events listed in Question 1. Research has shown that individuals who are young, time conscious, and with strong goal- and task-orientation, are likely to think that past events occurred more recently than they actually did, and frequently have their watches slightly fast. Those who are less time conscious, older, and with dominant people-orientation, tend to overestimate the time of past events, and often have their watches slow.

If you answered yes to Question 2, it is important that you read *BODY TIME*. You may be suffering from a recently identified affliction that psychiatrists are calling seasonal affective disorder (SAD).

A mark on the bar in Question 4 which lies to the outside of either 6 indicates that there is a significant need for change in your life. If some correction is not made, physical or mental health may eventually be affected. A thorough reexamination of lifestyle, work and goals is particularly important under these circumstances.

The following checklist can help you pinpoint time-related problem areas in your life:

> Time present and time past
> Are both perhaps present in time future,
> And time future is contained in time past.
>
> *T. S. Eliot*

	TOO MUCH	TOO LITTLE	ABOUT RIGHT
1. Time with your family and/or friends.	_____	_____	_____
2. Time feeling well.	_____	_____	_____
3. Time at work.	_____	_____	_____
4. Time by yourself.	_____	_____	_____
5. Time trying to catch up.	_____	_____	_____
6. Time traveling.	_____	_____	_____
7. Time bored.	_____	_____	_____
8. Time on vacation.	_____	_____	_____
9. Time doing others' work.	_____	_____	_____
10. Time in business meetings.	_____	_____	_____
11. Time on the telephone.	_____	_____	_____
12. Time following up on other people.	_____	_____	_____

	TOO MUCH	TOO LITTLE	ABOUT RIGHT
13. Time feeling alert.	___	___	___
14. Time doing household chores.	___	___	___
15. Time doing paperwork.	___	___	___
16. Time watching television.	___	___	___
17. Time correcting others' mistakes.	___	___	___
18. Time forgetting things.	___	___	___
19. Time being productive.	___	___	___
20. Time creating things.	___	___	___
21. Time putting things off.	___	___	___
22. Time spent organizing and planning.	___	___	___
23. Time managing others.	___	___	___
24. Time in conflict with others.	___	___	___
25. Time improving yourself.	___	___	___

The chapters in this book fall into three groups—*Time Facts*, *Time Planning*, and *Time Use*. The checklist above focuses on time planning and time use, and provides some pointers for you to use to save time in your reading access. It is not necessary to read this book from front to back. It may be more productive for you to first read those sections which can most significantly affect your personal time relationships, then browse through other sections as your interest and time permit.

Use the matrix below to relate your feelings about your time to the book's subject headings. Those activities which have been marked "About Right" should not require correction or change. They form your satisfactory time base, which should be expanded to a maximum. Those activities marked "Too Much" or "Too Little" should be ranked in terms of their importance to you, then the line or activity number noted. For example, if you feel that "time in business meetings" concerns you most, you would note line number 10. Then read down the 10 column in the following matrix index, and you will be guided to those sections which are most relevant to that interest or concern.

To get more time for desired activities, your time allocation pattern must change, or the wish must be abandoned. The choice is up to you. If you want to do something about it, the section to read first

MATRIX CHART

	1	2	3	4	5	6	7	8	9	10	11	12	13	14	15	16	17	18	19	20	21	22	23	24	25
BIORHYTHMS																									
BODY TIME																									
COLD TIME																									
COMMUNICATION TIME																									
CONCENTRATION TIME																									
CONFLICT TIME																									
CREATIVE TIME																									
DECISION TIME																									
DELEGATION TIME																									
DESK TIME																									
ELECTRONIC TIME																									
EXECUTIVE TIME																									
FILING TIME																									
GUARDING TIME																									
HOUSEHOLD TIME																									
JET LAG																									
LEISURE TIME																									
LISTENING TIME																									
MEETING TIME																									
MEMORY																									
MNEMONICS																									
PAPERWORK TIME																									
PROCRASTINATION																									
READING TIME																									
RECORDING TIME																									
SHORT-INTERVAL SCHEDULING																									
SLEEP TIME																									
STRESS																									
TARGETING TIME																									
TELEPHONE TIME																									
TIME AND AGE																									
TIME MUSEUMS																									
TIME PAYOFF ANALYSIS																									
TRAVEL TIME																									
VACATION TIME																									
WORD-PROCESSING TIME																									
WRITING TIME																									

is *TIME PAYOFF ANALYSIS*. It will help you to identify the time traps in your lifestyle, which are not worth the effort, and those activities in which you are least effective and likely to be wheel-spinning. Both are candidates for dumping. The time freed up may then be reallocated to the most important "Too Little" items. If you believe you can't dump *anything* (although that is rare), then it will be necessary for you to increase your productivity in one or more existing activities in order to find the elective time. The various rating tests throughout the book can assist in identifying the strengths and weaknesses in your activity skills, again pointing the way to improvement.

AUDIT TIME SCORESHEET

1. a. December 10, 1958, between New York and Miami.
    b. April 17, 1961.
    c. February 20, 1962, when Lt. Col. John Glenn piloted the Mercury capsule.
    d. January 22, 1973.
    e. March 28, 1979.
    f. May 25, 1980.

2. If you answered *yes* to this question, it is important to read *BODY TIME*.

3. People who keep their watches fast are usually more task-oriented than those who maintain the correct time or let their watches run slow.

4. Significant improvement in time planning and allocation should be sought by those placing a mark to the outside of either figure 6.

Please read text for explanation of headers in the table following:

	ACE	POLITICIAN	CZAR	SHEPHERD	BUREAUCRAT	ABDICATOR
5.	e.	b.	d.	f.	a.	c.
6.	a.	b.	c.	d.	e.	f.
7.	f.	e.	d.	c.	b.	a.
8.	e.	f.	a.	b.	c.	d.
9.	f.	a.	d.	b.	c.	e.
10.	b.	f.	e.	d.	c.	a.
11.	d.	c.	b.	e.	a.	f.

BIORHYTHMS

*Developmental background · Constructing
your personal biorhythm chart*

Many people believe that knowledge of their biorhythms can improve their daily effectiveness. This is not scientifically proven, but it may work for you. We do know that human beings' daily biological cycles vary remarkably. Some of us are habitually early risers, and operate better during the morning hours, while others are night owls who find it difficult to work effectively before noon. It seems to me that it is better to develop an awareness of one's energy/effectiveness cycle and adapt activities to it, than to try to buck what may be unalterable. Attempting to tinker with the body's intricate cyclical activity can cause serious health problems. (See *BODY TIME*.)

Wilhelm Fliess, after twenty years of research, established the first set of biorhythmic principles in 1920. He believed that there are four cycles that overlay the circadian, or daily, pattern of body time. There is an emotional cycle of twenty-eight days, a physical cycle of twenty-three days, an intuitive cycle of forty days, and an intellectual cycle of thirty-three days. The pattern is said to be created at the moment of birth, when the life clock starts ticking, and to remain unchanged until it stops. Biorhythm theory divides each cycle into two phases, the positive and the negative. These phases sometimes coincide and sometimes conflict. It is the varying effect of the cycles that may influence our success or failure in our daily endeavors. For example, one might avoid undertaking a tough mental exercise at a critical point in the intellectual cycle, or negotiation with a divorce lawyer during the emotional dog days.

To determine your position on any of the biorhythmic cycles, you must first calculate the number of days since you were born:

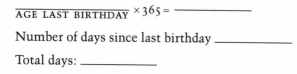

$\overline{\text{AGE LAST BIRTHDAY}} \times 365 = \underline{\hspace{3cm}}$

Number of days since last birthday _____

Total days: _____

The above figure must now be adjusted to take care of leap years that have occurred during your life. From the table below, count all the years in which you have lived, and add their total to your age in days.

1900	1916	1932	1948	1964	1980
1904	1920	1936	1952	1968	1984
1908	1924	1940	1956	1972	1988
1912	1928	1944	1960	1976	1992

My age in total days is: _____

To determine your physical cycle position, divide the above figure by 23. If there are no days left over, then you are on the first day of your physical cycle. If there are any days left over, they will indicate your position on the physical by counting from the start of the cycle. For example, suppose that your age in days is 11,689.

$$\frac{11689}{23} = 508, \text{ with 5 days left over.}$$
$$(23 \times 508 = 11,684)$$

This would mean that you are at the fifth day in your physical cycle.

Similar calculations will locate your positions on the other cycles. Divide your age in days by 28 to pinpoint your position on the emotional cycle; by 40 for the intuitive cycle, and by 33 for the intellectual cycle.

Monitor your daily progress to find the degree to which your biorhythmic cycles seem to impact your effectiveness and productivity. You may find that your cycles are affected by what you eat and drink, by the hours you work and sleep, or by the use of medication. Scientists are now convinced that gearing activities to natural body rhythms leads to better mental and physical health, and extended life. Get to know your body's time patterns, and act accordingly.

See also BODY TIME, JET LAG.

BODY TIME

*The internal human clock · Research
background · Circadian synchronization ·
The body rhythms · Continuing research*

Only within the last four decades has the scientific community given serious credence to the presence of an internal human clock that is capable of sensing energies from the cosmos to continually keep it correct and that blocks our naive attempts to meddle with it. The investigation of body time has been so neglected that we know more today about the life rhythms of fruit flies than why most babies are born during the first six hours after midnight, or why most people in the Northern Hemisphere are born in March.

Statistically, cycles fall into three categories. A *dynamic* or *endogenous cycle* is caused by one or more elements within a system. A *random cycle* is just what it says, and has no statistical significance. An *exogenous cycle* is caused by something outside of a system. A researcher, sent to investigate the abnormally high birthrate in a small country community, found an exogenous cycle. The daily milk train that regularly woke everybody up as it passed at 6 A.M. was the outside factor. As one resident explained, "It keeps waking me up when it's too early to get up and too late to go back to sleep."

Many of the rhythms in our body time are exogenous. They are linked to the magnetic and light emissions from the sun and the moon and, perhaps, to other cosmic forces still under investigation. We know, for example, that many animals are sensitive to ultrasonic energy, which is inaudible to us. Scientists theorize that there may be other body clock controls hidden in other parts of the spectrum of energy which bombards us as the earth hurtles through space.

How has our awareness of body time developed since Aristotle first noted the cyclical patterns of sea urchins over two thousand years ago? Very slowly, it seems.

In 1729, the French astronomer de Marain reported that the heliotrope plant opens its leaves in cycle with the rising sun and closes them at sundown, even when totally enclosed and not exposed to the sun in any way. Nobody paid much attention.

More than a hundred years later, in England, George Newport reported the disturbed activity patterns of bees during a partial solar eclipse. Some nineteenth-century botanists and biologists began to document the peculiar abilities of various plants, insects and animals to schedule their activities with a seemingly impossible knowledge of time.

In 1890 the Viennese psychologist Hermann Swoboda first noted and documented the biorhythmic behavioral patterns of his patients. Five years later the Swedish Nobelist Svante Arrhenius indicated the likelihood that body rhythms are influenced by cosmic cycles in atmospheric electricity. Interest quickened as better research techniques became available and in 1920 two Americans, Garner and Allen, showed that plants determine the time of the year by measuring the length of daylight. However, the Dutch botanist Antonia Kleinhoonte proved in 1929 that plants use an autonomous internal clock for daily leaf movement, rather than the effect of light and darkness.

A solar eclipse in 1936 permitted Syuiti Mori to document the synchronization of fruit fly activity with the loss of sunlight, while other life forms were not affected. Another biologist, N. A. Weber, recorded the selective effects of solar eclipse on various animals in 1952.

Then, the following year, James D. Watson and Francis H. C. Crick developed the theory of the DNA molecular structure, for which they received the Nobel Prize. Their breakthrough brought new excitement to the biological sciences, as the synchronization of molecular patterns began to explain the body's ability to keep time.

Other unsuspected animal clocks showed up as research intensified. In 1954 Gustav Kramer showed that birds achieve their accurate directional flight by relating the sun's position to an internal timekeeper, similar to the procedure followed by the navigator of an aircraft. A year later, biologist Semour Kety, noting the drop in blood circulation and oxygen consumption rate in the brain as we age, suggested that this may account for time appearing to go faster as we get older.

William Wolf, at New York University in 1952, outlined the importance of body rhythms and time in human biology.[1] Surgical

---

1. Rhythmic Functions in the Living System; Annals of the New York Academy of Sciences, Vol. 98.

In theory, one is aware that the earth revolves, but in practice one does not perceive it; the ground upon which one treads seems not to move, and one can live undisturbed. So it is with time in one's life.

Marcel Proust,
Remembrance of
Things Past

hemorrhaging, for example, is more frequent in the second lunar quarter than at other times.

The same year at Cambridge, Janet Harker showed that cockroaches carry an internal clock in their endocrine systems. When these clocks are disturbed, the insects rapidly die of cancer—a strong indication that time stress could be the root cause of sickness in man.

In 1964 the German botanist Erwin Bünning also linked lunar influences with internal clocks; he showed the persistence of fruit fly activity patterns without benefit of changing environmental conditions, and that a single, brief exposure to light during a dark period will change the rhythm of plant leaf movement.

Biologist Frank Brown, working with marine creatures in his laboratory at the University of Illinois, developed a then-controversial theory that internal clocks, the sun, the moon, and perhaps other energy forms such as magnetism all play a part in regulation of body time.

Nineteen sixty-seven saw Charles F. Ehret, at Argonne National Laboratory, advance his "chronon" concept with evidence that body time is maintained by life's basic component, the DNA molecule, working in conjunction with messenger RNA. The chemically related process, he surmised, is affected by temperature, which may explain why a sick person with a fever feels that time is going faster.

There has been intensive research into the possible presence of a body clock in the DNA string in recent years. Recognizing that Ehret's twenty-four-hour chronon would not have been correct aeons ago when the earth was spinning faster, Robert Kravitz has shown that the basic DNA-string body clock seems to work on three- or four-hour "quantil" units which can be added together to produce longer cycles. The body clock resets itself daily when strong light energy enters our eyes—at least 2,000 lux, or the equivalent of about fifteen 100-watt lamps. Ideally, the body requires 4,000 lux for several hours each day to establish the well-defined rhythms that make us operate and feel at our best. Unfortunately, all too few of us get it. Instead, we spend our days in homes, offices, and factories that are too dimly lit to affect body cycles. Researchers have linked this to poor mental and physical health. Without the all-important daily dose of intense synchronizing light, our complex body rhythms become weak and confused, resulting in an "out-of-sorts" feeling.

For most of us, sunlight is our synchronizing adjuster, so sitting close to a window is useful. Direct sun is best though, for its light level is so high that only about twenty minutes exposure is neces-

Time deals gently only with those that take it gently.

Anatole France

sary for body clock synchronization. The time of day at which this is undertaken is very important. Exposure to early morning sunlight advances body clocks; late afternoon sunlight retards them. People who have trouble waking up should get a shot of sunshine as soon as they get up. That means going outside *before* breakfast. Those who get sleepy early in the evening should get their exposure in the late afternoon.

If you are one of those to whom winter is a particularly depressing prospect, you may be suffering from the body clock problem christened *seasonal affective disorder*, or SAD, by psychiatrists. It is not something to be ignored. Unless corrected, it can bring dietary and sex problems, irritability, lack of energy, oversleeping, and social withdrawal. It was once believed to be a mental disorder, but the National Institute of Mental Health (NIMH) has now expanded the apparent cause to include lack of daily sunlight. Interestingly, some people who dislike high temperatures have been found to suffer from *summer* depression. It is conjectured that, because they need to stay indoors in an air-conditioned environment to escape the heat, they too are affected by the loss of the all-important circadian solar time check that their body clocks demand.

NIMH estimates the number of SAD victims in the United States to be about five million, with women outnumbering men four to one. Symptoms may appear as early as age nine, but usually do not become evident until the early twenties. One of the first signs to look for in children is an annual increase in bad temper and aggressiveness that comes with the shorter days of winter—often ascribed to being "cooped up," or to school problems.

As ongoing research strives to determine the possibility of genetic SAD inheritance, the only proven cure is light therapy. Lacking sunlight, SAD sufferers find that their symptoms are quickly relieved by daily exposure to strong, broad-spectrum artificial light, or by relocation to a sunny part of the globe. The severity of SAD has been shown to increase with distance from the equator.

The artificial light that is required to cure SAD must simulate that from the sun. That means looking at a bank of fluorescent sunlamps capable of emitting ten times more light than normal room lighting for 30–50 minutes daily. A direct nerve connection that bypasses the optical nerve has been found between the retina and the DNA clock, thus circadian rhythm is preserved even if sight is lost. Body exposure is unnecessary, and may, in fact, be harmful.

Now that we know that many human functions work on a daily timer, it is becoming obvious that intimate knowledge of our internal timekeeper is essential for good health care. The success of medical procedures and drugs can depend upon our biological rhythms, which control our tolerance levels. Laboratory tests on mice show how strong these effects can be. Antileukemics, administered at one time of day, brought an 80 percent recession rate. Given at another time, most of the mice died. It is well known that the human body is more easily damaged by alcohol during the late morning hours, but what about other substances?

We nonchalantly administer drugs and bombard our bodies with x-rays, ultraviolet and ultrasonic energy, and high-frequency lasers at any time of the day in spite of the evidence that exposure or dosage at the wrong time can be disastrous. The traditional "three times daily, after meals" is a prescription that belongs in the Middle Ages.

It is remarkable how well our bodies preserve their all-important time sense in spite of our attempts to put our biological clocks out of whack. We can be thankful that they do, for body clocks are not to be trifled with. They must stay in synchronization. Health spa operators know this; their rigid scheduling of eating and sleeping probably does more to restore the even beat of body time than their fad diets and unguents, although they doubtless make more money from the latter.

You'll be glad to learn that even the British penchant for tea at four o'clock is related to body time. Tea contains traces of a poisonous alkaloid called *theophylline*. It so happens that the body can absorb it more easily in the late afternoon than at any other time of the day.

Our body clocks also produce a low tolerance for proteins in the afternoon and evening hours, while tolerance for starch is low in the mornings. A Texas breakfast and an Italian dinner would thus seem to be the ideal diet for healthy people.

We know, too, that our sense of wellness is destroyed if we disrupt our body clocks by moving rapidly from one time zone to another (see *JET LAG*), or by making major time changes in our activity patterns. Research has shown that many workers suffer from irritability and increased error rates when they change shifts, and some simply cannot make the adjustment. Our body clocks are obviously very powerful. But what do we know about them?

The complex pattern of body time contains more than a hundred rhythms, evidenced in many ways:

The hypothalamus, for example, is triggered to control body temperature through a daily cycle, with lows between 2 A.M. and 5 A.M. Other low points in body rhythms at night include heart rate, blood sugar level, urine production and brain cell activity. Conversely, the senses are keener at midnight than at noon, and hormone secretion and blood clotting are at their peak then, too.

Adrenal gland activity slows gradually during sleep cycles and speeds up again prior to waking.

Blood corpuscle count drops in the early morning.

The kidneys reach a functional peak at noon each day, with urine flow increasing during the ninety minutes before and after noon.

Muscle power varies throughout a twenty-four-hour cycle. The hand can grip harder at 6 P.M. than at 3 A.M.

Women can drink more in the very early hours than men because their livers consume alcohol best at 3 A.M. Men's livers work best in the evening.

Cell division, or reproduction, increases between 8 P.M. and midnight. Each type of tissue cell also has a fixed reproductive cycle, so that the periodic renewal of entire organs is as follows:

Fingernail	180 days
Red blood cells	120 days
Gums	94 days
Scalp hair, per inch	60 days
(Shaving or cutting do not affect the growth rate.)	
Skin	26 days
Mouth lining	5 days
Duodenum and colon	4 days

The brain's alpha rhythm[2] electrical activity pulses between two and five times per second in small children, and increases to a rate of about ten cycles per second in adults.

Heart attacks most frequently occur around 9 A.M. and are least likely to hit at 9 P.M.

Human beings' daily biological cycles vary remarkably. It's easy to discover your energy cycle peak by checking body temperature periodically for a few days. When your temperature rises each day, as it will, your energy/effectiveness motor is humming along at its

---

2. Four types of electrical brain patterns are known. Alpha rhythms, about ten cycles per second, are generated by a state of nonconcentrated relaxation. Theta rhythms, about five cycles per second, stem from a state of drowsiness. Delta rhythms, about 1.5 cycles per second, are produced in the deepest sleep stages. All other electrical brain rhythms, including those connected with alertness or mental concentration, are called beta waves.

THE BEAT OF BODY TIME

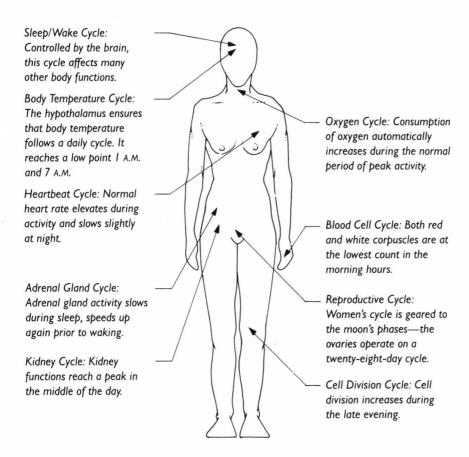

Sleep/Wake Cycle: Controlled by the brain, this cycle affects many other body functions.

Body Temperature Cycle: The hypothalamus ensures that body temperature follows a daily cycle. It reaches a low point 1 A.M. and 7 A.M.

Heartbeat Cycle: Normal heart rate elevates during activity and slows slightly at night.

Adrenal Gland Cycle: Adrenal gland activity slows during sleep, speeds up again prior to waking.

Kidney Cycle: Kidney functions reach a peak in the middle of the day.

Oxygen Cycle: Consumption of oxygen automatically increases during the normal period of peak activity.

Blood Cell Cycle: Both red and white corpuscles are at the lowest count in the morning hours.

Reproductive Cycle: Women's cycle is geared to the moon's phases—the ovaries operate on a twenty-eight-day cycle.

Cell Division Cycle: Cell division increases during the late evening.

greatest efficiency. Most people claim that they can even "feel" more productive at this time.

Continuing research in biorhythms is being conducted at Argonne National Laboratories. Dr. Kenneth Groh and Marijo Ready have determined that lithium is a phase-lengthener, and can have a devastating effect on the body. Their work also indicates that manic-depressives may be suffering from periodic dyschronic, or unsynchronized, body rhythms. Their symptoms wax and wane as their body cycles move in and out of synchronization.

The body clock may also answer some questions about drug addiction, as experiments have shown that four days after receiving phenobarbitol, the body cycles of laboratory rats are strengthened. Their phasing accuracy and amplitude increases. They become instant addicts. Human beings may react in the same manner, particularly those whose biorhythms are poorly synchronized. The feelings of wellness that come with drug-corrected body time can quickly build dependence, since maintenance of the condition demands continually increasing dosage until the body and mind are destroyed.

The correction and maintenance of body time is so important that it may well become a focal point of medicine in the future. Whenever drugs or other forms of therapy are used, their application must be linked to the body clock. We may even discover that the most efficacious way to maintain a healthy body is simply to support the internal defense mechanisms with well-managed body time.

CALENDAR TIME

*How our calendars developed · Cultural
calendars · The World Calendar*

The first attempts to make some order out of the chaotic heavenly bodies that ruled the days and nights were made some five thousand years ago by the Sumerians, who lived along the banks of the Euphrates and Tigris rivers. They devised a calendar based on their observation of the moon, with twelve lunar months of thirty days. But in each year there are 365.25 days, not 360, so they had a built-in error of more than five days. A letter written by King Hammurabi in the eighteenth century B.C. refers to this; five days were simply added to the calendar to bring it back in line. The sun was thereafter used as the basis for the calendar, giving a 365-day year, although lunar cycles were still used for religious calculations.

The Egyptian priests noted that the annual Nile flood, which the farmers depended on for irrigation and planting, coincided with the appearance of the star we call Sirius. A bas-relief, dated about 2,000 B.C., shows their goddess Isis, who represented the star, watering a fertile field of corn. They used this knowledge to "predict" the annual flood, thus insuring their continued employment. But as they had stuck with the 365-day calendar, Sirius' appearance slipped a day every four years, and they were forced to slip in an intercalary day to straighten things out. They covered up their problem by making the extra day a feast day, so nobody complained.

It took the Mediterranean civilizations many centuries to equate the solar and lunar calendars by discovering that the sun and the moon took 235 lunar months to assume the same relationship to one another. Things were further complicated by invading armies' habit of imposing their own calendar systems upon those they conquered. Throughout the six centuries prior to the Christian Era, invasion was a popular business. The Egyptians, for example, invaded the Persians in the sixth century, the Greeks in the third century, and the Romans in the first century. Further afield in Europe and Asia, things were even more chaotic as the Huns in the north and the Ch'in people in the Far East (who gave their name to China) used

chariots to blitzkrieg their neighbors and impose their systems upon them. A worldwide calendar was unimaginable.

But knowledge of the heavens slowly improved, and the various calendars were gradually corrected. The 300-day calendar with ten months that Romulus had given to the Romans in 753 A.D. was changed by Numa Pontilius to twelve months and three hundred and fifty-five days in 712 B.C. Then, unfortunately, the politicians got into the act. An extra holiday did wonders for the election returns, they discovered, so they began to add days at will to suit their selfish purposes. By 46 B.C., things were badly awry. The Roman calendar was three months ahead of the solar year, and the farmers were protesting because their crops were ripening at the wrong time. Julius Caesar determined that he had to fix the problem and halt the frequent calendar manipulations. He had become enamored not only of Cleopatra, but also of her Egyptian calendar. So, with the help of the Greek astronomer Sosigenes, he extended the single year of 46 B.C. to 445 days, to bring the Roman calendar back in line, and decreed the adoption of the Egyptian calendar of 365 days throughout the empire. The Egyptian priests quickly seized the opportunity to avoid having to explain away their extra day every four years, and it was officially built into the new calendar. We call the year in which the extra day occurs a leap year. The Julian calendar satisfied everyone for the next 1600 years. But there was an eleven-minute-per-year error in its calculation and as the centuries passed, the minutes added up to hours and days, like a ticking time bomb. It blew up in the sixteenth century.

While the Romans were sorting themselves out, the Greeks had created another calendar system called the Olympiad, based on the games held every four years at Olympia in honor of Zeus. The games became a system of dating in 760 B.C., and always began on the eleventh day of the new summer solstice moon (around July 2) which heralded their New Year.

Meanwhile, in Europe, the calendar used by the marauding Scandinavians was most commonly used when anybody cared. It had fifty-two seven-day weeks and no months. There were but two divisions, Summer and Winter, and each year started at the summer solstice which was celebrated with a week-long festival. They cared about that, and a similar one held at the start of Winter. But as the Roman armies moved north, Europe was converted to the Julian calendar, except in some isolated areas. In Iceland, for example, the old "week-year" was used as late as the nineteenth century. The Julian calendar remained in use for more than a thousand years, until the annual eleven-minute error had become a massive problem.

There is an hour wherein a man might be happy all his life, could he find it.

George Herbert

By 1545, the calendar was thirteen days late. The Vatican religious planners who had already erred by seven years in establishing the date of the birth of Jesus Christ couldn't afford another snafu. They realized that the way things were going, they would eventually be celebrating Easter at Christmas. Originally set at the vernal equinox on March 21 by the Council of Nicaea in 325 A.D., Easter was already back to March 11. They quickly passed the buck upstairs.

You can use a 1779 calendar in 1993 and 1999 with perfect accuracy.

Pope Gregory XIII convened the Council of Trent to deliberate the matter. After consulting numerous contemporary scientists, the Council recommended a ten-day correction, plus the removal of three leap years every four hundred years. (The year 2000 will be the next one.) A papal bull was issued in 1582 to initiate this change and also to move the start of the year from March 21 to January 1. This improved the calendar's accuracy to a one-day error in 3,325 years, instead of every 128 years, or about 25 seconds a year.

The Protestant countries were not about to go along with this Catholic bull, however, and stuck doggedly to their inaccurate Julian calendar. Reason eventually forced them to accept that this was not a subversive papal plot, but it took England two hundred years to convert to the new Gregorian calendar. Lord Chesterfield was successful in putting a bill through Parliament in 1751 to make it official. Even then, it produced a major social upheaval in 1752, with rioters demanding their eleven days back. With Britain converted, their colonies in America followed.

Most people around the world use the Gregorian calendar today, although some holdouts, like the Soviets, did not adopt it until right after World War I, and then not for long. With revolutionary zeal, the Communist party attempted to institute another new calendar system in 1929, with five days in each week, and new names for the days. It caused much confusion and many problems. After some abortive attempts to patch it up, a return was made to the Gregorian calendar in 1946. But other calendars are still around.

The Hebrew lunisolar calendar remains in use by many traditional Jewish people, although not in the form originated in the seventh century B.C. A month is reckoned according to the moon, and a year by the sun. This presents a problem, because the solar year is eleven days longer than twelve lunar months. The situation is corrected by the addition of seven additional months to the calendar over the nineteen-year lunar cycle. The calendar is further complicated by religious dictates that certain rites must not fall on certain days. The Day of Atonement, for example, must not fall on a Friday or Sunday. To work around this problem, a system of variable-length years is used.

The Islamic calendar is something else. It's dated from July 16, 622 A.D. by most Muslims, but not all. And the month begins whenever two upstanding citizens will swear before a *cadi*, or judge, that they saw the new moon. There's often argument about that, particularly when the sky is overcast. The names of the days vary from place to place; the Muslim day starts at sunset, and their Sabbath is Friday, counted as the first day of the week.

Even though it is simpler, the Gregorian calendar is now considered by many to have outlived its usefulness. In fact, a World calendar was proposed in 1834 by an Italian cleric, Abbe Mastrofini, and many others have surfaced since then. In 1930, the World Calendar Association was founded, and it recommended the universal adoption of the calendar.

WORLD CALENDAR

The World calendar proposed some years ago by the International World Calendar Association. Two undated days (*) are proposed as World Holidays, one following June 30, and one Leap Year Day, following December 30 in leap years.

1st QUARTER

	JANUARY								FEBRUARY								MARCH					
S	M	T	W	T	F	S		S	M	T	W	T	F	S		S	M	T	W	T	F	S
1	2	3	4	5	6	7					1	2	3							1	2
8	9	10	11	12	13	14		5	6	7	8	9	10	11		3	4	5	6	7	8	9
15	16	17	18	19	20	21		12	13	14	15	16	17	18		10	11	12	13	14	15	16
22	23	24	25	26	27	28		19	20	21	22	23	24	25		17	18	19	20	21	22	23
29	30	31						26	27	28	29	30				24	25	26	27	28	29	30

2nd QUARTER

	APRIL								MAY								JUNE					
S	M	T	W	T	F	S		S	M	T	W	T	F	S		S	M	T	W	T	F	S
1	2	3	4	5	6	7					1	2	3	4							1	2
8	9	10	11	12	13	14		5	6	7	8	9	10	11		3	4	5	6	7	8	9
15	16	17	18	19	20	21		12	13	14	15	16	17	18		10	11	12	13	14	15	16
22	23	24	25	26	27	28		19	20	21	22	23	24	25		17	18	19	20	21	22	23
29	30	31						26	27	28	29	30				24	25	26	27	28	29	30 *

3rd QUARTER

	JULY								AUGUST								SEPTEMBER					
S	M	T	W	T	F	S		S	M	T	W	T	F	S		S	M	T	W	T	F	S
1	2	3	4	5	6	7					1	2	3	4							1	2
8	9	10	11	12	13	14		5	6	7	8	9	10	11		3	4	5	6	7	8	9
15	16	17	18	19	20	21		12	13	14	15	16	17	18		10	11	12	13	14	15	16
22	23	24	25	26	27	28		19	20	21	22	23	24	25		17	18	19	20	21	22	23
29	30	31						26	27	28	29	30				24	25	26	27	28	29	30

4th QUARTER

	OCTOBER								NOVEMBER								DECEMBER					
S	M	T	W	T	F	S		S	M	T	W	T	F	S		S	M	T	W	T	F	S
1	2	3	4	5	6	7					1	2	3	4							1	2
8	9	10	11	12	13	14		5	6	7	8	9	10	11		3	4	5	6	7	8	9
15	16	17	18	19	20	21		12	13	14	15	16	17	18		10	11	12	13	14	15	16
22	23	24	25	26	27	28		19	20	21	22	23	24	25		17	18	19	20	21	22	23
29	30	31						26	27	28	29	30				24	25	26	27	28	29	30 *

This calendar has numerous advantages. Every year begins on a Sunday; the quarters are equal; the pattern of monthly start days is regular, and a universal holiday on the last day of each year perpetually stabilizes the counting system.

Although it makes reckoning easier, the calendar has been resisted by some religious groups, in spite of strong endorsement by the World Calendar Association. It seems that international adoption is unlikely until worldwide pressure to simplify our time planning forces the issue.

CLOCKS

Ancient timekeeping methods · Water clocks · The early mechanical clocks · The foliot and verge escapement · Balance wheels and springs · Pendulum clocks · The American clockmaking industry · Scientific clocks

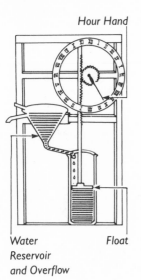

Diagram of water clock, c. 250 B.C.

Hour Hand

Water Reservoir and Overflow

Float

Cloudy days and nights made it difficult for the ancients to keep track of time, for neither their sundials nor their knowledge of the stars could help them when the skies were obscured. They turned to fire and water for their primitive "clocks." The first devices to record the passage of time, as distinct from sundials, were water clocks, or *clepsydrae*, known to have been in use in Egypt about 1400 B.C. and in most ancient civilizations. Their original simple form was an earthenware bowl with a small hole in the bottom, through which water gradually escaped. The passage of time was marked by the change of water level as it descended past a series of graduated marks.

The Romans and Greeks improved their clepsydrae and made them easier to read. Vetruvius, about 250 B.C., mentioned the use of Archimedes' cogwheel which, connected to a float, turned a single hand upon a dial. Arabic numbers were introduced about 780 A.D. and simplified the arithmetic needed for time calculation and recording. Ingeniously complicated clepsydrae were constructed, such as the one given to Charlemagne by Haroun-al-Rashid in 800 A.D. At each hour, a door opened to release the appropriate number of metal balls, which fell on to a drum to sound the hours. At noon and midnight, all of the doors were closed by mechanical figures in the shape of horsemen. History has ignored the ballperson, whose unfortunate job, presumably, was to lift all of the heavy balls back to the hopper twice a day.

Candles were marked to measure the time as they burned down. The containers of oil lamps were graduated to mark the time as the fuel was consumed. One enterprising Chinese "clockmaker" even made an alarm clock. He arranged for a tar fuse to burn through a rope holding a heavy ball. After some hours, the ball dropped into a metal bowl with a loud clang, which not only woke him up, but everyone else on his block. His invention was not popular.

Burning candles and water pots were not much use to the traveler, though, and there were a lot of travelers in prebiblical times, as sects were driven from place to place by the constant wars. It was this lack which is said to have produced the sand clock, or hourglass. Although its exact origin is unknown, it spread rapidly across the world, finding its way into pulpits for sermon-timing, and into our kitchens for egg-timing.

A mechanical water clock was not developed until the end of the eleventh century. The first we know of was constructed by Su Sung at K'aifeng in China in 1096 and used a number of small buckets arranged on the rim of a wheel. As a clepsydra filled a bucket, the wheel would rotate a controlled distance to bring the next bucket in line. Science historian Joseph Needham, at Cambridge University, was responsible for the early research on this device, and amateur horologist John Combridge has reconstructed working models, one of which may be seen at the Rockford Time Museum (see *TIME MUSEUMS*).

The first rudimentary contrivances in Europe were installed in monastery turrets, where they were used to alert the bellringers to sound the times of prayer. A large stone weight, in this case, provided the massive contraptions with motive power, slowly unwinding a rope which turned a wooden cylinder. The power was controlled by a swinging bar, or foliot, acting against a ratchet wheel. The foliot carried two weights to control the speed at which the bar rotated back and forth. This primitive oscillator pivoted on a verge with two tabs, or pallets, that alternately engaged with a toothed wheel. One tooth was released for each double-swing of the foliot.

The first known public clocks were installed in Exeter Cathedral and St. Paul's Cathedral, both in London between 1284 and 1286, and during the next hundred years, seventy-three more were constructed throughout Europe. They were monstrous iron contraptions which still depended upon a verge and foliot mechanism. With luck, they would be accurate to within about an hour a day; sufficient, since at the time, people weren't as time-conscious as we are today. But as the century progressed, tower clocks with one hand as well as bells were constructed. It took another three hundred years before minute hands were deemed necessary or practical.

In the meantime, not to be outdone by the churches, noblemen wanted clocks of their own, and Italian clockmakers of the early fifteenth century are credited with the first iron wall clocks designed for private residences. Deluxe models were later furnished with alarms and chimes.

Nuremberg's Peter Henlein was the first person to make a spring with which to drive clocks, based upon an idea of Leonardo da Vinci's. He gained the blessings of clock owners the world over in 1500 A.D. when he eliminated the chore of hauling weights back up. Unfortunately, his new spring-powered clocks got slower and slower as their springs wound down. Customer complaints led him to Jacob Zech, a Swiss mechanical genius, who in 1525 invented a cone-shaped pulley that was connected to the spring cylinder with catgut. Named a *fusee*, the pulley evened out the spring's power as it slowly unwound.

With the new spring-driven mechanism, clocks became smaller, and moved off the wall. Table or "drum" clocks were made for the next eighty years, usually about nine inches in diameter, and about five inches high. Some were furnished with a hinged lid to protect

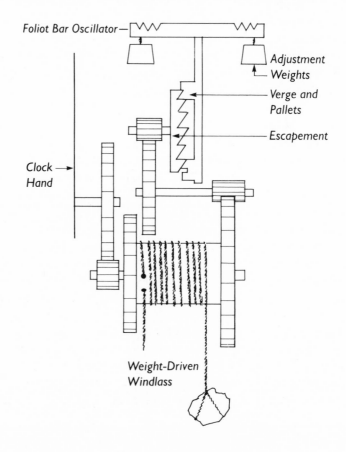

Foliot Bar Oscillator —
Adjustment Weights
Verge and Pallets
Escapement
Clock Hand
Weight-Driven Windlass

the hour hand, and most were intricately decorated to suit the whims of those who could afford them.

About 1560, the English clockmakers' work became popular. Demand outstripped supply, and the London clockmakers rushed to add apprentices to their shops. To protect their trade, they petitioned Charles I to grant them a trade union charter, which he did on August 22, 1631, establishing the Worshipful Company of Clockmakers. Unfortunately, their protectionism and refusal to accept new design and manufacturing techniques worked against them, but for more than two hundred years English clocks were sold throughout the known world.

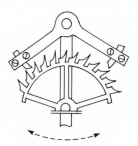

Pendulum (Anchor)
Escapement

While the London clockmakers were hard at work, so was a fellow named Galileo in Pisa, Italy. He was tinkering with a thing he called a pendulum. He had watched physicians checking pulse rates against the rhythm of a stone swinging on the end of a string. He probably was amused by the practice, until he found that those simple pendulums were a great deal more accurate than anything he and his fellow scientists had come up with. So he wrote about it in 1582, and, happily, Christian Huyghens, who lived in Holland, was smart enough to see how the pendulum might be used as a regulator in clocks, instead of the old foliot. Salomon Coster, who worked in the Hague, made the first one to his design for Louis XIV, which is now in the Amsterdam Rijksmuseum. Sixty years after Galileo's observations, the pendulum caught on and from 1657 onward, no clockmaker worth a ducat would foist a foliot on his customers.

By 1670 weight-driven, short-pendulum clocks were being made all over Europe, accurate within ten seconds a day. Under the influence of the French court, their styles began to reflect the artistic theme of furniture of the period. To grace the salons and halls of the Sun King's palaces, a spate of new designs in inlaid wood cabinets and ornate cases were produced in Versailles by craftsmen assembled from all over Europe. But the French Revolution, which began in 1789, removed the craftsmen's prime customer, Louis XVI, by chopping off his head. Most of the clockmakers saw this as a negative market indicator and rapidly departed for the sake of their health.

Then William Clement, an English clockmaker, realized that when the pendulum was lengthened, the regulation accuracy was so much improved that a clock might even be made capable of recording seconds. The idea was made more feasible through an improved anchor escapement invented a few years earlier. The anchor escapement not only controlled the powered escape wheel very well, but it also transmitted some of the power back to the pendulum, causing

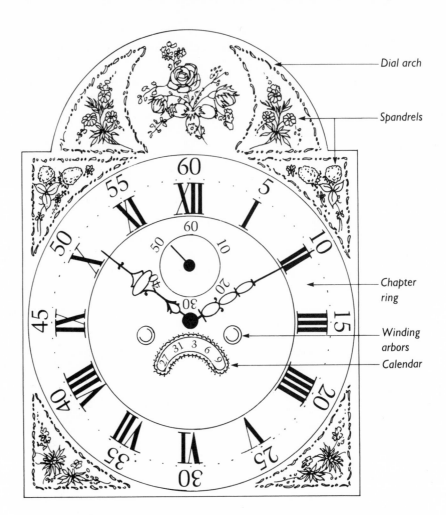

Dial arch

Spandrels

Chapter ring

Winding arbors

Calendar

Shown here, a painted iron dial made in England, commonly used after 1780 in America.

it to continue swinging. George Graham later corrected a problem in the anchor escapement that showed up if the pendulum swung too far, and the ingenious work of these men finally made precision clocks possible.

Although some European clocks were brought to America by wealthy settlers and officials during the seventeenth century, the first known American clockmaker was William Davis, who disembarked at Boston in 1683. He was soon followed by Samuel Bispham, Abel Cottey of Devon, and Peter Stretch of Staffordshire, among others. They began work in Philadelphia, took on apprentices, and by 1750 the town was recognized as a center of fine cabinetmaking and hand-crafted clock movements. The apprentices had to be dedicated young men. For seven years, their indentures forbade their absence without leave, day or night; they received no wages, could not marry or "commit fornication," and were not allowed to play at dice or cards, or "haunt" alehouses. Not surprisingly, newspapers often carried notices of runaways. But those who stuck it out were able to go into business for themselves, and upon their diligence the New World industry was built.

One of the young clockmakers was a genius named David Rittenhouse, who went on to become the country's foremost mathematician, surveyor, and astronomer. Thomas Jefferson said of him, "The world has but one Rittenhouse." His hand-crafted clocks are examples of the finest and most complex ever made.

Another craftsman, Thomas Harland, came to America with gear-cutting machinery on one of the ships that was involved in the Boston Tea Party. Finding things a little tense in Boston, he set up shop in Norwich, Connecticut, and built a properous business. He also designed and built a fire engine for the town. Ironically, the *Norwich Packet* reported on December 11, 1795:

> On Friday evening last, the clock manufactory belonging to Mr. Thomas Harland was discovered to be on fire; the destructive element was raging with such fury before it was discovered as to render all exertions for preserving any part of the building totally abortive.

Harland got his manufactory going again though, and operated it successfully until his death in 1807. His ideas for producing more than one timepiece simultaneously by using standardized parts were passed along to one of his apprentices, Daniel Burnap, who in turn taught them to a young Eli Terry. After the Revolutionary War of 1776, Eli began making clocks with hardwood mechanisms, using the primitive multiple-production methods he had learned. By the turn of the century, as orders increased, he harnessed water power to drive his rudimentary machinery, and his ingenuity soon allowed him to produce more than two hundred timepieces a year. His Plymouth, Massachusetts factory was the birthplace of American clock manufacturing. He sent out salesmen on horseback to sell his merchandise, reduced his prices, formed a partnership with Seth Thomas and Tom Hoadley, and increased his output to the unheard of level of two thousand clocks a year. To enable his peddlers to carry his clocks more easily, he reduced their size and was granted patents for a new style of shelf clock. His success enabled Seth Thomas, who sold his interest profitably in 1810, to start up in business for himself. He established the company that has survived to this day.

During the same period, between 1750 and 1820, Swiss and German craftsmen created remarkably intricate and decorative clocks for the rich, royal and famous in Europe. Many of them contained musical movements to sound the hours, in addition to recording the hours, minutes, and date.

In Massachusetts, new clock designs were proliferating, too. The "banjo" clock, patented in 1802 by Simon Willard, appeared at this time. Some were not as successful. In 1815, Joseph Ives patented his "wagon-spring" clocks, which used a powerful miniature leaf spring similar to those used today in automotive suspensions. Its strength was also its weakness, for it often wrecked the entire clock. Then Chauncey Jerome conceived the idea of making clock movements from brass instead of wood, and the industry grew apace. The stiff competition and hard economic times kept pressure on American clock manufacturers to invent new methods to reduce their prices. They were so successful in this that they were soon able to export inexpensive clocks to England, and over a period of twenty-five years, the industry in that country became practically extinct. By 1865, American clockmakers were exporting nearly one million dollars worth of clocks annually.

The English tower clocks were still the best available though. In 1856 Edmund Beckett, later Lord Grimthorpe, improved their escapements once again, to accommodate changing load conditions caused by snow, ice, and dirt. He built London's famous Big Ben in 1859, and his design has become a standard for public clocks. The name Big Ben actually belongs to the great bell which sounds the hours. It was named for Sir Benjamin Hall, commissioner of works. The first stroke of the clapper gives the exact hour.

For the remainder of the nineteenth century, clockmakers concentrated on making their products more accurate, reducing cost, and offering new features and designs to capture public taste. Weight-driven, tall clocks gave way to smaller, spring-powered models. Precision clocks were made in small quantities for scientific and institutional use. Seth Thomas, for example, produced a mercury-pendulum clock for astronomical observatories in 1890.

Although it had been available for forty years, the newfangled electric power was ignored. Nobody could have been more disappointed at the lack of public interest in electric clocks than Alexander Bain, an Edinburgh clockmaker who patented the first reliable electromagnetic clock in 1845, and Samuel Kennedy of New York who received a similar patent in 1867. They were both unsuccessful in gaining any public support, and their ideas languished in oblivion

TEMPUS AD LUCEM
DUCIT VERITATEM
*Time Brings Truth
to Light*

for nearly a hundred years before electric clocks were finally introduced in America in 1928. Their production was pioneered by the Hammond Clock Company of Chicago whose owner, Laurens Hammond, also developed the electric organ. Hammond electric-wound clocks marked the demise of the pendulum in household clocks.

The clock industry was rocked in March of 1929, when one of the industry leaders, the Ansonia Clock Company, announced bankruptcy and sold its assets to the government of the Soviet Union. Within ten years after moving the equipment to Moscow, the Soviets were producing millions of clocks and watches annually, while in America, the depression was cutting the industry to shreds.

Since the thirties, sixty-cycles-per-second alternating electric current has been reliably available in the United States, and most clocks produced in the last fifty years have used electric synchronous motors for their power, although some interesting special clocks have been developed for particular applications. The quartz crystal "talking clock," used by telephone companies, originally used three endless loops of sound film to produce the familiar, "At the tone, the time will be . . ." message before electronic voice-simulation replaced them. The Atmos clock has enjoyed some popularity. It uses changes in temperature, and the resulting expansion and contraction of its metals, to provide energy to its mechanism. But having sold production tools, equipment, and know-how to the Swiss, Soviets, and Asians, American clock production is now practically defunct. Seth Thomas has been displaced by Seiko as the leading seller of clocks in the United States, and clockmaking innovation today focuses primarily on case design. While nostalgia still sells a few high quality pendulum clocks, the current trends in mechanical clocks are toward clean, undecorated design or whimsical novelties, both types using mass-produced, battery-operated movements or digital electronic displays.

For scientific purposes, clocks started to become important in 1906, when the first electric master clock was developed to control a group of others through a timed electrical impulse. Later, the Shortt pendulum clock was used for standard time around the world. It was, in fact, two clocks, one synchronized by the other, with the pendulums sealed in pressure- and temperature-controlled cases. It was accurate to about thirty thousandths of a second per day.

In 1967, the cesium atomic clock, using the cesium atom's vibration rate of approximately .000000009 of a second, was installed for use at the National Bureau of Standards and the United States Naval Observatory. It maintains an accuracy of better than one sec-

The French à l'arme! (to arms!) became, in English, the word for the war cry or warning itself; thence for anything, such as a special clock, that sounds such a warning.

ond in three thousand years. A maser clock, utilizing the hydrogen molecule instead of cesium, achieves equivalent accuracy. After six hundred years of development, the most accurate clocks are now built upon atomic physical phenomena, rather than astronomical, because we have learned how variable time becomes when based upon the movement of the Earth in the universe. While most of us are satisfied by marking the passage of time between key events like coffee breaks and quitting time, scientists now use their super-accurate clocks to measure distance, using radar and Loran, and to make the split second commands that successfully control space-ship trajectories.

As more nations adopt the decimal system of measurement, it is foreseen that future clocks may have one hundred seconds to the hour, and ten hours to the day. This same system was tried in France in 1793, but the world was not ready for it. Whatever the future holds, however, clocks will continue to be nothing more than so-phisticated shadow sticks. Although their time-fixing function is essential to our daily living, the elasticity of time will remain an integral part of the cosmos.

COLD TIME

*Minimizing the time lost
through colds and flu*

More time is lost from sickness caused by the common cold than from all other diseases combined. There is, as yet, no cure-all because of the hundreds of viral mutations. In spite of that, Americans spend nearly five billion dollars each year on physicians and "remedies," and lose about the same amount in working hours.

There is something that can be done about it.

First, dispense with the idea that only those with low moral fiber call in sick when they have a cold. The stoics who persist in struggling into the office with runny noses and aching muscles do nothing but worsen their colds, while spreading millions of virus particles that infect many of those with whom they come in contact. Colds are spread through both aerosol (airborne) and tactile transmission, and not through cold, damp weather, in spite of the name. Do everybody a favor, and stay out of circulation when you have a cold. If you must go to work, use a hygenic mask as is the custom in many other countries.

Second, learn your own body's signals of respiratory infection and react immediately instead of trying to ignore them. There are seven primary forms of virus that attack our respiratory systems; one causes influenza, the others cause colds. Take influenza seriously, for it can kill you. Use the vaccines and drugs that prevent and control it. Cold viruses like a dry environment, about ninety degrees Fahrenheit. The body's temperature and the moist, antiviral conditions in healthy nasal passages will stop most of them, given a chance.

When a rhinovirus establishes a bridgehead, the human body starts a counterattack within minutes. It is the defense mechanisms that cause most of the discomfort. Nose and throat cells dilate to speed the passage of white cells to infected tissue. A protein called interleukin-1 is released to raise body temperature to counter viral reproduction. Left to itself, the body will dispose of the invader in about 220 hours.

Third, help your body to avoid infection by selecting and using preventative regimens that *seem to work for you.*

Practice good hygiene. Don't smoke. Maintain a low-cholesterol, high-fiber diet. Remember that it's been only a short time, developmentally speaking, since our species existed on nuts, fruits, and grains, with occasional low-fat game. Our scientific progress has far outstripped our bodily adaptation.

Counter tactile infection with frequent washing of the hands and face.

In spite of the controversy, ascorbic acid (vitamin C) does reduce cold symptoms for many, providing that the dosage is no less than two grams daily. Nearly twenty research studies, using this minimum dosage level, have now demonstrated its benefit.

A 1987 study in England has shown that zinc lozenges, taken every two hours, help prevent rhinovirus infection, speed cure, and reduce nasal and throat congestion for some people. Zinc may be toxic to others, and cause nausea. Try sucking zinc lozenges at the first sign of a cold, and see if it helps. If there's any nausea, stop.

Antihistamines are medically proven to be useless. They work for allergies, but not for colds. Don't waste your money on them.

Use the power of your mind. Studies at the Harvard Medical School have recently shown that antibody release is increased when we focus our minds internally, relax, and temporarily blank out the outside world.

Drink as much hot liquid as possible: chicken soup, tea, lemon and honey in hot water. This will help soothe inflamed areas, reduce congestion, and help the kidneys to dispose of viral waste.

Go to bed, or rest quietly. The body has to work very hard when fighting cold viruses. Physical energy should be conserved.

Cold time *can* be shortened, but only if one finds and applies the personal regimen that works. A Band-Aid approach is worthless. Try the approaches recommended, note those that bring relief, and swing into action the minute you detect the warning signals.

The inaudible and noiseless foot of Time.
William Shakespeare,
All's Well That Ends Well, Act V

COMMUNICATION TIME

*Using the right words effectively ·
One-on-one communication ·
Group discussion · Audience presentations
· Visual aids · Mistaken assumptions ·
Management communications time ·
Communications time-savers*

Whether at home or at work, we spend the greater part of our time communicating. But although we learn the tools of communication in school, we're rarely taught the art of using them properly. The frequent result, for most of us, is frustrating and time-consuming corrective activity and the need to repair hurt feelings. Expert communicators have studied the art in depth and use the following information and techniques.

VERBAL COMMUNICATION

Verbal communication is our primary tool, but because words mean different things to different people, it's almost impossible to convey *exactly* what we think or feel. The word "face," for example, has 47 meanings. "Round" has 73, and "run" has 832. In fact, the five hundred most-used words in the English language have 14,070 meanings, or an average of 28 per word. Of the more than half a million words in the language, only about a thousand are in the average person's vocabulary. No wonder we have problems.

At the other end of the scale, when bureaucrats add their obfuscation to the medley of meanings, the situation can get worse. The Ten Commandments used 297 words, but a U.S. government order to reduce the price of cabbages used 26,911. And the story is told of the plumber who asked his city water department if he could use acid to clear clogged drains. They replied, ". . . while the efficacy of hydrochloric acid as an anticoagulant is indisputable, the chlorine residue is incompatible with metal permanence." They would have saved everyone's time had they simply said, "Don't use acid; it eats pipes away."

Using the right words effectively is the first step in improving your verbal communication time. Start by getting rid of the bad habit clutter in your speech. Some words and phrases have an uncanny ability to put people on edge, raise their emotions, or persuade them to tune you out. Some of the words, according to psychologists, are:

management decision	strike
layoff	demand
price increase	yuppie
cheap	bigot
time-study	redneck
mother-in-law	mister
	sissy

and phrases like:

"What I mean to say is . . ."	"Shall we say?"
"If you see what I mean?"	"Notwithstanding the fact that . . ."
"As I just said . . ."	"Really?"
"Irregardless of . . ."	"So to speak . . ."
"Let me say . . ."	"Until such time as . . ."

There are probably some gems in your own vocabulary. Ask your spouse or a friend. They may surprise you. Remember, too, that people to whom you talk are constantly checking what they hear with what they see; most have an uncanny ability to sense true or false expression in a conversation. So say what you mean, say it truly, and say it intelligently.

ONE-ON-ONE COMMUNICATION

Because we spend so much of our time in conversation with one person at a time, it is worthwhile to use every skill we can muster to make the communication as meaningful as possible. Our parents and grandparents were better at this than we are today. Our reduced skills are probably the result of less interactive pursuits such as television that fill so much of our free time nowadays. (See *LEISURE TIME.*) The level of interesting and informed conversation one encounters at social gatherings is low, or narrowly focused on sports or business.

It is possible to become a good communicator, command a listener's attention, and achieve absorbing, interesting verbal interaction by adopting the procedures described below. The quality of your own time, as well as that of others with whom you converse, will benefit accordingly.

Whenever you are communicating with another person, be truly ready to listen, and *make it obvious that you're listening.* Pay full attention to the speaker, and watch his face and body to see if they agree with what he's saying. Mentally question the purpose underlying the conversation (he may not be aware of it himself!).

Keep checking on what you think you heard by asking clarifying questions. Summarize frequently to consolidate opinions and facts. Make mental notes of key points.

Use your eyes effectively. Look directly at your listener's right eye when you're talking. Watch his eyes for signals. A sudden shift to the right may presage a lie. If the eyes wander around, your listener is bored. When the pupils enlarge, there is increased interest. If he's sitting cross-legged, watch the suspended ankle. He will flex it unconsciously when the conversation becomes stressful.

Respect your listener's private space. Westerners like to have about three feet of space around them; Middle-Easterners need less. Private space intrusion and body contact are powerful moves that can easily offend. Use them carefully.

In verbal business communication, or whenever there is a specific objective to a conversation, it's important to develop an approach that matches the listener's probable train of thought. Whether you are selling ideas or products, there are usually eight factors to consider:

1. *Subject definition*   should be stated in the *listener's* terms.

2. *Need*   what are the listener's needs and priorities?

3. *Suggestion/idea*   must be stated concisely and smoothly. Hesitation or confusion implies that you haven't thought it through.

4. *Benefit(s)*   ranked in order of importance.

5. *Acceptance problems*   those thoughts that may be counter to your argument. Don't underestimate them.

It takes eight minutes for the sun's light to reach the earth. If the sun ever stopped shining, we would remain blissfully ignorant for eight minutes after the fact.

6. *Evidence/proof sequence* which of these six forms of evidence will be used:

Figures and Statistics: If statistical evidence is to be convincing, the source must be known and accepted. If an article has been printed, use it in conjunction with raw figures. Make figures easier to understand with visual graphics.

Facts: Using basic statements like "There must be hope on both sides of a good deal" can often add strength to a communication. Use well-known principles and information from respected sources, too.

Examples: The power of examples to form mental pictures has been known since the use of parables in biblical times. Use them as frequently as possible.

Analogies: Next to examples, analogies are one of a communicator's strongest tools. They stay in the minds of listeners longer than most things they hear. Example: "It's no use stoking the boilers unless we know where the ship is going."

Experience: The communicator's own experiences can be impressive and can build respect for "someone who has been there." Don't mix personal opinions with experiential description, and beware that listeners may have had conflicting experiences.

Experts: The use of experts' opinions, as long as they are known to be unbiased, is a valuable persuasive tool. Insure that their credentials are solidly established.

7. *Conclusion/reinforcement* repetition of key points and restatement of areas of agreement. As the ad executives say, "Tell 'em what they're going to hear, tell 'em what they're hearing, and tell 'em what they've heard."

8. *Action* invoke any physical action that can take place immediately, such as completing a worksheet, voting, or signing an order.

SMALL GROUP DISCUSSION

Business managers consistently place meetings and group discussions at the top of their time-wasters list, although they are supposed to aid communication. (This subject is dealt with in greater depth in *MEETING TIME.*) Check yourself . . . do you get ready beforehand, or do you wait for others to come into your office, then make them sit woodenly while you hunt for your papers or take telephone calls? Do you do your homework so that you know as much

Time is a storm, in which we are all lost.
William Carlos Williams,
Selected Essays

as possible about the subject before you start talking? If you do, you've made a good start. Keep things moving by:

Speaking slowly, with the best voice modulation you can achieve, especially when expressing disagreement. Get to the point quickly, and keep your words concise and relevant.

Avoid contributing to nonessential talk. Develop some tactful but firm phrases to get the discussion back on track. Deal with long-winded people courteously, but don't let them set the pace. Cut off the discussion as soon as it seems to have reached a noneffective level. Make your displeasure apparent if somebody starts a side discussion.

Allow a slight delay after someone has spoken before you reply or raise another issue.

AUDIENCE PRESENTATIONS

Use the eight-step procedure described above to prepare your material and presentation. The following techniques, used by many professional speakers, can help you polish your delivery.

Eye Control: The eyes are capable of providing information to the brain faster than any other sense organ. In fact, 85 percent of what we learn is gathered through our eyes. Glance around a room, then shut your eyes and recall what you saw. The amount of information you gained in one glance is evidence of the incredible power of the eye-brain combination.

The brain favors the eyes when determining the level of attention it will give to competing demands. One cannot communicate effectively if one's eyes are occupying too much of the brain's attention. This is Problem One. It is under these circumstances that speakers lose their train of thought, and their audience. Unskilled communicators allow their eyes to wander around the room, picking up visual images at the rate of about three per second. This massive amount of data is fed to the brain while the speaker tries to concentrate on his or her information output. The result is nervous tension and poor delivery.

Problem Two. To get a message across to an audience, it's essential to control their eyes as well as their ears. This is easy to do in a one-on-one situation, but more difficult when there are many eyes on you. Nonetheless, your goal is to have each member of your audience develop the same mental image or concept that you have.

The answer to both of these problems lies in the way in which you use your eyes when addressing a group. You should establish eye contact for at least five seconds at a time with each member of your audience. This will be tough at first, but it soon becomes comfortable with practice. Concentrate on each audience member. The benefits can be remarkable.

- It will reduce the visual input to your brain and, thus, improve delivery control.
- It will command the attention of each listener, giving them a feeling of importance and individuality.
- It will provide response and reaction feedback.
- It will build audience involvement.

This technique is the foundation of effective communication in meetings and should be practiced constantly. It will significantly increase the impact of your presentations and make your meeting time more valuable.

When speaking to an audience, don't waste their time with clichés like: "I'm sure you all know more about this than I . . ." "That reminds me of a story about . . ." or "Did you hear the story about . . ." (*They probably did.*) "I'm not much of a speech-maker, but . . ." (*It may be obvious, but don't make it worse.*)

Dionysius, as long ago as 400 B.C., put it well. He said, "Let thy speech be better than silence, or be silent."

VISUAL AIDS

The importance of reinforcing verbal communication with visual aids is universally understood. Translating the principle into effective action is not. All too often an audience finds its time wasted with a boring, poorly-managed series of visual and sound images that invite sleep rather than attention.

The audience's first visual impression is the way the speaker presents himself or herself. Personal visual skills involve the use of gestures, motion, and facial expression. They are important in all communications, but more so before an audience, because the special dynamics require one to be "larger than life." That is, if one is to capture and hold the listener's attention.

Use video to check your personal mannerisms if possible. While the eye-contact technique will help you to speak more slowly, it won't control other communication problems. Check the use of nonwords—the "ands," "er's," "y'know's," and others that may have become a habit. Get some excitement into the voice, and learn to maintain it throughout the presentation. Many speakers start off in good voice but quickly degenerate into a monotone. Learn to pause so that the audience has a chance to absorb what you've said. Write PAUSE in your notes at the appropriate places as a reminder.

The audience's second visual impression will come from your slides, transparencies, or flipcharts. These suggestions can improve their effectiveness:

> If possible, set up your presentation, then sit at the sides and rear of the room to check sight-lines before your audience arrives. Try never to give visuals pride-of-place in the center of the presentation area. That belongs to you. The left side is preferable because our eyes naturally move in that direction when reading.

> Make visuals simple and readable. If they cannot be seen from the rear of the audience, they will annoy rather than inform.

> Use color. The extra cost is worth it. The use of red to excite and cool colors to highlight tables, etc. is valuable and effective. People respond to color.

> Use pictures and symbols. Keep text to an absolute minimum. No more than five words on a slide is a good target. With too many words to occupy them, an audience will tune out the speaker. Never let visuals upstage you.

> Reveal information a step at a time. If necessary cover part of a visual until it should be seen. Set up your audience with anticipation before you put anything on a screen or board.

> Build involvement into visuals. Draw in circles and lines yourself. Write in a total figure to add impact to it.

> Don't risk foul-ups in the organization of your notes. Rehearse, and write yourself lead-in phrases. Guard against fumbling with pages sticking together by folding and unfolding their corners.

MISCOMMUNICATION

Miscommunication gets people into trouble more often than they may admit. Here's a typical scenario, related to me by the president of an electronics company. He had to participate in a meeting while expecting an important telephone call from a major customer. On the way to the meeting, he told the receptionist, "If Jack Barnes calls, I'll be in the staff meeting." Two hours later, when the meeting broke up, he told the receptionist that he was surprised he didn't hear from Barnes. "Oh, he called," she said, "and I told him you were in a meeting, like you said." I'll bet you can tell a similar story.

Much of the time wasted in both verbal and written business communication stems from the *assumptions* people make in their exchanges. Inferences and biased judgments take the place of reality more frequently than most of us realize. Logically, a statement can only be true, indeterminable, or false. The ability to perceive these values accurately is a constant challenge. Test your own skill. Read this short paragraph, then rate the following series of statements as true, false, or indeterminable. Read the paragraph as many times as you wish, until you're confident you understand it. Then rate the statements in the order given. Don't jump around or change answers.

> Paul Harper, the engineering manager of a large electronics company, ordered a crash program to develop a new microchip. He gave two of his supervisors the authority to spend up to $10,000 each without the need for approval. He sent one of his best men, Williams, to the London laboratory to work on the program independently. In six weeks, Williams came up with a promising new approach to the problem.

Now cover the above information, and complete the following rating sheet:

STATEMENTS	RATING		
Harper sent one of his best men to England.	T	F	?
Harper overestimated Williams's competence.	T	F	?
Williams did not produce anything new.	T	F	?
Williams could spend money without approval.	T	F	?
Only two of Harper's men could spend money without approval.	T	F	?
Harper had a high opinion of Williams.	T	F	?
Two men were given authority to spend up to $10,000.	T	F	?
Harper was an engineering manager.	T	F	?
The story refers to only four people.	T	F	?
Williams was part of Harper's research team.	T	F	?

To check whether you have injected any assumptions into your understanding of the given information, turn to end of chapter.

In productivity studies, communication always tops the list of problems for professionals and managers. That's not too surprising, when on the average their incoming communications soak up about nineteen hours every week, and their outgoing communications about seventeen hours. Here's how a manager's time is generally spent in upward, downward, and lateral communications:

Superiors

2.5
2.1

Hours per week (36.6 hours)

5.4
6.3

3.6
2.9

7.1
6.7

Associates

Subordinates

People outside the organization

The choice between verbal and written communication is often difficult. Two-way discussion often produces better understanding, but a memo can communicate in a fraction of the time, and provide a record, too. Ask yourself the following questions to determine your best mode of communication.

Will my presence help to bring matters out that might otherwise stay hidden? If it will, talk, don't write.

Do I want the personal interaction that can give me a "feel" for a situation? This can only come from face-to-face communication.

Do I want to be questioned about the communication? If not, stick to the letter approach.

Should I write a general memo, or make a verbal statement in a group meeting? It depends. Large meetings bring one-way communication; small groups are tough to manage. If you determine that discussion is preferable, read *MEETINGS*.

What sort of stimulus does the recipient react to? From bitter experience, some managers have learned that their correspondent's habit patterns have to take priority.

Should I communicate at all? Not responding can often deflect unwarranted interference, without your actually telling someone to mind their own business.

Although our most popular mode of communication is oral, written communications still consume a significant slice of managerial time. In a survey of more than seven hundred midwestern executives, a typical day's communication time was split as follows:

Direct verbal communication	2.8 hrs.
Telephone communication	1.2 hrs.
Reading letters or memos	.9 hrs.
Reading reports, etc.	.6 hrs.
Creating internal correspondence	.9 hrs.
Creating external correspondence	.8 hrs.

Here are some techniques that savvy executives use to salvage some of this time. You may be able to use a few of them to your own advantage.

Make handwritten replies to internal memos whenever possible. Print all names and odd trade words. Use form memos whenever possible if you don't have electronic mail facilities.

Check out voice messaging (see *TELEPHONE*). It may be a good time-saver for you.

Force yourself to limit your replies to two paragraphs. If it has to be longer, use clerical assistance. Give them the gist and let them handle it, or use an electronic dictation unit.

Write on the original if you can. Only make a copy if you must.

Require a summary face sheet on all reports over four pages long.

Practice "wastebasketry." Throw more stuff away.

When you pick up a written piece of communication, *do something with it*. Move the matter ahead somehow. Deal with it completely, if possible, and get rid of it.

Use rubber stamps to save time. For example, use a follow-up stamp reading:

REMINDER

I would like to have your response
to this correspondence.

Think of other stamps that you can use to save repetitive writing. Stamps are cheap and carry a sense of urgency, especially if you use red ink.

Only write formal letters when essential. Remember they cost more than ten dollars apiece these days.

A few years ago, I modernized paperwork communications in a large court system. They realized how far things had gotten out of hand when I showed they had seventy-six linear *miles* of records spread throughout eighteen warehouses. And across the U.S., in spite of our advances in electronic data storage, there are more than seventy million file cabinets, and about three million people shuffling their contents daily. Think about that. Do these people really *want* to spend their time like this? And are you a contributor? If you want to save time, take an oath *never* to buy another filing cabinet.

If you must write, make your letters short and crisp. Try and write in the same way that you speak. Don't get pompous. Use the first person singular and active voice. (If you do much writing, read *WRITING TIME* for more ways to make written communications effective.)

The human communication process has undergone an enormous amount of research since World War II. Theories of the Neolithic origins of language include the "bow-wow" theory, which allies it to the imitation of animal sounds; the "ding-dong" theory, which relates sound and substance; and the "pooh-pooh" theory, which ties it to feelings. It may also have originated to accompany and emphasize gestures. We really don't know.

Modern studies have focused upon *syntactics* (sign relationships), *pragmatics* (causal relationships), and *semantics* (word and

There are certain spots on the earth where extreme longevity seems to be the rule, even allowing for exaggerated reports. These include Hunza, in the Himalayas, and the famous Caucasus region of the USSR. Constants seem to be mountain living, a meager diet, and a lack of enemies.

sign meanings)[1] as the basis of a communications science. Psychological theories of perception, cognition, attitude formation, and behavioral effects have been added. But it is clear that human beings are resilient to any form of brainwashing in communications, and the mass media achieve no more than reenforcing or confirming what a listener or viewer thinks or wants, except in times of social upheaval or instability.

Mass communications may be the cement of society, but on a personal level, your communication time will be best utilized when you know who you are and what you want, and assume that the world knows neither until you *let* it know.

See also *READING TIME, WRITING TIME, MEETING TIME.*

ASSUMPTIONS TEST ANSWERS

STATEMENTS	RATING
Harper sent one of his best men to London. *(That is what the story says.)*	T
Harper overestimated Williams's competence. *(The story gives no information on this.)*	?
Williams did not produce anything new. *(The story says he did.)*	F
Williams could spend money without approval. *(Williams's spending authority is not described.)*	?
Only two of Harper's men could spend money without approval. *(ONLY is the key word. The story does not say whether others had the same authority.)*	?
Harper had a high opinion of Williams. *(Maybe it's suggested, but it's not specified.)*	?
Two men were given authority to spend up to $10,000. *(We don't know whether they were men or women.)*	?
Harper was an engineering manager. *(Correct. It says so.)*	T

---

1. Charles Morris first incorporated these within his proposed semiotic science in *Signs, Language and Behavior*, 1946.

The story refers to only four people.   ?
(If Williams was one of the two authorized to
spend $10,000, this would be true. But we don't
know that.)

Williams was part of Harper's research team.   F
(He was specifically sent away to work
independently.)

We all have beliefs and assumptions, and we all make inferences
and judgments. They will be better if they are not based on invalid
facts. Sorting out what is true, false, or unknown is not always easy;
the alternative usually costs more time.

CONCENTRATION TIME

*Consciousness control · Daydreaming ·
Time fragmentation · The working
environment · Concentration techniques*

Concentrated attention is a form of consciousness control. It is a limited, energy-consuming resource, but its effective application can shape an entire life. Conversely, the inability to focus attention can produce inner stresses. Undirected, attention will vacillate between whatever outside stimuli it senses. The result can be a sense of guilty ineffectiveness or a feeling of being overwhelmed. The tension between competing demands and limited attention may even cause behavioral problems.

Feelings, wishes, and latent ideas become real only when attention is directed to them. It's like taking an item out of our mental closet and holding it up to the light. William James, the famous psychologist, said, "My experience is what I attend to. Only those items I notice shape my mind—without selective interest, experience is utter chaos."

Unfortunately, even with well-focused attention, our conscious minds can only handle a small amount of data at once. It thus becomes important to discern the components of a problem correctly, as well as determining in what depth, and for how long they should be examined.

Dreaming is brain activity of which we are conscious, but unable to direct. When we daydream, we elect not to direct the stream of conscious thoughts that flow through our minds.

What does influence the direction and effectiveness of our attention? There appears to be a small group of factors. Enjoyment of the subject is one. A sense of threat or danger is another. But in addition to those stimuli, we have a strong need to apply our skills to solving challenging problems. We will concentrate hard when we believe the results may prove that we *matter*, that we are not impotent or nobodies. There is a heady sense of being in control, and fulfilling one's destiny. Those who learn to concentrate experience one of life's great pleasures.

Managers would do well to note these factors. People at work, even when doing something less enjoyable, will try harder and succeed better given two conditions: (1) their skills must be matched to their task, and (2) they must be able to concentrate on and exercise some control over their work. Workers report feeling more alert, free, active, and satisfied when these two basic requirements are met. The opposite also applies. People who are prevented from concentrating or directing their attention voluntarily will become impatient, careless, and depressed, or will retreat into daydreaming and fantasy.

The president of a multinational Silicon Valley company used to complain to me about his lack of time. When I visited with him at his office and talked to some of his associates, the reason became obvious. His working day was fragmented into a stream of impulse-driven activities that did more to disrupt his subordinates than to help them. He had a compulsion to drop into meetings unexpectedly and to ricochet through the office to "keep up on things." His inability to concentrate on any one task long enough to deal with it in depth made his managerial effect superficial and drove his employees up the wall.

With some self-analysis (see *TIME PAYOFF ANALYSIS*), he came to understand that his concentration energy could not be spread so thinly and that he could not afford to permit distractions to rule his workday.

Although you may not have the same problems as my friend, your ability to concentrate will play a major part in your business success. Andrew Carnegie recognized this when he said, "Concentration is my motto." If you feel a compulsion to do *something*, even when caution is indicated, or feel impatient when a conversation exceeds ten minutes, slow down and start changing things.

First, set up your working environment, whether at the office or at home, to feel comfortable. Invest in a good chair, for example. There are many who will spend $3,000 on a personal computer, yet begrudge $100 for a decent, human-engineered seat. Make sure that you have good lighting and enough work surface to spread things out.

When you've got your workplace under control, take a look at your tools and supplies. Having to get up and hunt for a roll of tape is just the type of interruption that can ruin concentration. Pay attention to your writing instruments. They'll serve you better when you like the way they feel. Don't give yourself any excuse to break your thought process.

Figure out how to cut yourself off from the world. Unplug the telephone. Put a "Do Not Disturb" sign on the door. Turn off the radio. Get rid of all the distractions. If you can't do it at the office or at home, go someplace else—maybe your local library. But don't let lack of privacy cover up for procrastination in tackling a problem.

Start in on the easy stuff. Ease into gear by breaking the issue into segments and dealing with the simpler ones. If your mind tries to wander, haul it back. Remember, you're the boss. As you work, your mind will absorb the details and store them in memory, helping your brain to get deeper into the guts of the matter. When you start to roll, stay with it. Don't worry about the time; keep the creative juices flowing as long as you can.

Please come back at

_____

CREATIVE TIME

Creative thinking techniques and self test ·
Presenting ideas · Synergistic factors

I n spite of its superior ability to manipulate enormous amounts of data, the electronic computer cannot compete with the human brain's ability to relate facts creatively. It is this facility, coupled with our natural curiosity, which has produced most of our scientific progress, beautified our environment, and allowed us to contemplate the very meaning of our existence. Yet most of us devote little time to truly creative activity, in spite of the fact that it is the most valuable of all. Creativity can bring remarkable rewards, not only in the benefits of solving problems in new ways, but also in the sense of personal value that accompanies the search for solutions.

Michael Faraday, the English physicist, said, "The creative thinker is a man willing to listen to every suggestion, but determined to judge for himself. He should not be biased; have no favorite hypotheses; be of no school; and in doctrine have no master. He should not be a respecter of persons, but of things. Truth should be his primary objective."

Creative thinking, according to the Greeks, comprised four elements: scientific, aesthetic, political-economic, and ethical-moral. We seem to have made progress in the first over the last two thousand years but, arguably, not in the others. The problems with this uneven development are on every side today. The controversies over nuclear energy, genetic manipulation, and abortion are causing social disturbances in all of the advanced nations. Wars over political-economic issues continue to kill millions. There is worldwide distrust of the ethical-moral standards displayed by our leaders. Hopefully, the postindustrial society will focus intelligently on these problems, and our schools will begin to educate our children to better standards. They may even start to teach that creative thinking can be fun, instead of a grind. James Barrie put it well. He said, "The

most gladsome thing in the world is that few of us fall very low; the saddest is that with such capabilities, we seldom rise high."

Creativity does not depend upon advanced education. All of us are born with it, to some degree. For it to survive, however, a great deal of self-confidence is required to counter the various social and educational systems which will suppress it. There is much to be done to foster the natural curiosity of children, dulled by poor schools and lack of parental support. If only their innate curiosity can be preserved, there is no boundary to their possible achievement. Progressive business corporations are actively seeking creative people and have developed some tests to identify those with well-developed abilities. The selection which follows[1] is from one based on several questionnaires used in creativity studies, including the Meyers-Briggs Type Indicator, the Cree Questionnaire, the California Psychological Inventory, and others. You may like to try it. Turn to the end of the chapter to check your answers.

TEST YOUR CREATIVITY
Word Hints

The object of this test is to find a fourth word that is related to *all three* of the listed words. For example, what word is related to these?

cookies   sixteen   heart   _____

The answer is "sweet." Try one more example:

poke   go   molasses   _____

The answer is "slow." Now try these words:

1. surprise	line	birthday	_____
2. base	snow	dance	_____
3. rat	blue	cottage	_____
4. nap	rig	call	_____
5. golf	foot	country	_____
6. house	weary	ape	_____
7. tiger	plate	news	_____

---

1. Reprinted by permission, *Nation's Business*, June 1965. Copyright 1965, U.S. Chamber of Commerce.

8. painting	bowl	nail	_____
9. proof	sea	priest	_____
10. maple	beet	loaf	_____
11. oak	show	plan	_____
12. light	village	golf	_____
13. merry	out	up	_____
14. cheese	courage	oven	_____
15. red	star	house	_____

There are several other tests which were not designed to measure creative ability, but which have nevertheless been successful in differentiating between more and less creative individuals.

One of the best known among these is the Strong Vocational Interest test, which asks the subject to rate likes and dislikes of four hundred items. Also valuable is the Study of Values test developed by Allport, Vernon, and Lindsey. It contains forty-five items which measure the relative dominance of six basic interests or motives.

Whatever your test scores, it is possible to increase your creativity by using one or more special techniques. Alex Osborn is remembered as one of the first to systematize the ideation process. He called his method "Brainstorming." It uses small groups of people in short, intensive sessions to develop as many ideas as possible, with all criticism or judgment withheld. That's applied later. Brainstorming sessions work best when the rank of all participants is equal and they share similar backgrounds and interests.

Other systems include Gordon's "Operational Creativity," in which a group first discusses every conceivable aspect of a problem before attempting solutions. For example, to devise a new can opener, "opening" might be the focus of discussion. The group would explore all meanings of the word and all applicable examples that occur in nature and science. This process can reveal unusual approaches that may be overlooked when using conventional thought processes.

Drawford's "Attribute Listing" suggests that the problem solver break down a problem into separate attributes. For example, to improve a screwdriver one might list the attributes as (1) round wood handle, (2) steel shank, (3) wedge-shaped flat end to engage screw slot, (4) manual operation, and (5) torque provided by twisting.

To devise a better tool, each of the attributes would then be ad-

Time, which changes people, does not alter the image we have retained of them.

Marcel Proust,
Remembrance of
Things Past

dressed separately. The round handle might be changed to a hexagonal shape, so that a wrench could be used to increase the torque; plastic may be substituted for wood, to eliminate splitting, etc. Many other variations may be developed as each separate attribute is considered.

Charles Whiting proposed a "Forced Relationships" approach. To use it, a manufacturer of office furniture would list the items currently made—desks, chairs, file cabinets, etc. The first relationship probed might be that between the desk and chair. Free association of ideas might suggest a legless chair connected to the desk by a swivel-bar, or the use of space beneath the chair seat to house a minicomputer.

Dr. Gerald Nadler recommends the construction of a "System Framework" for creative analysis. The system description, he says, should include function, inputs, outputs, sequence (what happens when inputs are changed to outputs), the environment, physical catalysts, and human beings.[2] An "ideal" system is conceived from scratch, rather than attempting to improve on any existing system. This approach, it is claimed, will produce better solutions because mental constraints, such as comfort with traditional methods, are avoided. Once the system elements are identified and described, a ten-step process is applied to eliminate, simplify, or improve them.

You may want to try the "Dynamic Thinking" approach I have used successfully for many years.

1. *Define the problem.* Establish clear objectives and determine the conditions that the solution must fit.

2. *Get the facts.* Question every detail. Ask questions about the purpose, necessity, location, time, methods, and the people involved. Ideas will start coming as you do this. Note them, but don't stop to work them out at this stage.

3. *Build your idea bank.* The more ideas you can develop on how to solve the problem, the better the solution will be.

4. *Classify and rank your ideas.* Separate the best overall ideas and list supplementary ideas under them.

5. *Select the best alternative.* Consider the changes that will be required; list the benefits; list the liabilities and risks; consolidate, and include any supplementary ideas.

---

2. Nadler, Gerald. *Work Design: A Systems Concept.* Homewood, Ill.: Richard Irwin, Inc., 1970.

6. *Sell the idea.* Treat this as a separate problem and use your creativity to develop a persuasive approach to getting your plan accepted. Focus on the benefits that it will bring to others—not just yourself. Make it easy for others to say "yes" by thinking through every objection likely to arise. Be ready with answers to show that you've anticipated and prepared for any circumstance.

Think about the environment and time of day that can make your creative time more effective. Here's a checklist of items that have been proven to generate creative synergism:

- Easy access to the fullest possible source(s) of information appropriate to the problem.
- External stimulation from people, displays, and media.
- Compatible surroundings with colors, temperature, noise, space, and aspect conducive to positive feelings.
- Personal freedom to choose hours, dress, and working place.
- Easy access to required materials and equipment.
- Access to support specialists, when required.
- Encouraging leadership from respected persons.
- Appropriate reward and recognition.

Nobody has yet been able to determine what triggers the spark of creativity, but it will occur more frequently when the above conditions are met. The subconscious mind can become part of the problem-solving process when it is not distracted and can assist in making your creative time rewarding.

For further reading:

Ackoff, Russell L. *The Art of Problem Solving.* New York: John Wiley & Sons, 1978.

ANSWERS TO WORD HINTS TEST

1. party 2. ball 3. cheese 4. cat 5. club 6. dog 7. paper
8. finger 9. high 10. sugar 11. floor 12. green 13. make
14. Dutch 15. light

Creative individuals get 75 percent or more of these items right.

The words are based on the Remote Associates test developed by Dr. Sarnoff A. Mednick of the University of Michigan and Dr. Sharon Halpern of the University of California, Berkeley. The actual test consists of thirty such series, and the individual is given forty minutes to complete the test.

Dr. Mednick defines creative thinking as "the forming of associative elements into new combinations which either meet specified requirements or are in some way useful. The more mutually remote the elements of the new combination, the more creative the process or solution." He also maintains that the richness or the number of associations the individual can marshal to the requisite elements of a problem increases the probability of a genuinely creative solution.

The test has proved helpful in identifying IBM engineers and scientists rated as more creative. Extensive experimentation with this test on engineering, scientific, and managerial personnel has been and is being carried on also at General Electric, Lever Brothers, Dow Chemical, and several other firms.

The test is not published commercially as yet. It is available for research use by qualified psychologists in industry and elsewhere.

CYCLES IN TIME

*Noteworthy natural and economic time
patterns that have been recorded*

Cycles in time that recur with a pattern that belies happenstance are turning up more and more frequently now that scientists can use computers to search for them.

According to the *Financial Times*, British taxpayers exhibit a "conscience pattern" which peaks every 3.5 years and brings in a spate of unexpected and voluntary tax payments.

The lynx, snow rabbit, cinchbug, and salmon all have a 9.6-year population growth cycle.

In the western United States, volcanos seem to have a 65-year eruption cycle. Mount Lassen erupted in 1850 and 1915. Mount St. Helens followed in 1980.

The fastest reproductive cycle of human body cells occurs in the rectum, where cells divide every 13 hours. The longest cycle is that of body hair, excluding the scalp, which takes 5.5 months for renewal. (See *BODY TIME*.)

Church membership in the U.S. peaks every 9.5 years.

An 18.3-year real estate cycle brings peak real estate values, building starts and construction costs, and property-transfer activity.

The solar eclipse cycle, when the moon passes between the sun and the Earth, occurs every 18.6 years. Industrial strikes and electric power production both appear to reach a crest every 7.5 years.

A thirty-seven-year cycle has been traced in wheat prices since 1265, cotton since 1731, railroad stocks since 1831, and industrial shares since 1871.

Grosbeak finches invade New England in alternate years and have now maintained the cycle for more than 60 years.

The longest recorded life cycle of living creatures on Earth is:

Fish:	Sturgeon	152 years
Mammal:	Man	115 years
Reptile:	Turtle	85 years
Bird:	Raven	69 years

There is evidence of an 11-year cycle in human "excitability," reflected in warfare, uprisings, and revolutions. Historians have also noted a relationship between sunspot activity and human proclivity to fight.

The shortest gestation period in mammals is that of the platypus, which bears its young 12 days after impregnation. The longest cycle is that of the camel, at 400 days.

Meteor debris fields move around the sun, and eight of them lie in the Earth's orbit. Our planet passes through the core of most, with consistent "shooting star" activity from year to year, but the passage through the Perseids varies, producing an activity peak every 33 years, when 100,000 burnouts an hour have been reported. The cyclical periods for meteor showers are:

Quadrantids	January	1–4
Lyrids	April	19–22
Aquarids	May	1–13
Perseids	July	27–August 15
Orionids	October	15–25
Andomedids	November	26–December 4
Geminids	December	9–13

Planetary rhythms, which determine the length of their years, are shown under *YEARS*.

DAY TIME

The length of the days in the solar system ·
Clock days and solar days · The equation
of time · Sidereal time · The United States
Naval Observatory standard

From primordial times, man has used the solar day as his basic unit of time. It governed his life long before hours, weeks, months, or years were conceived. It's not surprising that our ancestors worshipped the sun, with their utter dependence upon it for light and heat, and the sense of well-being that it imparted. Little did they know or care how elastic the day is, not only on this planet but on all those in a solar system. The rotational speed and direction, orbital speed and axial inclination of all planets (in relation to their suns) give them vastly different days. Here's how the days of the planets in our solar system compare.

PLANET	AVERAGE LENGTH OF DAY (ROTATION PERIOD)		
Mercury	58 days	16 hours	0 mins.
Venus	243	0	0
Earth	0	23	56
Mars	0	24	37
Jupiter	0	9	50
Saturn	0	10	14
Uranus	0	20	0
Neptune	0	21	0
Pluto	6	9	0

Then, if we look in a dictionary, we find two meanings for "day": the interval of time between two successive nights, and the amount of time it takes for the Earth to make one complete revolution around the sun. They are equal in time only four times annually. There are two reasons for this. First, the Earth is moving around the sun in an elliptical orbit. Second, the Earth's axis is tilted 23.5 degrees, so the sun's apparent movement varies in respect to the equator. These little complications cause more than sixteen minutes variation each year.

In olden days the sixteen minutes was no problem, but as we got smarter, it was realized that something had to be done on a worldwide basis. For if each country made their own corrections, chaos would result. So, on October 21, 1884, the Prime Meridian Conference was held in Washington, D.C. By some incredible means, the international delegates were able to agree when minutes should be added or subtracted from each day to keep things in line, and the mean solar day was established throughout the world. They didn't do quite as well when it came to time zones. There has always been some confusion around the world as to when the day should begin. In biblical times, Middle Eastern countries began their days at sundown, and this practice still remains among Israelis who cling to the Hebrew calendar. The international conference plan was rejected by Mongolia, Afghanistan, and Saudi Arabia. As a result, the minds of some visitors to Mecca are boggled by the sun setting at noon.

Our tilted axis affects the day in another way—at least for all of us who don't live on the equator. It means that the length of the day keeps changing as we wobble around, so we have longer days in summer than in winter. The longest day is June 21, called the summer solstice and the shortest day is December 21, the winter solstice.

With all this complication, astronomers realized that they needed to check our "day" against something other than the sun. The relative movements of the Earth and its star made accurate measurement too difficult. They looked out to the stars in other galaxies, selected about two hundred that were suitable, and began to measure the exact time each took to cross a hairline in a telescope. The transit time can be established with great accuracy. The United States Naval Observatory now constantly checks about fifteen stars, using a photographic zenith tube camera. The result is that our day is now accurate to less than three-hundredths of a second in what is called *sidereal time*.

Sidereal time is slightly different from solar time. Due to the relative Earth/sun rotations, the sidereal day is shorter than the solar day by 3 minutes and 55.909 seconds. This adds up to one day per year, so the sidereal year is 366 sidereal days or 365.25636 mean solar days, and that varies a bit from the tropical year, measured from one vernal equinox to the next, which is 365.24219 mean solar days. That should make your day.

Our day-names can be traced to the various gods worshipped by pre-Christian Europeans. The above drawing comes from a seventeenth-century woodcut of the sun, honored on Sunday.

dried system that may simply be injected into any business organization.

On the other hand, there are some prime benefits that come with delegation:

- Delegation increases results from what a person can do, to what he can control.
- Delegation develops initiative, competence, skill, and knowledge in others.
- Delegation maintains decision making at the correct level.
- Delegation releases time for activities that only the delegator can perform.

What does it take for it to work well?

1. The delegator's management style and beliefs must be conducive to co-operative task sharing for delegation to work effectively.

Delegation has been described as "having the courage to stand back and let other people make mistakes." Whether it's lack of courage, or some other excuse, there are managers who just don't like to delegate. How do you feel about it? How good a delegator are you? Do you challenge your people and expand your group's accomplishments to the limit? The self-assessment questionnaire that follows will test your attitudes toward delegation. It's important for a manager to believe in delegation, because he will eventually be forced into using it.

WHAT ABOUT DELEGATION?

This questionnaire will assist in exploring your attitudes about this important management tool. Mark the statements as TRUE or FALSE, then compare your answers with those at the end of this chapter. An additional delegation test may be found in Appendix A.

	TRUE	FALSE
1. A good manager must "keep his hand in" by frequently handling operational tasks.	____	____
2. Everyone must know the details if work is to be accomplished properly.	____	____

3. A manager who regularly delegates is insecure. _____ _____

4. You shouldn't delegate until you're experienced in the job yourself. _____ _____

5. It's not worth delegating when you can do it better yourself. _____ _____

6. My people like me better when I don't load chores on them. _____ _____

7. We can't afford mistakes, so I can't afford to delegate. _____ _____

8. My staff likes me to make the decisions on everything. _____ _____

9. Delegation won't help my subordinates to improve themselves. _____ _____

10. Decisions are too critical to leave to others. _____ _____

11. If I can delegate jobs, then my people don't have enough to do. _____ _____

12. It takes too long to explain every detail. _____ _____

13. Things are too urgent to permit the luxury of delegation. _____ _____

14. None of my staff have time for my left-over jobs. _____ _____

15. If my subordinates do my work, there's no need for me. _____ _____

16. There are enough mistakes made without asking people to handle more work. _____ _____

17. When I delegate I expect to lose control. _____ _____

18. My boss could move me tomorrow without hurting the organization. _____ _____

19. I always prepare my own correspondence and memos. _____ _____

20. Approval of plans can sometimes be usefully delegated. _____ _____

21. In an emergency, delegation can be a
valuable technique.   _____   _____

22. My assistant can always represent me,
when necessary.   _____   _____

23. Total authority must be transferred if
delegation is to succeed.   _____   _____

24. I don't want my people to have to work
as long as I do.   _____   _____

25. When I delegate a job, I don't want to
hear about it again until it's done.   _____   _____

2. Skill in deciding what to delegate and what not to delegate is
essential.

Many elements of time management focus on accomplishing
more in a set time period. Delegation is intended to help a manager
to do less. Then he may have more elective time at his disposal
which can be used for a better payoff. (Read *EXECUTIVE TIME* for
information on "managing" versus "doing.") Delegation will not
save time for an organization, but it will allow the delegator to tackle
new and progressive activities to the organization's overall benefit.

DO DELEGATE	DON'T DELEGATE
Fact-finding and analysis.	Policy and goal selection and approval.
Policy and goal formulation.	Resource commitment to plans, projects, and programs.
Plan development for any goal or project.	Tasks with fuzzy goals.
Execution of managerial decisions.	Hiring, disciplining, and firing of direct or staff subordinates.
Drafts of papers, reports, speeches, etc.	Tasks with tight time deadlines, or emergencies.
Meeting representation.	One-shot affairs.
Anything somebody else can do better.	Confidential matters.
Tasks which will develop subordinates without excess risk.	
Routine, well-defined tasks.	

Selecting those tasks that will best lend themselves to delegation can be simplified by using the following matrix chart. It recognizes the four criteria for delegation: what to delegate, the control
required, the level of task importance, and the task urgency.

Rate each task you do, and enter the rating scores in the Delegation Analysis worksheet on the following page. An additional Delegation Plan Worksheet may be found in Appendix A.

DELEGATIVE CRITERIA

1. I MUST DO IT Nobody else can.	2. DELEGATE SOME Subordinates can handle some subtasks.	3. DELEGATE ALL Subordinates can do it all.	4. DELEGATE ALL Sub-subordinates can do it all.

ORGANIZATION CRITERIA

1. DAILY CONTACT	2. FREQUENT CONTACT	3. REGULAR CONTACT	4. RARE CONTACT

IMPORTANCE CRITERIA

1. VERY IMPORTANT Must be done!	2. IMPORTANT Should be done.	3. SOMEWHAT IMPORTANT Useful, but not essential.	4. UNIMPORTANT Can be eliminated.

TIMING CRITERIA

1. VERY URGENT Now! Now!	2. URGENT Must be done soon.	3. NOT URGENT Long range.	4. URGENCY IS NOT A FACTOR

3. Insure mutual understanding of authority and responsibility.

Consider first those tasks that have the highest rating scores. For each, determine to whom the task may be delegated, and the delegation plan, which defines the scope of subordinate decision making, or the delegated control. An appropriate control-level should be selected from among the following:

Level 1: Complete the assignment with no further contact or feedback.

Level 2: Complete the assignment, but inform what was done.

Level 3: Analyze the problem, inform what action is planned, and proceed unless advised not to.

Level 4: Analyze the problem, inform what action is planned, but wait for approval before taking action.

Level 5: Analyze the problem and outline all possible alternatives with supportive reasoning. Recommend one for approval.

Level 6: Gather and organize all pertinent information on a matter, and present for analysis and "next step" decision.

Pick the right person, then insure that delegation is made with appropriate authority and that the delegatee has the necessary time

DELEGATION ANALYSIS WORKSHEET

SUBTASK DESCRIPTION	DELEGATIVE	ORGANIZATION	IMPORTANCE	TIMING	TOTAL	DELEGATE TO	LEVEL	HOW? WHEN? (DELEGATION PLAN)

and resources. If it is a short assignment, hand it out at the start of the day so that things will get under way as you handle other tasks. Define the task and the goals thoroughly.

Strive to delegate every possible task that is nonmanagerial, and retain only those in which there is clear advantage. Be prepared to delegate tasks that you can do, but others can too. Don't ever delegate tasks which involve decisions about change or are related to discipline or morale. Routine meetings, communication responses, and tasks aimed at maintaining stability are the best candidates.

With a delegation plan in mind, add notes to pinpoint any barriers to delegation that may need to be removed. Think, too, of times when somebody may *have* to fill in for you. Like it or not, it's important to determine who will fill your shoes in certain circumstances.

4. Match levels of competence with assignments.

Delegated tasks fall into four categories:

Basic tasks Straightforward, concrete, and easily understood, requiring little or no intiative.

Training tasks Where subordinate development is as important as shifting workload.

Interactive tasks Although simple in themselves, scheduling and balancing factors require creative thinking and initiative.

Complex tasks Those that demand intelligence, knowledge, creativity, and diligence.

Some managers have found it helpful to make a list of their subordinates and to rate them according to those categories that they can handle. Assign the same ratings to the list of delegable tasks, and you have a valuable matching system.

5. Use an appropriate management style for achieving results through others.

With delegable tasks and assignees lined up, it only remains to put plans into action. The important factors here are:

1. *Don't* be "willing to let others make mistakes." Why should you? Mistakes should only be tolerated as part of a learning process and should be correctable.

2. Pick the most receptive assignee, but allow extra time if it's an inexperienced person or one with a heavy existing workload. Delegate to *everybody*.

3. Complete definition and understanding of the task objectives. Focus on results rather than process.

There is a tide in the affairs of men,
Which, taken at the flood, leads on to fortune;
Omitted, all the voyage of their life
Is bound in shallows and in miseries.
William Shakespeare, Julius Caesar, Act IV

4. Equitable task distribution, so that the worst (or best) assignments don't always go to the same person.

5. Appropriate contact and explanation to all those likely to be involved. Don't let an assignee work without backing.

6. Avoid abdication. Shifting the workload does not shift the responsibility. Be available if the assignee needs to ask questions, *but don't let him shift the job back to you.*

7. Joint appraisal of the finished product or result.

IMPROVING THE DELEGATED SKILLS OF OTHERS

Management educators repeatedly warn that, in spite of the mass of literature underscoring the benefits of delegation, all too few executives do more than pay it lip service. One of them may be your boss. That gives you a sensitive educational task.

Start by assessing your boss's pressure points—the tasks he likes least, the tasks with tough deadlines, the problems he would like to tackle if he had more time. Make it clear that you understand them.

Present evidence, subtly or directly, that you might tackle some of the tasks *without compromising or neglecting your own job.*

Insure that your performance on the first delegated task, however trifling or complex, is exemplary. If it calls for recommendations, make them clearly and succinctly.

Deliver on time. Only ask for more time when it is warranted, and before it's too late—and justify your request.

If your boss delegates too much, give him the list of tasks and ask him to prioritize them. He will probably delete some.

If this approach doesn't work, try and assess whether your boss is fundamentally unable to delegate because (a) his ego is involved, or he's a perfectionist, (b) he's a work addict, (c) he is too insecure, or (d) he's inexperienced.

Ego problems can sometimes be solved by pointing up the *increased* gains in status that he may achieve through better utilization of his subordinates' abilities. Let him have as much credit as possible. Acknowledge his value and expertise, but let him know that his planning and directing is more important than operating functions.

Dealing with work addicts requires different strategies. Try talking about the things he's missing because he works so hard—partic-

A week is a long time in politics.
Harold Wilson, British prime minister

ularly those which he enjoyed. Help him out when it's obvious he's going to miss a deadline. Workaholics usually resist self-development, so some education may have to be subtly administered. Use conversational opportunities to explore the differences between managing and doing. Tell him you need some stimulation in your own job, and show an appropriate level of dissatisfaction. Workaholics can rarely change their ways, so about the best that can be done is keep pushing to help out in some of the worst pressure areas. Or find another job.

Inexperienced bosses are concerned that people will spot that they're green if they expose themselves too much, so they generally avoid personal contact and the teamwork that delegation demands. If they have been recently promoted, they may have problems in handling old relationships at their new level. Give a new boss time to realign and construct supportive relationships; take every opportunity to let him know that you'll keep him up to date with detail, and that he need not bother with it himself; suggest that you handle one or two projects "until he has a chance to get to them." As his newness wears off he will gradually come out from his shell, particularly if you show a willingness to support him and evidence of dependability.

The insecure boss is probably the worst problem because, for whatever reason, he tries to insulate himself from others. It's worthwhile attempting to break through to him in an informal manner at first, with lunchtime or after-hours conversation. But avoid talking about your own aspirations; never bypass him in your communications, and try to soften his insecurity by being available to help out when needed. Insecure bosses usually make poor managers, so don't get your hopes up that he will change. Perform your function as effectively as possible, and keep your fingers crossed that *his* boss will deal with the problem.

Monday is the moon's day. This personification of the moon is based on one which appeared in a seventeenth-century almanac.

REVERSE DELEGATION

"Dumb is smart"—seek help to solve your problems, but don't rush to solve those of subordinates or you may become a victim of reverse delegation.

One has to be aware of the constant "upward migration" of functional responsibility that takes place in all organizations. It often occurs caused when a concerned manager "fills in" for a subordinate who has dropped the ball. And once it's in his lap, he never manages to get rid of it. Or, as they walk together to a meeting, the ballplayer says to his boss . . . "you know, I think maybe we've got a problem with . . ." The "we" is the giveaway. If his boss gets at all involved at that point, he's hooked. Reverse delegation causes and cures include:

CAUSES	CURES
A subordinate:	
Wants to avoid risk.	Ask, "What's *your* recommendation?"
Is afraid of criticism.	Offer constructive criticism.
Lacks self-confidence.	Give developmental assignments.
Lacks information.	Don't delegate without it.
A manager:	
Wants to feel needed.	It can't be hidden. Get rid of it.
Can't say "No."	Learn to say "No" gracefully.
Has his opinion taken as decision.	Keep emphasizing subordinate responsibility.

There are some occasions when upward delegation can have positive benefits. Reward or praise for one of your subordinates will carry more weight if you ask your boss to handle it. It also makes it clear that you don't keep things to yourself.

If somebody you are about to hire will work with your boss part of the time, invite your boss to participate in the selection process.

Don't hesitate to involve your boss if he has special expertise that can be helpful in solving a problem.

If you plan on making a new policy announcement, either ask your boss to make it or be present when it is made.

Subordinates have a keen sense of what's right and wrong in their delegation system. It's wise to listen to them. This author's studies often disclosed some hard-hitting truths:

"The boss is the biggest time-waster here . . . he talks too much about unimportant stuff . . . he spends too much time checking details . . . you can never get to see him when you need to . . . he has us going round in circles because he keeps moving the goalposts . . . you can never understand his instructions . . . he likes to keep people waiting on him . . . 'Hurry up and wait' is the word around here . . . nobody ever knows where he is . . ." How do your delegation habits stack up?

There comes a point in every manager's life when delegation is the only answer to getting the job done. The red flags are the bulging briefcase that's toted home all too often, the lonely extra hours at the office, the pile of unread literature, the lack of time to plan . . . they're the warning signals that your delegation approach or system is not working. Don't overlook the fact that delegation does not have to be utter or complete—apply only the level that is appropriate. Some managers use a time-saving transmittal slip with papers that indicates what they want:

```
FROM: _____ TO: _____ DATE: ____

PLEASE TAKE ACTION:   No further contact needed

                      Report on results

PLEASE INVESTIGATE:   Report facts only

                      Report facts and recommend
                      action(s)

PLEASE RESPOND BY:    _____
```

Many CEO's consider that effective delegation is the distinguishing factor that has led them to select certain executives for promotion, those with the ability to leverage their time, giving the best possible return on corporate time.

WHAT ABOUT DELEGATION?
TEST ANSWERS

All the statements are false.

DESK TIME

The office environment ·
Planning desk functionality · Desk tools ·
Scheduling desk work

Desk organization, or lack of it, has a major impact on effective time use. Long gone are the days when everybody had to use a rectangular box with drawers. There are important differences in the type of desk needed by an administrator, a manager in sales, and an engineering executive. Workplace design has come into its own and ergonomics, or human-factors engineering, is now permitting manufacturers to produce furniture and workstations that excel in convenience and time-saving features, even for executives who want the ultimate in decor.

Determination of normal work patterns should precede desk and chair selection. To avoid fatigue and back problems, it's important that the chair you use is "human-engineered," as well as being aesthetic. If the lower back is not well supported and pressure is not removed from the thighs, backache and discomfort will slow you down. A high-priced, genuine leather chair is a poor investment unless it adequately supports the body. So is the cheap office chair that has no facility for adjustment.

If you are setting up a new office, consider the entire area, not just the workplace itself. To help in your planning, use a plastic scale layout template (Koh-i-noor 850610 or equivalent) from your stationer.

From which direction will daylight come? Computer screens that reflect windows are tough to work with. Check the possible impact of light on your other tasks too.

How can vertical surfaces be utilized most effectively? Trend charts, marker boards, planning networks, and similar graphic communicators may be placed where they are easily visible . . . and they can act as a focal point for staff meetings, replacing handouts. If necessary, put up a drapery track to cover them and add a softening touch to your office at the same time. Take a good, hard look at your walls; how can you make the best use of them?

What provision must be made for storage of books and files? Inconvenient storage facilities breed cluttered desks and time is lost in searching for mislaid materials.

How will the major tools of your work be accommodated, such as a computer, fax terminal, conference surface, telephone, desk calculator, etc., and how will their electric power cords be handled? How long has it been since anybody *really* studied your needs and matched them to available equipment?

Finally, don't forget the little details: the trashcan, a place for your briefcase, coat, and personal gewgaws (which should *not* be on the desk).

Desk workplaces should be arranged so that eye contact with passers-by is avoided, in order to discourage drop-in visitors. Consider your normal work patterns. They should be integrated with the general area plan and be detailed in advance so that the desk design selection is not made on a purely aesthetic basis. If you organize your workplace in a logical and systematic way, your thinking will follow the same pattern.

Don't wreck a desk's functionality. The area that lies within your reach (about thirty inches) should be protected from the clutter of memorabilia and temporarily stored papers and files. It's too valuable. There's certainly a place for personal items in everyone's habitat, but putting them on the desk is equivalent to putting grandmother's photograph on the kitchen stove.

Next, think about the desk drawers. The pencil drawer can quickly become a catchall because it's the handiest place to stash stuff you don't know what to do with. Avoid that squirrel complex, and keep the junk out of it. Don't start your own office supply operation either, trying to keep a stock of everything ever invented. Use the pencil drawer to put papers out of sight when visitors arrive or for temporary storage of special project materials. For those with computers, the space may perhaps be better used for a retracting keyboard.

Side drawers lend themselves to many creative uses. Sliding letter-trays within them can replace stacked in and out boxes for interaction with a secretary. Sloping compartments can provide easy access to pads, forms, and papers. Transverse file spaces are good for short-term storage of in-process tasks. If necessary, keep a drawer free for papers that you're unable to move forward. If you review

Chinese fire-clock

them weekly, you'll probably find that most of them can get the old heave-ho. Those that can't should be dealt with there and then.

Desk filing must accommodate ten basic categories of materials:

Today   materials that demand immediate attention.

Soon   materials that can be dealt with within a few days.

Never   stuff that may be immediately trashed.

Read   information that is not time critical. (Bulky items, magazines and books may have to go on a shelf or in a cabinet.)

Transmit   papers to go to others with verbal explanation, or with delegated tasks.

Secretary   interactive papers and instructions.

Hold   materials that require more information before they can be processed.

Project   materials for special-purpose activities.

File   materials that must be kept for reference or record.

Whatever your style of workplace, there are some basic operating procedures that can improve the time spent at it. I do *not* recommend those of a senior manager with a reputation for efficiency who was lunching in the corporate cafeteria. A colleague asked, "How do you manage to keep your desk so clear? Mine always seems buried with junk."

"No problem," was the reply. "When I get too much in my in box, I just write 'Refer to Johnson' across it, and send it out. That's the last I see of it, usually."

"That won't work for me, I'm afraid."

"Why not?"

"I'm Johnson."

A better approach is to try and avoid the omnipresent in basket. Have your assistant put new material directly in front of you, and deal with as it arrives. Information materials should come to you in folders. Quickly sort the incoming paperwork into these five categories explained above—*Today*, *Soon*, *Hold*, *Transmit*, and *Never*. Get rid of the last two, and put everything but the *Now* papers into their designated drawers. Don't hold anything that can be gotten elsewhere, if needed. Now you can focus on the urgent stuff, rank it by importance, and deal with it.

It's a good idea to go through your desk once a month and reor-

> Nine-tenths of wisdom consists of being wise in time.
>
> *Theodore Roosevelt*

ganize it to reflect *current* job needs. There is a constantly changing work pattern in everybody's life, and it's important to adjust to it.

Desk Tools

Almost everybody has a desk diary. Some have the company-issue some a Christmas present, and some the one they purchased on impulse the last time they were in a stationery store. Those who work with PCs may have an electronic version. (See *ELECTRONIC TIME*.) Few people make a careful analysis of their job needs before selecting one. Yet the desk diary is one of the most important and essential business tools.

Schools don't teach us how to use diaries to organize our lives effectively. Most of us only note appointments, birthdays, and clothing sizes. Diaries should link career and personal goals, both short- and long-term.

I recommend that you give your desk diary a lot of thought before you buy it, and consider its interaction with a pocket diary. There are numerous diary systems available today, and I would urge you to invest in one that seems suited to your activities and style. Read *PLANNING TIME* for ideas on planning your activities.

Do something about your writing instruments, too. Treat yourself. Go to a good stationery store and find a style of writing instrument that you really like. It doesn't have to be expensive. Make that your standard, and throw out the heterogeneous mass of pens and pencils that quickly fill every recess in the pencil drawer but rarely work right when you need them. (While you're at it, make a note in your pocket diary of any necessary refill numbers.)

Think about all of your tasks in detail, and write a list of the tools needed to perform them properly. Make provision for storage of tools according to their frequency of use. For example, if you often collect and need to refer to business cards, get a card file instead of throwing them into the desk drawer. If you frequently want to file papers in three-ring binders, make sure you have a paper punch close at hand. Get a dispenser for Post-it notes. Then, with desk and workplace organized, you can start taking control of the work flow.

Clean up notes on scrap paper. Transfer them to a plan sheet and assign a task priority. Add new tasks stemming from incoming materials or your own initiative. Cross them off as completed, and enjoy the feeling of accomplishment as you work through them.

I wasted time, and now doth time waste me;
For now hath time made me his numbering clock;
My thoughts are minutes.
   William Shakespeare,
   King Richard II, Act V

If you are forced to interrupt a task, collect up the relevant papers *and put them away*. Fight the tendency to simply place them aside.

Use some type of timer when working at your desk. If your watch does not incorporate an elapsed-time beeper, purchase a small electronic desk timer or a desk clock with such a feature.

Schedule desk work to your advantage. For certain people, the early morning hours are more effective for making telephone connections; others may find the midafternoon preferable. (See *TELEPHONE TIME*.) Getting rid of a few minor matters can get the day off to a good start.

Late morning, for most, is when mental abilities peak. Get a feel for your own internal clock, and tackle the most demanding tasks when your mind is at its best.

Use the late afternoon for planning and interactive activities. One or two days a week, adjust your schedule so that you work beyond five o'clock, adding an extra hour or two of work when everything is quiet. Some executives claim that they do some of their best thinking at those times.

ELECTRONIC TIME

*The development of electronic watches and
time-keeping · Frequency standards ·
Integrated circuit technology · Electronic
time-savers · Personal computers ·
Modems · Information utilities · Facsimile
machines · Cellular telephones · Electronic
pagers · Electronic organizers*

I f one were to have constructed an electronic digital timekeeper
in 1960, it would have filled a closet with a mass of transistors,
six hundred vacuum tubes and other components, and would
have consumed ten kilowatts of power. It was, fortunately, the same
year that Texas Instruments and Fairchild produced integrated cir-
cuits (ICs) using semiconductors, and the electronic watch began to
move from the pages of science fiction toward practical reality. Miniature circuitry was only part of the solution though, because an
electronic device capable of calculating time is useless as a watch
unless it can also "tell," or communicate, the time. That meant
some form of readable display was necessary. The hunt began with
renewed investigation of liquid crystals, which had been discovered
in 1888 but neglected for decades because they used too much
power. While research on that problem continued, scientists at General Electric laboratories discovered a way to convert the infrared
light emitted by gallium arsenide diodes to visible light. The first
light emitting diode (LED) watch displays were developed by George
Theiss and William Crabtree and introduced under the Pulsar name
by Hamilton Watch Company in 1969. In spite of their bulk, they
were commercially successful. Then, in 1971, James Ferguson, a scientist at Kent State University, solved the liquid crystal power problem. He applied the phenomenon of light polarization to make his
tiny liquid crystal display (LCD) work at very low voltages, and the
new age of electronic timekeeping took off.

Electronic watches depend on a frequency standard for their accuracy, in exactly the same fashion as their larger clock brothers, used in international time measurement. (See *CLOCKS*.) A tuning fork oscillator was used in the first Accutron watches, driving a tiny ratchet wheel. A higher-frequency quartz oscillator later became the industry standard. Its high-speed oscillation of about 32,000 times per second is electronically reduced to a one-per-second impulse by an IC.

The balance-wheel oscillator has been used as the frequency standard in mechanical watches since 1790 (see *WATCHES*), controlling the gear train which moves the hands. The tuning fork oscillator uses a ratchet to drive the gear train. Analog watches using quartz oscillators employ a stepping motor to move the hands. Digital electronic watches provide all their information electronically, using a segmented display panel.

Quartz crystals are used as oscillators because they have the remarkable capability of converting their mechanical vibration into an electrical signal. They are called *piezoelectric* crystals. Contrary to some advertisers' claims, quartz watches can become inaccurate due to mechanical shock, just like a fine balance watch. The quartz crystal will recover from a light blow, but dropping a quartz watch four feet onto a hard surface can cause damaging shock.

Integrated circuit technology, which revolutionized the electronics industry in the sixties, is the heart of the electronic watch. Starting in 1965, manufacturers began to supply ICs using a metal element sandwiched between layers of silicon. An area south of San Francisco Bay became the home of the metal oxide semiconductor, or MOS integrated circuit chip, and was promptly christened Silicon Valley.

The ICs not only reduced the oscillator frequency to a useful one-pulse-per-second rate, but also made all of the calculations necessary to display minutes, hours, day and date, etc. Since 1975, this has been accomplished with only one chip, including the "smart" calendar, which automatically recognizes the correct number of days in each month. With little extra circuitry, arithmetic, stopwatch, and other functions can be added.

The IC chip's ability to perform so many tasks perhaps persuaded some manufacturers to go overboard in their watch design. The story is told of the Swiss watch manufacturer who wanted to sell his product to the Soviets. He traveled to Moscow to meet the State Purchasing Commission, and on the way to their office stopped a passer-by in the street to ask the time. Putting down the two heavy cases he was carrying, the man gave the time and then proudly reeled off a mass of additional information about the sun, the moon, the tides, astrological aspects, and the current Five-Year Plan. Impressed and dismayed at the extent of the data displayed by the Russian watch, the Swiss merchant watched as the Muscovite picked up his cases and started on his way. "Those cases sure look heavy," he remarked. "Da. Is batteries, you know," said the Russian.

Fortunately, the advance of technology now makes it possible to operate a watch-function IC with less than one ten-millionth of a watt of electrical power. A watch battery will continuously deliver about forty-millionths of a watt over twelve months, usually lasting at least two years. It is important, by the way, not to substitute hearing-aid batteries for watch batteries, even though they are the same size and can deliver the same voltage. The reason is that hearing-aid batteries are designed for a shorter working life and may leak if their duty-cycle is extended.

The designers of the latest Seiko AGS electronic watches have perhaps moved closer to the perpetual motion machine. They have used the self-winding technology of the mechanical watch to drive a microgenerator that stores electrical energy in a capacitor. In turn, that capacitor powers the quartz oscillator. The result is a "lifetime" watch that will never require a battery.

The first electronic watch displays suffered from poor visibility in low-light conditions. Initial attempts to make them readable by using subminiature light bulbs were a failure. Light-diffusing panels were better, but still used a lot of electrical power. Finally, the radioactive gas tritium was used to energize a phosphor screen, and this provides most of the modern display readouts.

ELECTRONIC TIME-SAVERS

The pace of electronic technology shifted into hypergear as IC miniaturization brought a spate of new products to the marketplace.

Unthinkable a decade ago, today senior executives are working directly with computer terminals, instead of leaving it to others. The personal computer has been groomed through two decades of formative development to become a sophisticated, easy-to-use tool that cuts the time needed to produce, store, and communicate information for everyone. In fact, we are entering an era in which a return to the decentralized pattern of business is again becoming feasible, which may offset some of the negative elements inherent in the separation of workplace and home. (See *LEISURE TIME*.)

The operating speed of PCs now makes software simpler to use, and there is such a wide selection of programs available that anyone who wants to improve their time payoff should invest in a system. It means investing time as well as money, though. A learning process is necessary, not because small computers are difficult to use, but because they can do so many things. The hunt-and-peck method may have been satisfactory for some when typewriters were in vogue, for the difference in output between a trained typist and an amateur was offset by the convenience and neatness of the product, but that does not apply to PCs. Their inherent sophistication is such that, if one is not prepared to put in a minimum of a hundred hours of practice, their value will never be fully realized, and a lode of capability will lie unused. With some time investment, though, a new window on the world will open.

The basic software to manipulate numbers and text are usually the new PC user's first software purchases. For my money, *Lotus 1-2-3*, *WordPerfect*, and *Microsoft Word* are the best if you want the ultimate. But be prepared for the learning process necessary to use their power. Simpler programs are available that may be adequate. The best sources of information on the mass of available programs are computer magazines. You'll waste your time if you expect to get accurate, or even informed, help from most computer stores. Use your local library's index system to locate comparison feature articles in back issues of magazines like *PC World*, *Personal Computing*, etc., and you'll get some quick, concentrated education. You might also read John Bear's *Computer Wimp*.[1] As he puts it, he was "an otherwise intelligent, sensible human being, who was turned into an unhappy, frustrated wimp by his first ten years with small computers, and who has now written a book to spare others his fate."

There are also PC user groups in most communities, comprising knowledgeable individuals who have banded together for self-protection, and their friendly help can save much wasted investigative time.

The recent and continuing improvements in PCs, and particularly in portable, or laptop models, have made them a remarkable tool for better time management and greatly increased productivity. The Compaq SLT/286, for example, is as powerful as most desk-bound machines but is an easily portable, 14.5 lb., battery-operated marvel. It provides 640 kilobytes of memory, a 20-megabyte hard disk, a 3.5-inch disk drive, a backlit VGA screen that displays eight shades of gray, and the convenience of a detachable keyboard.

Like as the waves make towards the pebbled shore,
So do our minutes hasten to their end.
William Shakespeare, Sonnet 60

---

1. Bear, John. *Computer Wimp*. Berkeley, CA: Ten Speed Press, 1983. Revised edition, 1990.

Toshiba has also gained much popularity with their wide range of laptop models, including the new T5200, which will out-perform most desktop computers; the compact 20mb T1600, which weighs only 11.6 pounds but will run large spreadsheet and text programs; and the gutsy little T1000 which, although limited by its one 3.5-inch drive, is still quite powerful.

Armed with one of the many laptop powerhouses, one can continue work at home or on a trip with ease, saving a great deal of time. Accessories that make them even more useful include:

Battery Watch a valuable program that helps users know when batteries are about to die.

Desk Link which quickly transfers data at 19,200 baud between a laptop and another computer.

Expansion bases to convert a laptop into a full-feature desktop PC, with a printer port, accessory slots, and full-size monitor connector.

Miniature copiers such as the Ricoh MC50 which, although only book-sized, will instantly copy anything put beneath it.

Fax capability, to transmit and receive data via telephone. (Ricoh IM-F50.)

Modems

The real power in personal computers today lies in the ability to communicate, via telephone lines, with any other computer system in the world. The device that performs this data transfer, called a modem, may be housed within a microcomputer (with a modem "card") or connected externally. Hayes Smartmodem series is the industry standard, offering 1200- and 2400-baud transmission speeds at modest cost. Higher transmission speeds are also available, with attendant savings in telephone costs.

With a modem installed, you can access a wide range of valuable, time-saving services:

Local authorities and libraries are using modem communication to save time for community residents. In Palo Alto, California, for example, the public library system index can be searched from one's home, allowing the caller to determine availability of any book in the collection. Some communities' city halls are providing direct interaction for residents, eliminating time-consuming personal visits, and, of course, making it easier to pay utility bills and local taxes.

Public Access Message Systems (PAMS), often called "bulletin boards," are run by thousands of computer aficionados across the world. Their telephone numbers are usually to be found in the back of computer magazines or at your local computer store. When you dial and log on to a bulletin board, you can exchange messages with others, copy useful file data provided by another user, browse classified "for sale" and "wanted" lists, engage in keyboard debates, and ask for assistance; all this for the price of the call. The *sysop*, or system operator, will usually provide any information you need on the bulletin board. Most PAMS serve computer users with similar hardware because their program commands all work the same way, but that's not necessary when you hook up to an information utility.

Information Utilities, or *videotex*, are on-line computer services which charge an advertiser or a user for their use. Passive utilities simply allow one to access information; interactive utilities permit user input too. They can provide a wealth of reference information, shopping and banking services, electronic mail and national special-interest group interaction, games, and education at on-line rates of about $12.50 per hour. WARNING: They can be addictive, particularly if young people use them, and telephone bills can become astronomical. Most utilities require a one-time membership fee, but if properly used, it buys a lot:

Communications
Send letters, documents, and files by electronic mail.
Browse national bulletin boards.
Get help with computing problems.
Participate in debate and discussion.

Business Services
Information databases.
Business management information.
Data-processing services.
Engineering data.
Media services.
Legal services.

Financial Services
Market quotations.
Company information.
Banking and brokerage services.
Economic forecasts.
Insurance.
Financial news.

Education Services
Encyclopedia reference.
Government information.
College databases.
Educational games.
Handicapped services.
Services for parents and students.

Computer Services
Hardware and software
forums.
Electronic magazines.
Software catalogs.
Data processing.
User-support services.
New product
announcements.

Entertainment Services
Adventure games.
Multi-player games.
Trivia games.
War games.
Board games.

Travel Services
Travel information.
Airline reservations.
Hotel information.
Tour and cruise information.
Road information.
Travel news.

News Services
Wire service news.
Business news.
Sports news.
Entertainment news.
Weather news.

Home Services
Food and wine information.
Health and fitness guidance.
Personal finances.
Home shopping.
Hobbies.
Arts/music/literature.
Automotive information.

A new service first offered by Prodigy Ineractive Personal Services in 1988 is jointly owned by Sears and IBM. The display screens, as one might expect, are organized like a series of department stores.

The "floors" in the Prodigy Information Building contain a group of different services. Selecting EXTRA EXTRA gives polls, close-ups, and people news; CONSUMER gives product ratings for appliances, automobiles, electronic products, and food items; WEATHER gives a national weather map, plus regional forecasts; SPORTS gives news, scores, and statistics; BUSINESS gives industry and market news, and stock quotations; NEWSROOM gives national and local news briefs; and LOBBY gives information about Prodigy services and membership.

Selecting a "floor" will bring up another screen with detailed information on the selected subject or will permit interactive communication through the Prodigy Message Center. One can, for example, ask a question about movies and receive an expert answer, or make an airline travel reservation through the EEASY SABRE system after scanning national airline schedules. The Prodigy system is constantly being expanded, so program descriptions may

```
INFORMATION

                      New Floor:

                      To move to another
                      level in this building
                      use [TAB]. At the desired
                      floor, press [RETURN]


 EXTRA EXTRA
 CONSUMER              New Building:
 WEATHER
 SPORTS               To move to another
 BUSINESS             building, select [MENU]
 NEWSROOM             and then press [RETURN]
 LOBBY

        MENU PATH JUMP              EXIT
```

The "floors" in the Prodigy Information Building contain a group of different services. Selecting EXTRA EXTRA gives polls, close-ups and people news; CONSUMER gives product ratings for appliances, automobiles, electronic products, and food items; WEATHER gives a national weather map, plus regional forecasts; SPORTS gives news, scores, and statistics; BUSINESS gives industry and market news, and stock quotations; NEWSROOM gives national and local news briefs; and LOBBY gives information about Prodigy services and membership.

change. Call Prodigy Membership Services (1-800-759-8000) if you want the latest information.

Facsimile (Fax) Machines

Fax machines, which use telephone lines to speed exact duplicates of documents from one location to another, have actually been around since the turn of the century, but until recently were so bulky and expensive that they were used only by businesses with high-volume needs.

In the last decade, IC technology has brought their cost and size within almost everyone's reach, while improving their speed and reliability. Today, there are more than 2.5 million fax machines worldwide, and a million of them are in use in the United States.

Manufacturers such as Ricoh, Sharp, Murata, Savin, Pitney-Bowes, and Canon offer a range of time-saving products:

Ricoh's RF900 is an integrated desktop fax/telephone unit with an additional copier function and a seven-page memory that acts as a backup for incoming transmissions and provides document storage to reduce sending time. It will transmit an $8\frac{1}{2} \times 11$ page in twenty seconds.

By connecting the Ricoh DX-1 external adaptor unit between an IBM AT, PS/2 or MacIntosh computer, one can extend the capability of a basic fax machine to serve additionally as a computer printer, image scanner, and optical character reader. A page of printed text put into the fax machine thus may not only be transmitted at user-specified times, but also may be directly transferred to a computer with full editing capability. This time-saving feature is accomplished through conversion software from Pattern Analytics.

Ricoh's MC50 portable copier/digitizer with the IM-A image controller/scanner.

For business travelers, Ricoh's Portable Digital Information System is worth investigating. It's a book-sized portable reducing/enlarging copier (MC50), with accessories that will also fax and transfer documents to an IBM or compatible computer graphics file. It weighs just three pounds, including the rechargeable battery. A portable 9.8 lb. fax/telephone/copier with optional carrying case is also available from Ricoh, with the same transmission speed as the RF900. The telephone can be programmed for manual or unattended reception and has a fifteen-number memory with autodialer. A built-in timer may be used to transmit during low-rate night and weekend hours, and the unit maintains an automatic record of use and transaction confirmation.

The Sharp UX350 provides two separate lists of twelve numbers which may be stored in the autodialer, contrast control, unattended operation and the option of connection with an answering machine, ten-page document feeder, sheet cutter, and activity and transaction reports.

The Canon FaxPhone 15 is an 8.4 lb. portable unit featuring speed-dialing, last number redialing, on-hook dialing, monitor speaker with volume control, five-sheet document feeder, and activity and transmission reports. It has a sheet transmission speed of thirty seconds.

The Savin SB-2000 permits an IBM or compatible personal computer to become a fax machine, with ability to transmit text and graphics, through the installation of an expansion card. This reduces time by permitting the transmission or receipt of a document without the necessity of printing it. With an accessory scanner (Savin SP-2100), a document may be transferred to the PC memory, viewed in graphics mode, and transmitted. Using the computer printer, incoming documents may be printed on bond paper.

Another Savin product, the SX-1500, has an open platen instead of a sheet feeder, which permits the copying and faxing of bulky materials such as books and magazines.

The Murata M1600 is a lower-priced basic fax/telephone/copier with thirty-number autodialer, monitor speaker, sheet-fed copier, and transmission and activity reporting capability.

Pitney-Bowes 7100 is a high-quality, compact unit with outstanding print quality, a five-sheet feeder, and unattended automatic operation. It can communicate with other Pitney-Bowes office equipment to automatically distribute fax transmissions to nearly one hundred recipients.

Cellular Telephones

Since the FCC authorized the use of cellular telephones, drivers have switched from personal grooming to communications as they hit the commuter lanes. The ability to use travel time more usefully has become so popular that the FCC recently increased the number of channels available to 832. That means that, unless one wants to wait in line for an open channel, one should now only buy a mobile cellular telephone with a full channel capability. The Tandy/Radio Shack CT-101, at about $800, is one of the lowest-priced automobile units available with acceptable quality. Other, more expensive units offer complete portability with rechargeable battery operation. Although cellular phones can save a remarkable amount of time, calls are expensive, particularly when one dials out of the local area and a "roam-rate" is applied. To combat these costs, the Oki Phone 700 offers registration in the two areas between which most calls will be made, to escape the roam surcharge. A call timer is also provided.

The first triple-use cellular phone is available from Audiovox, the people who install the phones in BMWs. The Audiovox CTX-5000 is a powerful 3-watt mobile phone in the car, with hands-free operation. As you leave the car, it may be quickly disconnected and slipped into a briefcase, where it operates with built-in battery power at 0.6 watts. For use in a cottage or boat, a transportable battery-pack boosts its power back to 3 watts.

For those whose lives and pocketbooks have become so filled that they need the ultimate cellular phone, relief is only four figures away. That will buy a GoFax Spectrum Cellular phone/fax unit. The GoFax 88 is a compact 9 lb., 12 v./110 v. unit that will transmit a page in forty seconds at 4800 baud. An internal battery allows it to be unplugged and carried with you as you travel.

Electronic Pagers

Mobile executives now have four kinds of electronic pagers to choose from: those that simply beep, requiring a call to obtain the caller's number; voice pagers that beep and transmit a brief message; numeric pagers that display a number to call; and alphanumeric pagers that can receive, store, and display a message. Some pagers may be used to provide personal alert signals by dialing in a call to yourself to be sent at a certain time.

Some of the most sophisticated pagers are obtainable from companies such as Cue Nationwide Paging, which covers the entire United States. Their units start paging with a quiet tone which becomes louder until answered or a flashing light. A code number is displayed which categorizes the caller, followed by his or her telephone number. The number is retained in memory and may be used for automatic dialing by holding the pager to a touch-tone phone.

British Telecom's Metrocast system provides a range of message options, unattended message reception and storage, and a personal alarm feature.

National Satellite Paging, although their system does not cover the entire country, uses a signal which can penetrate office buildings better than many of its competitors. Their services also include voice-messaging, wherein one dials an 800 number to leave or receive a stored voice message.

Electronic Organizers

Small, battery-powered voice recorders have been used by busy executives for many years to simplify note-taking, and permit them to capture ideas and conversations on the spot. One of the most popular units is the Olympus S930, which features voice-activated control, an easily-readable LCD status display, and the ability to automatically encode recording time and date. For many, these handy idea-traps are adequate, but for those who want more in their pocket, one of the new electronic organizers may be the thing.

First introduced in 1987, these new organizers are actually pocket-sized microcomputers, designed specifically for those whose time is at a premium. They can store more information than you can believe, as well as providing other time-saving features.

The Psion Organizer II/CM, measuring only 3 in. wide by 5.6 in. long by 1.1 in. thick, packs an 8K random access memory to handle personal filing, appointment scheduling, and special programs; a 32K ROM containing the operating system, OPL language and applications software, diary, calculator, and clock with nine alarm presets; a two-line, sixteen-character display; a thirty-six-pad multi-function keyboard; two miniature "datapak drives"; interfaces for RS232 9600 baud COMMS-LINK, barcode and magnetic card reader, and 9 v. battery giving up to six months operation. (An AC adapter is also available.)

The system is unique in that it permits one to plug in any two of a series of miniature solid-state program modules, which perform the same function as a floppy disk and provide unlimited storage of programs and data. They may be edited or erased. The optional program modules include:

> *Travel-Pak* comprising a language translator, expense record, world time clock, itinerary tracker, international dial codes, metric/U.S./ imperial conversion, clothing-size and currency conversion, and personal data file.

The race is not to the swift, nor the battle to the strong, neither yet bread to the wise nor yet riches to men of understanding nor yet favor to men of skill, but time and chance happeneth to them all.

Ecclesiastes 9:11–12

Spelling Checker with a 24,000-word database from the *Oxford English Dictionary.*

Diary Link to exchange diary information with any IBM compatible PC, interfaces with Borland's *Sidekick.*

Formulator providing more than 250 formulas used in finance, mathematics, physics, chemistry, electronics, navigation, plus a hexadecimal converter and faculty for custom formulas.

Spreadsheet a full-function 99-row by 26-column, *Lotus 1–2–3* compatible spreadsheet utility.

Finance Pak containing a series of programs covering banking records, expense control and allocation, interest rate and NPV calculation, bond yields, mortgage and APR calculations.

Portfolio created for the private investor, enables recording and updating of all securities, and complete portfolio management with preset buy/sell indicators, price tracking and trading position information.

Accessories include a COMMS-LINK to connect the Organizer II with printers, modems, Apple/IBM and compatible personal computers, and a directly-connected thermal printer.

The Sharp WIZARD Organizer (OZ-7000) delivers a wide range of functions, including a calendar, appointment book, telephone directory, calculator, memo pad, and world clock. Integrated circuit cards provide additional software for language translation, a thesaurus/dictionary, and a time/expense manager. The Wizard features an eight-line, sixteen-character liquid crystal display, and permits data transfer to another Wizard, a printer, or personal computer.

The Casio BOSS Organizers (SF-series) feature wide thirty-two-column, six-line screens, 32K or 64K RAM, depending on model, and two keyboard styles. Although not programmable, built-in programs include telephone directory, business card library, memo storage, schedule tracker, calendar, world clock, and calculator. Interface with an IBM or compatible PC requires a separate accessory module.

The British AgendA organizer is a slim, power-packed product that uses a new "microwriting" feature in addition to a normal keypad. Ingenious combinations of finger pressure, based on the shapes of letters, speeds up data entry on a five-key ergonomic pad designed to fit the fingers and thumb of the right hand. To microwrite an L, for example, the thumb, first and fourth fingers are used. High-speed data entry is possible with a little practice.

The AgendA provides telephone/address and other data files that can be searched by any word they contain (and the files may be transferred and printed out in any format required through connection to an external PC and printer), an appointment diary and daily action list with audible alarms, and a built-in word processor for notes and letters.

The AgendA electronic organizer.

Special program cards are available to convert the AgendA into a language translator or a number-crunching, programmable calculator for sophisticated amortization and cash flow procedures. For security backup, the entire database can be copied onto a tiny memory card in a few seconds for safe storage. In case of loss or damage to the AgendA unit, all data can then immediately be replaced.

Dimensions: 6.9 in. long; 3.375 in. wide; .75 in. thick. Weight: 11.5 ozs. Internal 9 v. NiCad rechargeable or disposable battery power supply. (Removable RAM security storage cards have long-life lithium batteries.) 80-character (4 lines × 20) display. 32K memory, expandable to 64K. Internal 100-year clock/calendar with audible alarms. Parallel and RS232C serial interface cables.

Although too big for a pocket, the Laser PC3 is a miniature portable computer with an impressive range of features, including address/telephone directory, expense account file, appointment and scheduling diary with four audible alarms, word processor with spelling checker, automatic telephone dialer, typing tutor, and PC interconnect capability. Weighing slightly over one and a half pounds, the Laser PC3 measures 10 in. by 7.6 in. by 1.3 in., with a 40-character, two-line display, 32K memory, serial and Centronics parallel interface, and cassette backup interface. Power is provided by four AA batteries or AC adaptor, and expansion program cartridges are available.

Now that electronic technology has put these time management tools into our hands, it brings closer the vision of Yoneji Masuda, the Japanese architect of the Plan for an Information Society. He described time management as "painting one's design on the invisible canvas of one's future, and then setting out to create it."[2]

By all means, let us simplify the means of controlling time and the myriad details of our lives, but let us vigorously preserve our responsibility to direct our lives toward *human accomplishment*, rather than the pure accumulation of information. That's the challenge and promise of electronic time.

See also *SCHEDULING TIME, LEISURE TIME, ORGANIZING TIME, TIME PAYOFF ANALYSIS.*

---

2. Masuda, Yoneji. *The Information Society*. Washington, D.C.: World Future Society, 1980, p. 3.

EXECUTIVE TIME

*Executive work patterns and time use ·
The basic elements of time allocation · The
differences between "managing" and "doing"
with self test · Function analysis · Activity
patterns and functions · Secretaries ·
Executive body clocks · Communications
time · Executives' time-wasters*

On any morning, as they drive or ride to their offices, thousands of executives are worrying about more effective use of their time. Take, for example, George Baker III who is president of U.S.A., Inc., forty-seven, and a college graduate. On a typical working day, he drives seventy-five minutes to and from his place of business. His work consumes fifty-three hours of his week. Although he sometimes works at home (about five hours each week, on the average), he also fits five hours of leisure, exercise, or educational activity into most days. He's reasonably satisfied with his balance of work, play, and sleep.

His working day is not so well organized. Since he has never kept track, George is not able to say exactly where his day goes. He worries that he never seems to have enough time for the things that he knows are important, such as long-range strategic planning, building support in the financial world, and foreign market penetration.

Although he is most productive when left alone, he can't seem to get enough uninterrupted work time. The telephone constantly disrupts his concentration, even though his secretary does her best to prevent it. Meetings seem to drag on too long and accomplish too little. As most of his employees are leaving for the day, George is often to be found wading through paperwork, trying to figure out where the last eight hours went, and kidding himself that he works better when there's nobody around.

This morning, he parks his car, and walks briskly into the office. He unloads a bulging briefcase, calls in his secretary, and together they start on the urgent correspondence. In the middle of the second

letter, his thoughts are interrupted by a telephone call that should have been given to his engineering VP. But as he's connected, he answers it. The ensuing discussion takes ten minutes. His secretary waits patiently until he hangs up, then they start in again. After a few minutes' work, she reminds him that the sales meeting should start, and he dismisses her to check his "must do" list for the day before everyone arrives. A dozen calls to make, two meetings, and lunch with the new marketing director. Not scheduled, but weighing on his mind, is the need to go over the third-quarter figures. As nobody has yet come in, he grabs the opportunity to quickly return an urgent call, only to become frustrated while they try to find his man; his visitors file in and sit awkwardly in silence. Annoyed, he hangs up with an apology. The meeting, set up to plan an upcoming trade show, is diverted while the budget director blows off steam about late quarterly budget forecasts . . . and the day is off, with its usual complement of crises, disappointments, and successes.

If the scenario sounds familiar, it isn't surprising. To learn more about executive time usage, I surveyed more than six hundred midwestern and western executives. The results reflect the opinions of 14 board chairmen, 358 presidents, 142 vice-presidents, and 121 general managers, representing most major industries. For instance I discovered that nearly a third of the younger executives say that they work ten or more hours a day, but less than 10 percent of those in their sixties put in the same amount of time.

Not surprisingly, travel or commuting time was a problem for most executives, and travel delays were particularly aggravating, especially for the seven out of ten who drove to work.

The data also showed that the top executive rarely gets enough time alone; he spends more than half of his business day listening or talking to somebody, yet his meetings often seem unproductive. His average time between interruptions is about seven minutes. He's concerned about people problems, subordinates' errors, their tendency to underestimate time and resource requirements, and the resulting crises. These are the interfering elements that cause seventy-two out of a hundred executives to express serious concern about their lack of time to think and plan.

> Time is dead as long as it is being clicked off by little wheels; only when the clock stops does time come to life.
> *William Faulkner*

EXECUTIVE TIME CONTROL AND ALLOCATION

Analysis shows that, despite a functional title that suggests the opposite, all too many executives do not, in fact, control as much of their own time as they think they do. It breaks down into three basic elements:

System-controlled Time   Time spent playing ball with the internal and external systems with which the business is linked and operates.

People-controlled Time   The unavoidable time demands imposed by directors, bosses, customers, subordinates, etc.

Self-controlled Time   The time when an executive finally gets to use his or her brain to the utmost. The amount of time that is moved to this category distinguishes the successful executive.

It becomes necessary to reverse Parkinson's Law,[1] and squeeze the first two time categories, in order to create more self-controlled, or discretionary, time and to make one's work *contract* to fit the available time. The best use of training and experiential skills is only obtained by controlling one's working day.

Peter Drucker, author of *The Effective Executive*, says that he has seldom found a senior executive who controls *as much as 25 percent of his time*, and he believes that the higher they are on the totem pole the worse it gets.

The problem often stems from the fact that the line between "managing" and "doing" has become faded or erased. People and the system have both invaded the executive function to the point that it is hardly recognizable. Managing and operating functions are spelled out below.

The average person is in a fairly good mood when they get to work in the morning, but that mood rapidly deteriorates, hitting a low between 10 and 11 A.M. Although spirits improve at lunchtime, the cycle repeats itself as soon as work is resumed, becoming more intense until the worker reaches absolute bottom at 3:30. Some companies have experimented with piping in lively music to counteract the blahs.

The Management Functions

Planning   Forecasting, developing strategies, setting objectives, budgeting, and establishing policies and schedules.

Organizing   Building the organization structure, defining relationships, describing functional positions and their criteria for qualification, and identifying resources.

Staffing   Selecting, orienting, training, and developing.

Directing   Delegating, motivating, coordinating, and managing changes.

Controlling   Establishing a database and reporting system, setting performance standards, measuring results, taking corrective action, and rewarding performance.

---

1. "Any given task will expand to fill the time available."

Decision Making Fact-gathering, problem definition, goal-setting, determining alternatives, evaluating consequences, choosing courses of action and implementing them.

Communicating Transmitting information, testing reception, clarifying meanings, checking feedback, developing internal and external constituencies, investigating, and monitoring.

The Operating Functions

Production Production planning and control, plant engineering and maintenance, industrial engineering, purchasing, manufacturing, and quality control.

R & D Basic and applied research and development in products and methods.

Marketing Research, planning, sales, advertising, and distribution.

Finance Resource control, tax management, credit, collections, and insurance.

Control Accounting, budget development, auditing, and systems and procedures.

Personnel Administration Employee services, compensation administration, training, industrial relations, and organizational planning and development.

External Relations Public and investor relations, civic affairs, and association and community affairs.

Legal Corporate legal affairs, patents, and board of directors' activities.

After you've read the list of functions, you can check the clarity of your understanding with the *MANAGING vs DOING* test that follows. Then you may want to review your own activities and weed out the tasks that you should really not be doing. Most business manuals point out the dangers of "reverse delegation"—the uncanny ability of subordinates to delegate their tasks *upwards*. Others describe the apparent inability of some executives to quit doing the things that they liked as they climbed the managerial ladder, but which don't belong on the top person's desk.

"MANAGING" VERSUS "DOING" TEST

Examine the tasks described below, and check whether you think they are "managing" or "doing" in the columns provided. Then compare your answers with those at the end of the chapter.

1. Explaining to one of your people why he or she is getting a raise.   MANAGING   DOING

2. Calling on a customer with one of your people to demonstrate that the company's top management is interested in their customers.   MANAGING   DOING

3. Deciding whether to add a staff position to your organization.   MANAGING   DOING

4. Reviewing periodic reports to find out how progress toward specific objectives is being achieved in your area of responsibility.   MANAGING   DOING

5. Deciding what the financial budget should be for your area of responsibility.   MANAGING   DOING

6. Interviewing a prospective employee referred to you by a friend.   MANAGING   DOING

7. Attending an industry conference to learn about the latest technical developments.   MANAGING   DOING

8. Meeting with a consultant to design a new profit-sharing plan.   MANAGING   DOING

9. Asking one of your people his opinion on an idea you have for his department.   MANAGING   DOING

10. Entertaining the president of an important supplier.   MANAGING   DOING

11. Making a speech to the Jaycees about your company's plans for the future.   MANAGING   DOING

12. Approving a request for a routine expenditure.   MANAGING   DOING

13. Explaining a bonus plan to your people.	MANAGING	DOING
14. Calling some of your business friends to gain their opinions on a new marketing idea you've developed.	MANAGING	DOING
15. Determining the date on which the move to a new plant will take place.	MANAGING	DOING

THE EXECUTIVE
PARADOX

Executives have nothing
to do because they
only tell others to do
things, listen to the
reasons why they can't
be done, discover they
haven't been done, in-
sist that they're done,
then discover that
they've been done
wrong. They realize
that they could have
done them in half an
hour instead of spend-
ing two days trying to
figure out why others
took two weeks to
achieve nothing, but
that, of course, would
give them something
to do.

Undoubtedly, for whatever reason, there will be some pruning that you can do in your own bailiwick, and there's no better time than the present. Don't be afraid of excising something essential. It rarely happens, because most of us tend to overrate our importance and think that we are the only ones who can do certain things. If you do overprune, correction can be made quickly.

The scope of an executive function may also be fuzzy because there are different sights that may be trained upon it. First, there is the job as it really is now; second, what you think it is; third, what others think it is; and fourth, what it ideally should be.

The person at the top has the responsibility of running the ship, but if one dithers between the bridge and the boiler room, one may find that the head of steam created is only propelling one's vessel in circles. Get your job back in focus at least once a year, and keep only the absolute essentials. If there's still too much to do, hire somebody.

Start by defining the *real* ends toward which your efforts should be directed. If you wish, you can use the Function Analysis Worksheet (a reproducible form will be found in Appendix B). It's a useful analysis tool that can help in achieving a better payoff on your time. If you've never tackled this sort of thing before, it may not be easy. But it will be well worth the effort.

On the worksheet, list all of your functional responsibilities and/or goals and if possible, get other people's input and comments. You may also find it useful to read *TIME TARGETING* before you begin. Be realistic in describing responsibilities, and avoid idealistic goals that stand little or no chance of accomplishment.

Discern between the things you do personally, and those you accomplish by managing others. Don't confuse responsibilities with activities. "Participate in budget review meetings" is not a valid entry; "Insure that budgets stay within 5 percent of forecast" is. Keep in mind that if there is no apparent way of measuring the result of an activity, it is not worth doing. The measurement factors are all-important.

The work load in most functions varies in direct relationship to business cycles, and it's often useful to get a fix on this. (One interesting recent discovery, by the way, is that accountants' cholesterol levels rise as April 15th approaches.) With the list of responsibilities that contribute to a crunch period before you, it may be possible to move one or two of them and even out the load. The columns marked D (daily), W (weekly), M (monthly), and A (annually) are for this purpose. Applying the appropriate multiplier to the "totals" line will give you a reading of your estimated total work load.

The VALUE column is used to rate the importance of each listed item. Rate them from 1 to 5, with 1 indicating those items that would be useful if you had time for them, intermediate numbers for different levels of "ought to do," and 5 for essentials.

If you have some control over distribution of responsibilities in your organization, the LIKE/DISLIKE column will help in pinpointing items that could be prime candidates for delegation or elimination.

The D column permits one of three entries: DUMP, or eliminate; DELEGATE or spin-off; or DO, meaning that nobody but yourself can bear that particular responsibility.

When you have your functions outlined (and it may need more than one attempt before you have it down to your satisfaction), take the appropriate steps with those items you will dump or delegate, and transfer the remaining DO responsibilities or goals to the *TIME PAYOFF ANALYSIS* chapter which will provide the time-allocation guide necessary for their attainment.

> To lose time is most displeasing to him who knows most.
> *Dante*, The Inferno

EXECUTIVES' BUSINESS MEETINGS

Although the executives in the group surveyed averaged seven major business meetings each week, there was a wide individual range, with some respondents participating in more than twenty.

Correlation between the number of people present and overall meeting time shows that meetings with a small number of participants take up less time, in general, than those with more than six participants. The implication, as the relative importance of the meetings was judged equal, is that too many people are invited to too many meetings for too little purpose. See *MEETING TIME* for more exploration of this subject.

EXECUTIVE SECRETARIES

It appears that the delegation of letter-writing to secretaries is not practiced by a majority of executives, although more do it in larger companies than in small firms.

SECRETARIES WHO WRITE LETTERS
FOR THEIR BOSS
By Company Size

COMPANY SIZE	RARELY	OCCASIONALLY	FREQUENTLY
Under $250,000	45.8%	45.8%	8.3%
$250–$500,000	41.4	44.8	13.8
$500–$1 Million	41.2	41.2	17.7
$1–$5 Million	37.3	43.9	18.9
$5–$10 Million	40.8	42.1	17.1
Over $10 Million	33.3	43.3	23.3

This does not tell us whether or not the secretarial function tends to be dictated by tradition rather than need. It's worthwhile to explore the redefinition of the "executive support task" beyond the technological replacement of typewriters with word processors.

The escalating costs of hard-copy correspondence—nine dollars or more per letter today—make the alternative means of electronic communication well worth serious investigation. *COMMUNICATION TIME* will provide more information.

EXECUTIVE BODY CLOCKS

Scientific studies continue to underscore the importance of understanding one's "body clock." A surprisingly large number of executives in the survey claimed that they work best in the very early morning—between 6 and 9 A.M. This is not necessarily due to bio-

PERIOD DURING WHICH EXECUTIVES
FEEL THEY WORK BETTER

A.M.			P.M.		
12–6	6–9	9–12	124	4–8	8–12
0.68%	28.60	48.28	9.38	8.46	4.57

rhythmic influence, as most people operate better between 9 and 11 in the morning, but early risers feel they get a head start on the day before the usual pattern of interruptions begins. You will find *BODY TIME* and *BIORHYTHMS* cover this interesting aspect of time. It makes sense to handle tasks that don't need a lot of brain capacity when mental energy is at a low ebb, when your mood is bad, when you have only a few minutes, and when risk of interruption is high. That's the time to deal with the no-brainers waiting in your file drawer or your reading file.

EXECUTIVES' TIME LOGS
AND SCHEDULES

Although an accurate picture of where one's time is going would seem to be an important step in improving functional effectiveness, evidence continues to show that a very large number of business men and women deceive themselves about their time allocation. The survey explored this, disclosing that those executives with higher educational levels, and those working in larger companies, are more likely to use some form of time recording. Recommendations in this area may be found by reading *RECORDING TIME*.

EXECUTIVES' COMMUNICATIONS

More than half of all executives surveyed complain that the way the telephone is used continues to "disrupt their schedule or decrease their efficiency." Most of the problem stems from the *timing* of calls, which more often than not interfere with periods of concentration, rather than *length* of calls. Higher-level executives are generally quite skilled in curtailing time-wasting pleasantries while on the phone. *TELEPHONE TIME* deals with this in greater depth.

In spite of the "open line" policy promoted by telephone companies, many executives ask their secretaries to control their telephone traffic.

HOW SECRETARIES HANDLE EXECUTIVES' TELEPHONE CALLS

	SECRETARIES SCREEN INCOMING CALLS	SECRETARIES PLACE OUTGOING CALLS
Rarely	27.3%	3.2%
Occasionally	21.2	5.7
Frequently	14.2	15.0
Almost Always	37.3	76.1

Executives' written communications show a much higher level of longhand content than might be expected, although the traditional dictation methods are succumbing to the inroads of electronic technology and local area computer networks.

EXECUTIVES AND MEETINGS

Although meetings are essential to the conduct of any business, a high proportion of the executives surveyed had poor opinions of them, no matter what size of company.

What frustrates executives in meetings? The table on the following page indicates their feelings clearly. It might be worthwhile circulating the list within your own organization.

The planning and review functions are regarded by most executives as those which depend primarily on meetings. The tables on the following page show the frequency of such meetings in various-sized companies.

HOW MEETINGS BOTHER EXECUTIVES

	FACTOR	EXECUTIVES WHO ARE "BOTHERED A LOT"
BY:	Length of time taken	60.0%
	People drifting off subject	82.7
	People not participating	51.1
	Emotional outbursts	41.3
	Participants lack of preparation	77.2
	People's wordiness	62.1
	People not listening	67.5
	Questionable effectiveness	73.9

FREQUENCY OF REVIEW MEETINGS
By Company Size

	NEVER	DAILY	WEEKLY	MONTHLY	QUARTERLY
Under $250,000	3.2%	28.6%	27.0%	11.1%	1.6%
$250–$500,000	3.8	38.5	42.3	11.5	3.8
$500–$1 Million	2.8	26.4	48.6	19.4	2.8
$1–$5 Million	0	30.8	43.8	18.8	6.7
$5–$10 Million	2.7	33.3	48.0	13.3	2.6
Over $10 Million	5.4	28.9	46.3	17.4	2.0

FREQUENCY OF PLANNING MEETINGS
By Company Size

	NEVER	DAILY	WEEKLY	MONTHLY	QUARTERLY
Under $250,000	2.2%	15.6%	28.9%	37.8%	15.6%
$250–$500,000	11.3	11.3	32.1	26.4	18.9
$500–$1 Million	2.9	13.0	29.0	33.3	21.7
$1–$5 Million	2.0	5.9	28.3	36.6	10.2
$5–$10 Million	1.3	6.5	32.5	32.5	27.3
Over $10 Million	4.0	8.7	27.3	32.7	27.3

EXECUTIVES' TIME-WASTERS

Here is a ranking of the things which the surveyed executives believe contribute most to reducing their effectiveness:

How executives rank those things that reduce their personal effectiveness:

1. Smoothing over "people problems"
2. Other people's refusal to make decisions
3. Having to correct subordinate's work
4. Having nobody to whom details can be delegated
5. Underestimating task/time requirements
6. Coping with unanticipated demands
7. Local travel delays

Conversely, these items are considered most important in upgrading executive effectiveness:

What executives believe improves their lives:

1. Capable subordinate managers
2. Careful personal planning
3. An efficient secretary
4. Getting good reports
5. Shutting off the telephone
6. Keeping visitors at a minimum
7. Becoming skilled in dictating
8. Getting away from the office
9. Taking work home
10. Using public transportation

The higher up the corporate ladder an executive is, the harder it is to make judicious use of his or her time. They have to balance community responsibilities and ceremonial responsibilities, like inspection tours and awards presentations. They have to bear responsibility for any problem that arises, digest reports, establish policies and communication channels, settle conflicts, and provide for organization renewal. They must also keep up with the industry, improve innate skills, think, plan, and initiate.

Allocating the right amount of time to these complex, interlocking responsibilities is the greatest challenge. If one tries to apportion time by some sort of intuitive "feel," it will endanger one's success and that of the organization. And if one believes that one can accomplish it all by simply investing more energy, one should look up the statistics on executive ulcer and heart attack rates.

Executives have one principle that can make their time-allocation task easier—that of the famous Vilfredo Pareto. His observation that "the significant items in any group constitute a relatively small percentage of the total" works in time management, as well as in countless other situations. It means that 80 percent of results will come from 20 percent of your time. The rest of your time will be absorbed by trivialities. The challenge, of course, is to know one from the other, and the information and tools described in this book will help.

The usual distribution of executive time today is shown in the pie chart. But we live in an ever-changing business world, and there's no reason to believe that the pace of change will slow. By keeping an eye on time allocation, you can make these changes work for you.

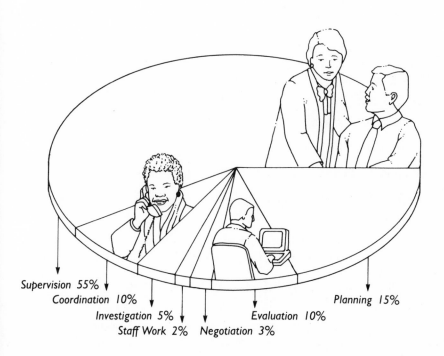

Supervision 55%
Coordination 10%
Investigation 5%
Staff Work 2%   Negotiation 3%   Evaluation 10%
Planning 15%

Simplification of communications, constant activity review, insulation, and delegation hold most of the answers, once an escape from people-imposed and system-imposed tasks has been accomplished. Keep decision making simple and don't involve more people than necessary. Pay what it takes to get good staff support. The difference in cost between a semi-skilled secretary and a top-notch administrative assistant is far outweighed by the cost of your wasted time. Insure that delegated tasks are completely understood before they are begun.

Executives may have problems controlling time use, but they also have the autonomy and opportunity to do something about it.

"MANAGING" VERSUS "DOING" ANSWERS

It's not easy to separate managing from doing in the normal day's work. Here's what the experts say about the list of tasks that you have analyzed:

1. *Managing* This is a motivating activity, and is part of the *directing* function (which also includes delegating, coordinating, and managing changes).

2. *Doing* Although perhaps necessary, this type of a call is not getting results through others, but rather a direct selling or public relations activity.

3. *Managing* This is a part of the *organizing* function of management, focused on the structure of the business entity.

4. *Managing* This is evaluation.

5. *Managing* Developing a budget is part of the *planning* job.

6. *Doing* The final decision to hire a new employee, *after* the screening and evaluation has been done, is a managerial task.

7. *Doing* The work "technical" gives the clue here, that the executive will get better results him or herself than through others.

8. *Doing* Designing a profit-sharing plan is a staff activity. Its approval would be a managing activity.

9. *Managing* This is part of the managerial *communicating* function, aimed at developing a program. It also has motivating elements.

10. *Doing* This is a *communicating* function.

11. *Doing* This is part of the *external relations* function.

12. *Doing* Since the expenditure is "routine," its approval should be delegated, and an appropriate audit procedure established to periodically insure that correct procedure is followed.

13. *Managing* Another example of the *communicating* function which, in this case, also permits the testing of reception, and the clarification of possible misunderstanding.

14. *Doing* Market research should be left to external or staff experts.

15. *Managing* This is part of the *decision making* function, and sets a specific course. (Other elements of this function include data-gathering, problem definition, goal-setting, selection of alternatives, and implementation.)

FILING TIME

The hidden costs in filing · File systems time and cost analysis · Subject classification methods · System management · Personal filing · Archival storage

Anybody who has started a business from scratch with a trial-and-error filing system rapidly learned what a time trap it can become. There are 1.2 million sheets of paper filed per minute in the United States, and our first-timer probably contributes by quickly setting up an A–Z file. *Wrong.* They probably hit the local office supply store and then, jolted by the prices, settle for the cheapest four-drawer file cabinet and file folders they could find. *Wrong again.* They end up with the most expensive file system they could buy.

Unfortunately, these mistakes are made not only by budding entrepreneurs, but also by very large organizations. Manufacturers know that space issues usually govern the purchasing decision for file systems, while in actuality space is only a minor part of the cost of storing and maintaining records and information. Keeping the lid on the cost of filing means keeping an eye on file maintenance time.

CHECK THE HIDDEN COSTS IN FILE EQUIPMENT

Work studies have shown that there are significant differences in access and retrieval time between plain or hanging files and lateral color-coded systems. It may be worth your time to compare the cost of your filing system, using the worksheet on the following page. Linear file-inch (LFI) costs to operate a four-drawer file system are around $20.50 per year; a seven-level databox file costs $7.00. Multiply those figures by the total LFI in your office, and it can add up to a staggering difference. For example, it takes four times longer to

FILE SYSTEM TIME
AND COST ANALYSIS WORKSHEET

(All figures are calculated on an annual basis.)

	PRESENT SYSTEM	LATERAL SYSTEM	_____ SYSTEM

FLOOR SPACE
Floor space cost per square foot: $_____
Floor space cost per file cabinet............ $_____ $_____ $_____

EQUIPMENT
Cost per file cabinet divided by the
number of years used to amortize capital
equipment = cost per cabinet per year:
$_____ × number of cabinets = total
equipment cost .... $_____ $_____ $_____

SUPPLIES
Use average number of folders per cabinet,
and factor the cost, based on purchase cost
× number of folders per cabinet............ $_____ $_____ $_____

SUPERVISORY TIME
Supervisor annual salary + benefits: $_____
divided by total number of cabinets in area
supervised = supervisory cost/cabinet .... $_____ $_____ $_____

FILING TIME
File clerk's annual salary + benefits: $_____
Time cost, based on the number of filing-
inches* handled (_____) = $_____
Divide by the number of filing-inches per
cabinet to get cost per cabinet .... $_____ $_____ $_____

TOTAL ANNUAL COST
PER FILE CABINET................. $_____ $_____ $_____

Divide by individual cabinet capacity, in
linear filing-inches (LFI) to obtain LFI cost
per year: .... $_____ $_____ $_____

---

*File-handling capability is generically reckoned as follows:

4-drawer cabinet - 1,300 LFI   6-level lateral file - 3,000 LFI
5-drawer cabinet - 1,625 LFI   7-level databox file - 4,500 LFI

locate and pull a file folder from a drawer file than it does from an open lateral file.

SUBJECT CLASSIFICATION

Next to the wrong file equipment, the big time-waster is usually the file classification system. It is remarkable how few businesspeople know anything about classification systems, and the problem with the standard A–Z system is that it mixes up a wide variety of different *types* of information simply because they happen to have similar initial letters. There are many better ways to do it, although an A–Z file may well be a useful *part* of an information storage system.

The two most-used subject classification systems are the Library of Congress system (LC), used by large libraries, and the Dewey decimal system (DD), used in smaller libraries.

LC classification is organized like this:

A	General
B	Philosophy, Psychology, Religion
C	Historical Sciences
D	History, General
E–F	History, American
G	Geog., Anthrop., Recreation
H	Social Sciences
K	Law
L	Education
M	Music
N	Fine Arts
P	Language and Literature
Q	Science
R	Medicine
S	Agriculture
T	Technology
U	Military Science
V	Naval Science
Z	Bibliography, Library Science

DD classification is organized like this:

000	General
100	Philosophy
200	Religion
300	Social Sciences
400	Language
500	Natural Sciences
600	Useful Arts
700	Fine Arts
800	Literature
900	History

This allows libraries to maintain their collections in blocks of similar or related subjects. You may want to take a leaf out of their book, as it were, and use the same approach. A typical business file system might be broken down like this:

001–999	SUBJECT FILES All types of reference information on business-related subjects. If necessary, subdivide, e.g., RESOURCES, COMPETITORS, MATERIALS, etc.
1000–1499	FINANCIAL RECORDS Operating statements, balance sheets, invoices, bank statements, etc.
1500–1999	CUSTOMER RECORDS An A–Z file can work well here. Regional or discount subdivision may be valuable.
2000–2499	OPERATING INFORMATION FILES Equipment service records and catalogs, real estate records, capital inventory, employee personnel records, etc.
2500–2999	LEGAL RECORDS Business licenses, permits, corporate documents.
3000–3499	MARKETING INFORMATION Advertising copy, graphics originals, mail lists, brochure samples, marketing data, etc.
3500–3999	COMMUNICATIONS RECORDS Correspondence files (one alpha and one chronological), telephone call reports, telegrams, fax copies, etc.

The file numbering system is not arbitrary, of course, and a logical alphanumeric system may be used, if desired, for smaller file systems. For example:

C1 COMMUNICATIONS
    C1A–Z Correspondence

C2 CUSTOMER RECORDS

C2A Eastern Region
    C2A1 Wholesale
    C2A2 Retail
C2B Western Region
C2C Midwest Region

F1 FINANCIAL RECORDS

L1 LEGAL RECORDS

M1 MARKETING INFORMATION

O1 OPERATING INFORMATION FILES

S1 SUBJECT FILES

The same file codes should be maintained throughout an organization. File subdivision may become the responsibility of the functional head, but a central file register is essential. The file register may be kept in a card file (if it's not extensive, it can go at the back of the telephone index), showing the file cabinet number and the number of records within it. Larger systems are usually organized with a record card for each file. With a well-conceived classification system, anybody can find the information they need at any time, without dependence on the presence of the person who put the stuff away. Confidential file cabinets should be locked, of course. This basic time-saver plan may be adapted to any type or size of business and can be expanded as necessary.

SYSTEM MANAGEMENT

In any size organization, the effective management of records and database files is a key factor in time management at every level of operation. While file locations may be decentralized, file management should not be. Many businesses have enormous duplication of records yet, at the same time, cannot create management information reports which would support the intelligent direction of the business. Frequently records management becomes, by default, part of the financial executive's function, either because he has the mainframe computer or because management figures that anyone who can crunch numbers for the federal tax system must be able to manage an information system. I believe that this is the wrong approach, and that any major information system, to be fully responsive to user needs, requires an experienced, dedicated manager at the VP level. It's that important. The alternative is a patchwork quilt of nonintegrated files, with various individuals jealously guarding their file domains and employing a time-wasting horde of protective clerks.

When an information system is integrated, the various operating functions will cooperate more closely, the information database will be used more fully and effectively, and the associated time and costs will be reduced.

PERSONAL FILING

Businesses aren't the only ones who can save time this way; good filing habits can also reduce lost time for the individual. These suggestions may be helpful:

Use the same file codes for your books as your business files. If you find a library book that is valuable, note the reference information on an information locator (see Appendix C), and file it. A personal computer file can be created to do the same job.

Use the information locator as you skim-read magazines, or strip out the pages with the information you want, number and file them with appropriate cross-references. Don't take the time to read everything. File it until you need it, *then* read it. Clean out subject files annually.

Use a time-indexed file in your desk, keyed to your appointment calendar for papers that will be needed at a specific time. This includes memos and letters that must be answered.

Create a separate file subsection for special projects. If there are many, color code them for fast access. When the project is complete, purge the files and transfer them to the primary filing system.

Insure that you have a time file in your desk, with day and month sections. File incoming materials according to action needed. Each evening, check the day file for the next day and schedule related activities in your calendar. If there won't be time, move them forward, shift something else to make time, delegate them, or if possible, eliminate them.

Create a trip file, indexed by city, with useful local information. Include restaurants' numbers and maitre d's names, data on local business contacts, etc. Use it to hold itinerary sheets, tickets, and hotel confirmations when you leave.

Use a telephone index for fast file-code access. Note the code you want on papers to be filed, if you don't want to leave the entire task to a secretary.

Avoid multiple handling of papers. When they are picked up, it should be with purpose rather than for an idle scan. Act on them, pass them along to somebody else for action, or file them for specific future action. If you don't know what you want to do with them, stop and figure it out then and there. Procrastinating by putting them back in the in basket won't help.

Tuesday was named for the Norse god, Tiw. He is depicted here as in a fifth-century carving of Tiw with the wolf-god, Fenris.

FILE STORAGE

At least once a year, insure that all files are purged, and their contents destroyed or stored. Some retention periods are dictated by federal agencies:

Receipts, Invoices, and Ledger Entry Records The IRS requires that these records be retained for three years. Ledgers and summary records should be stored permanently.

Freight and Shipping Records The Interstate Commerce Commission requires all records relating to goods moved by common carriers to be kept for two years.

Personnel and Payroll Records The U.S. Department of Labor requires that these records be kept for three years.

Postage Records Postage meter users are required to keep their daily register records for one year, according to the U.S. Postal Service.

The manner in which business information is filed and maintained is a mirror of an organization's effectiveness. It may be worthwhile creating a task force to review how well your organization provides information essential for decision making to the right people at the right time. If necessary, hire an expert to help, as the technology that is available today, and its appropriate application, is a complex and specialized science.

See also *PAPERWORK TIME*.

GUARDING TIME

*Controlling interruptions · Dealing
with unexpected visitors · Guarding
appointments · Terminating
meetings · Junk mail*

Those who succeed in organizing their own time effectively are usually faced with the need to preserve it. Executive surveys indicate that, on the average, 7.4 percent of managerial time is taken up with unwanted and unnecessary interruptions. The time wasted can be three times greater than their actual duration, too. That's because the mind, when jolted from the heart of a problem, cannot quickly return to the point at which it was disturbed. It has to return, step by step, layer by layer, until the thread is regained. It is not surprising that some managers find it tough to do any real thinking in the office where, in many cases, they are interrupted once every eight minutes. Check your own interruption frequency; you may be surprised at the way that your time is chopped up. (See *RECORDING TIME.*)

The effectiveness of time spent with unexpected visitors is low. Studies show that, after all of the apologies for interruption and protestations that "It's quite all right" are made, the unplanned encounter uses only 20 percent of the total time for the core subject.

While total accessibility is wrong, so is utter inaccessibility. There are occasions when a few minutes of conversation can save hours of a subordinate's time. The "open door" policy does not mean that anyone with the slightest urge should be able to barge into your office unannounced. It means that the door is open *under certain conditions* to those who need access. If you have a secretary or administrative assistant, he or she should know those conditions and screen visitors accordingly. For those without staff, a group discussion on the subject is recommended. Some of these techniques may be considered:

A series of "quiet times" may be set up throughout the day, during which interoffice visitation and telephone calls are restricted to emergencies.

In an office without a door, a red marker, such as a small flag, may be placed on the desk when interruption is discouraged.

A vertical wall-mounted paper-holder may be placed on or near the office door, into which notes and documents can be placed to be easily visible, without the necessity of actually entering the office.

A practice of closing office doors to signify the need for privacy should be universally adopted to be effective.

Desks should be placed so that eye contact with passers-by is not possible.

Guard your appointment time. If people are late, reschedule them. It will be a good learning experience for them. Avoid the trap of trying to squeeze one more meeting into a morning or afternoon. Those that "shouldn't take very long" are the ones that can wreck a complete day's schedule. Be firm, and resist the squeeze play.

Use your watch to signal visitors silently. If you take it off and place it on your desk face down, it will signify that you're putting no time restrictions on them. If you place it face up, it indicates that you're concerned about the time. If you need a more intrusive audible signal, use an alarm watch, and set it to beep when you want a meeting to end. It's useful to tell your visitor at the start of the meeting how much time you have, so that he can organize his conversation accordingly.

Use body signals to terminate a meeting. Let silences enter the conversation and move forward to the edge of your chair. If that doesn't work, stand up. If your visitor still has not taken the hint, walk around your desk and stand by your door. If absolutely necessary, put your arm on his shoulder and gently propel him out.

Unexpected junk mail, like unexpected visitors, can steal your time. It's rarely worth reading. If you are truly pressed for time, remove the temptation to explore the attractive packages and envelopes by tossing them, or having your secretary do the same.

The planet Earth is about 5 billion years old, and has a life expectancy of 12 billion years (based on the projected life of the sun). That means that we have 7 billion years before we have to worry about the sun exploding and incinerating the planet.

HOUR

*The history of man's attempts to divide
the day into hours.*

The Sumerians were the first people we know of that divided their day into smaller time units. They created twelve *danna*, each of thirty *ges*.

The first twenty-four-hour day was devised by the Babylonians, whose numerical system had a base of twelve. Daylight and night hours were of different lengths, which changed with the seasons. Then, as water clocks came into use, the unequal hours became difficult to mark, so each hour was made the same fraction of a day.

The ancient Egyptians also made twenty-four divisions of the day. Their word for "hour" meant "priestly duties," and with an added hieroglyph, "star watcher." The star-watching priests measured the passage of time by noting the appearance of twelve specific stars on the eastern horizon through each night. They set up ten daylight periods, and added two "twilight" hours at dusk and dawn. But, groping for help from the stars and the sun they, like the Babylonians, finished up with hours of different lengths. They later changed to a twelve-hour day, measuring it from noon to noon, and managed to live with the puzzling equinoxial variations.

Other civilizations tried different approaches. The Romans in 160 B.C. decided to split the day into five periods. Then, in 605 A.D., Pope Sabinianus added two more periods to the Roman day divisions, creating the seven "canonical hours" for prayers: matins (morning), lauds (praise), prime (first), tierce (third), sext (sixth), nones (ninth), vespers (evening), and complin (complete). But as towns began to form, with populaces lacking the farmers' natural time markers, more precise marking of the days became necessary, and the logic of the twelve-hour day spread across the world.

Attempts have been made in the recent past to implement a ten-hour day. Perhaps the most serious was that of the leaders of the French Revolution, who created a "Calendar of Reason" on that basis. Confusion and public outcry was so severe, however, that the

There's not a man that lives who hath not known his god-like hours.

William Wordsworth

plan was dropped, although its adherents continued to press for its adoption for over twelve years.

Scientists now describe the hour as either a mean solar hour or a sidereal hour. Astronomers call it a unit of angular measurement in the equatorial coordinate system equal to fifteen degrees of right ascension.

Hour angle is that between the hour circle of a body in the Earth's celestial sphere and a reference hour circle. The celestial *sphere* is the observable sky that surrounds the Earth, with opposing "poles" that are extensions of the Earth's poles. An *hour circle* is any circle drawn on the celestial sphere which passes through both poles.

HOUSEHOLD TIME

Household records system · Domestic time analysis · The family time planning process · The kitchen and mealtimes · Cooking and shopping time · Cleaning time

Too much time spent on cleaning, shopping, and home maintenance chores can steal a lifetime. That's why household time management is as important as office management. That is, if one wants to have more disposable time for hobbies, friends, family, and relaxation. Family households are in the minority today. Only 6 percent of Americans now live in the traditional family of two children, a working husband, and a wife who is a full-time homemaker. The demands of a family with two working adults make it essential to use a lot of thinking to get household tasks under control. Smart homemakers take a look at their methods, materials, tools, equipment, and working areas to find more effective and productive ways of getting things done.

Start with a "planning center." It doesn't have to be elaborate, but it's essential to have an appointed place for household records and planning. If you can, create a home office; it's one of the strongest trends in home design today.

Get your household records straightened out and you'll save a week's time every year. Make a point from now on of keeping a loose-leaf binder organized for each part of the house. Make a section for each room as well as the garage, the garden, etc. Use the binder as a central record and diary, with essential information and the date of all changes that you make in the home, including:

> Installation of appliances, with model and serial numbers, and dealer and warranty information. Punch holes in instruction manuals and add them to the binder.

What reason and en-
deavor cannot bring
about, often time will.
Dr. Thomas Fuller, 1732

Painting and decorating records, with paint and wallpaper identification numbers, names, and sources.

Plumbing and electrical wiring information: the location of the
main cutoffs, meters and fuses; your lawn sprinkler layout plan,
etc.

Room dimensions, with lists and/or photographs of furniture and
effects.

You'll find that these records will become invaluable in continued home maintenance. It will help others to cope if you're away, and
when you want to sell your home it will impress prospective buyers.
Your record center should also include:

Your own "yellow pages" telephone directory, listing local stores
and services under their own categories. It can be invaluable when
an emergency occurs and time is critical, and it will become increasingly useful as you develop preferences among vendors.

A pocket-sized notebook containing family records and information. Include birthdays, clothing sizes, color preferences, hobbies,
etc. Grab it when you're going to a shopping center. Try and buy
Christmas gifts throughout the year, and check off your successes
as you go.

A shoebox for decorating samples. Put pieces of tile, carpet, drapery
materials, paint chips and so on in it. When you need to shop for
something new, or to replace a damaged item, take your sample box
along to match colors and textures.

A key organizer. Pick up a ready-made kit or make a simple one
yourself. Don't ever put a key in it that isn't identified. Get duplicates of essential keys before it's too late. Record the numbers of
your car keys—in case of loss or theft, it will help your auto service
shop to replace them quickly.

With a workplace and records at hand, start to *plan* your home-
making time, using the time planning system in the Appendix. For
many people, the biggest hurdle is to correctly identify the time
thieves that are stealing valuable hours. Penetrating their disguise is
the first essential step. Find out how you *really* spend your day with
some household time analysis.

HOUSEHOLD TIME ANALYSIS

A household Time Record worksheet will help in recording the way
in which time is spent. The basic task categories, described below,

may be expanded to fit your particular lifestyle, using the chart in Appendix E.

Regular Meal Preparation   day-by-day preparation of food for meals eaten within the home; for packed lunches and/or picnics, and for babies and invalids. These tasks normally take about 15 percent of the homemaker's day. Mealtimes are frequently governed by outside factors such as office and school hours for family members, so other tasks must be scheduled to fit around the food preparation activities. Meal planning should be included with home management.

Special Meal Preparation   includes holiday meals, party food, and special occasion meals. The time taken by these tasks can be reduced by cooking or baking some items ahead of time, as part of the regular food preparation activity.

After-meal Cleanup   includes clearing all dishes and pans, manual dishwashing, dishwasher-loading, leftover storage, garbage disposal, and the cleaning of kitchen equipment not accomplished during the food preparation activity. Exclude dishwasher operating time.

Regular Housecleaning   includes cleaning and putting things in order—the tasks which are normally done more than three times weekly.

Special House Care   should include big cleaning jobs (like washing windows) that are not done regularly; and house maintenance tasks such as painting, replacing worn tile, or making home furnishings.

Yard Care   covers the upkeep of lawns, paths and driveways, gardens and patios. A Special Yard Care category should be used, when needed, for extensive garden work, such as installing a sprinkler system.

Family Care—Physical   includes bathing, dressing, and feeding any family member, and accompanying them to a professional health service such as a hospital, a dentist, or an optometrist.

Family Care—Nonphysical   covers all activities related to social and educational development of family members, and should include reading to children, chauffeuring, helping with schoolwork, etc.

Pet Care   includes all food preparation, exercising, and cleaning activities related to your pets.

Car Care   should include washing, polishing, and minor maintenance performed at the house, plus the time used to transfer the car to a garage or gas station for service.

The alarm clock as we know it was invented in 1787 by an industrious New England clockmaker. He never patented the design, mass-produced the clock, or made any money on it. He just wanted to be sure of waking up at 4:00 every morning.

Clothing Repair   covers sewing, mending, and alterations to the clothing (or footwear) of any family member.

Laundry   includes hand-washing; collecting, loading, unloading, and storing clothes laundered by automatic washers and dryers; travel and waiting time involved in the use of a coin-operated or full-service laundry or dry cleaning establishment.

Ironing and Pressing   is self-explanatory, and may be included within the laundry function if desired.

Shopping   whether for food, clothing, household supplies, or other items should include travel time to and from stores and the time spent putting things away; telephone or writing time when purchasing by these methods; and time given to home sales presentations.

Home Management   is frequently underrated as a time consumer, because it is often mixed in with other activities. Home management functions may include separate tasks like tax preparation, party planning, and household budgeting. But don't overlook the time taken in the training and supervision of others in performing household tasks; locating needed goods and services; price comparison reading; arbitrating children's social conflicts; and day-by-day scheduling activities.

Travel   in most households, travel time is involved in numerous activities and, where possible, should be included with them. Only travel time that is not assignable should be included here.

Reading, Letter-writing, Social Planning   may be a mixture of leisure and/or obligatory activities. Separate them appropriately.

Leisure Activities   may be difficult to identify in some cases, because what is leisure to one person may be work to another. Use your own judgment in determining how much leisure time you have, based upon your feelings of motivation, satisfaction, and relaxation.

With some facts in front of you, you can then start to gain control of your time, using some of the following tips:

First put down the time blocks dictated by your *external* living demands, such as picking up children from school or your spouse from the station.

Follow this by recording the time blocks essential to your *internal* family routines: mealtimes, children's bedtimes, etc. Only after you have satisfied these system- and family-imposed time demands can you exercise your own control. It's a good idea to keep them to a minimum.

Now that you know how much elective time you have, you can begin to plan it effectively. Figure out the best time to shop for groceries, when the store will be least crowded, and arrange to do it then. Go by yourself if possible. If you're an apartment dweller, use the same technique for the laundry room. Plan major cleaning jobs. Don't let them creep up on you and suddenly become a crisis.

Get your family involved in the planning process. Sit down with each of them, singly or as a group, and identify the time problems that they each cause. Make joint plans to eradicate problems and finish up with some *written* house rules. Introduce intelligent methods to share the household work, assigning tasks according to age and ability. For example, a small child may be given the job of keeping all of the soap dishes and tissue dispensers full, and emptying wastebaskets. Older kids can take on heavier tasks. But make their assignments as easy as possible, give them the right tools, and praise them for jobs well done. Team effort in home maintenance builds closer relationships and teaches respect for other people's time.

Save time every day by using these tips:

Check your kitchen storage system and cut out unnecessary steps. Organize storage around "action centers"—baking, fruit and vegetable preparation, beverage preparation, etc. For example, store coffee- and teapots, cream jugs, mugs, and coffeegrinder in the same cupboard as the beverages, or close to them. Create a baking center to store supplies and utensils. If necessary, invest in some time-saving storage devices.

Think ahead to save time in meal preparation. Plan meals on the day that food ads appear in your local paper, and allow for use of leftovers. Buy and cook in quantity whenever possible, and freeze meals in labeled, ready-to-use packets. You can even store a week's worth of prewrapped lunch sandwiches in the freezer. Work on meals one day ahead. Prepare everything possible and refrigerate it. You'll often get a bonus in enhanced flavor, as well as making the cooking task easier.

Back up your cookbooks and recipe collection with a Menu File. Use a three-ring binder and a set of index tabs. Figure out a weekly menu plan, and add notes on where to find each recipe. Use your Menu File to help in making up your weekly shopping list. Rotate Menu File pages for repeated use.

Buy food and household supplies in bulk. You'll get a double benefit of reduced overall shopping time *and* lower cost. If you have the space, stock up on a year's supply of hard goods (such as toilet paper, laundry detergent, and so forth) when they go on sale at the supermarket or at warehouse discount stores.

Make your own food store checklist. List the items you usually buy in the same order that they may be found in the store. That way, you'll avoid backtracking as you shop. Photocopy your list for repeated use. The government says that the average U.S. family spends more than $3,000 annually for food purchases, so some spend much more than that. The packagers and advertisers successfully confuse shoppers, it is calculated, so that they spend about 15 percent more than necessary. Beware of the big red star, the "$1.00 OFF!" A dollar off *what?* Many supermarkets raise their price about a month before holiday periods so that they can claim "reductions" as the heavy buying takes place. Experts say that only 20 percent of food shoppers buy intelligently. The majority don't take the time to compare and evaluate keenly. An extra half hour at the supermarket, when traffic is light, can mean real savings.

Use these time-savers with fruits and vegetables. Next time you use lemons or oranges, grate the peel and measure it into teaspoonfuls, then store them in twists of plastic wrap in your freezer. They'll be ready for use in cakes and sauces whenever you need them. Need a few drops of lemon juice? Don't cut the fruit in half. Just stick a toothpick into it, squeeze out the juice you need, and put the fruit back in your refrigerator.

To make tomatoes ripen faster, put them in a plastic bag with a very ripe apple. The apple releases a ripening chemical.

Remove the silk from corn ears quickly by rubbing them with a terry cloth towel.

Reduce cooking time. When you're cooking on a range top, use a pressure cooker to speed things up. You'll save energy costs too. When using a double boiler, add a small amount of salt to the water in the lower pan to cut cooking time.

Use a garlic press to smash wrapped bouillon cubes before putting them in water. They'll dissolve in half the time.

Microwave cookery is getting better as convenience food suppliers introduce new technology to avoid the hot-but-soggy dishes that have plagued microwave oven users. New packaging will give brown crusts and crisp coatings. It uses a thin layer of aluminum powder laminated in the package wall to provide high browning heat where it's needed. "Ready indicators" will take the guesswork out of cooking time. Entrees that need no refrigeration will be available. Check out a microwave oven. It might be for you.

Manage messes before they occur. Cut cleanup time in the kitchen by lining baking utensils with foil, or using nonstick spray. Catch oven spillovers with a cookie sheet or foil liner. Keep a sink or bowl full of sudsy water while cooking, and put used pots and tools in as you go. Protect trays and serving pieces with doilies or napkins. Put mats under pet food containers. Cut *two* layers of paper to line cupboards and drawers; throw out the top one when soiled. Move clutter-catchers, like small tables, away from entrances. Make sure there's a wastebasket in every room.

Pour excess cooking oils and hot fat into a used container, then throw it out with the garbage. You'll avoid the primary cause of drain stoppages. Use the range fan regularly; it will dispose of two hundred pounds of grease annually that you won't have to clean up. To cut oven-cleaning time (if you don't have a self-cleaning appliance), leave a saucer of ammonia in the oven overnight, or apply a cloth soaked in ammonia to soften burned-on spots. You can use a razor blade scraper to remove bad spills. It won't harm porcelain finishes.

Save time in personal care. Manicure right after showering or washing dishes to eliminate the need to soak cuticles. Stop nail polish tops sticking by putting a little face cream on the screw threads when you first open the bottle. And refrigerated nail polish won't thicken and become useless so soon. A small marker dot on the back of a necktie will take the guesswork out of where to start the knot.

Save time in the yard. Clean up cooled barbecue grills by tying them in a plastic bag with hot water and half a cup of detergent for several hours. Clean rusted garden tools with a wet cork dipped in scouring cleanser. Keep a bucket of sand mixed with used engine oil in your garage or toolshed. Stick used garden tools into it and they'll come out clean and oiled.

Keep rosebuds fresh longer by searing the ends of the stems with a lighter or match just before putting them in a vase of water. Cut flowers will last longer in a solution of half SevenUp and half water, with one half teaspoonful of chlorine bleach added. Remove all leaves below the waterline.

When seeding a lawn, a little flour mixed with the grass seed will mark the areas covered. Save your seed from the birds by soaking it in laundry bluing, which doesn't harm germination.

Rub drill bits and saw blades occasionally with a soap bar. They'll cut faster and smoother. Make a tool holder by nailing an old leather belt in loops at the top of your ladder. When your painting chore is interrupted, wrap the brush in aluminum foil and put it in the freezer. It won't harden for days.

In eternity, everything is just beginning.
*Elias Cannetti,
Bulgarian writer, 1945*

Keep all cleaning products and equipment together in a handy place. Set up a "cleaning center" to make silver cleaning and shoe polishing go faster. Store cleaning supplies and tools together, with a convenient work surface. Add your flower vases and knife sharpening materials too, if you wish. After cleaning, wrap silverware in plastic wrap to slow tarnishing, or put antitarnish strips (available from the 3M Company) in your silver storage container.

Organize a mobile cleanup tote that you can carry or push around. In addition to your cleaning supplies, include a soft-bristled paintbrush to get at grooves and crevices, a brown felt-tip marker to cover scratches on wood furniture, a reliable spot remover (lighter fluid is a good one, but test it first), and a feather duster with an extending handle.

Avoid running back and forth when cleaning. Work through the home with a definite plan, and avoid wasted motion wherever possible. You'll find it's faster to make beds from left to right. Clean the bedside tables at the same time. Keep a small dispenser with cleanser in your pocket and fix carpet spots as you vacuum. Hit the finger marks on the door on the way out. Try timing yourself when cleaning, and try to establish a speed record. It adds some interest to chores, and pushes you to find intelligent shortcuts. One of my neighbors found one recently. Cleaning her baby's high chair took a lot of time until she carried it to the shower, closed the door, and let the hot spray do the job. It drip-dried beautifully.

Sneak up on your chores. Picking up will take less time if you cultivate the habit of carrying things back to their proper place as you move around the house. Practice doing more than one thing at a time. Put in a "hands-free" telephone, and the manicuring job can be done while you talk to mother. Put slots in the lid of a large aluminum foil box, then stack gift ribbon spools side-by-side inside. Feeding the ribbons through the slots will keep them under control. Sew on a missing button while you're watching TV.

The search for better ways of doing things has been going on since the birth of mankind. It's in your own self-interest to reduce fatigue and time in your daily tasks. Use these sources for further reading and ideas:

Rhoads, Geraldine, and Edna Paradis. *The Complete How-to for the Busy Housekeeper.* New York: Viking Penguin, 1988.

Rubbermaid Home Service Center, Dept. CT, Wooster, OH 44691.

JAPAN TIME

*Asian time concepts · Pretrip planning ·
The Japanese businessman's cultural
and societal structure · Saving time with
the right "form" · Japanese vacations ·
Punctuality in Japan · Do's and
don't's while in Japan*

United States trade with Asia has, ever since 1978, far outstripped that done with Europe. Western businessmen, however, find that their time concepts and attitudes are not reflected by their Asian counterparts, particularly in Japan, which has now become the hub of the Pacific Basin marketplace. The billions of U.S. products sold in Japan, and the fact that together the United States and Japan account for more than one-third of the world GNP, make it impossible to ignore the potential of the Japanese marketplace. These tips, gathered from many experienced business travelers, can save an enormous loss of time, or even a totally wasted trip, for those attempting to negotiate in Japan.

PRETRIP PLANNING

Get a copy of Japan Airlines' publications, *A Businessman's Guide to Japan* and *Executive Guide to the Orient.* They are among the best around.

Check out the many federal government publications that are available free, or at modest cost. Start with the Department of Commerce, Japan Division (202-377-4527), and the Government Printing Office, but don't overlook these other valuable sources of time-saving information:

> Request the Congressional Research Service's *CRS Update*, a free catalog of background research conducted for members of Congress. Your representative can get you anything available on Japan; you cannot get it directly.

Call the Office of Trade Information Services (OTIS) (202-377-2432). Ask for their free catalog of Japanese market research reports and order what you need. If you want financial references on a Japanese firm, they can provide that too, although it costs $75.

The Bureau of Labor Statistics keeps track of labor costs, earnings, and living standards throughout the East. Call them at 202-523-1327.

Time, you old gypsy
 man
Will you not stay
Put up your caravan
Just for one day?
         Ralph Hodgson

Purchase the State Department's *Diplomatic List* ($3.75, available from the Government Printing Office) to get current names of people in the Japanese Embassy's commercial departments.

Call Japan's External Trade Organization (JETRO), which maintains offices in San Francisco and New York, and represents many Japanese trade associations. The Manufactured Imports Promotion Organization (MIPRO) is located in Washington, D.C. at 220-659-3729. They will also assist you in tackling the Japanese market.

The Japanese Clock and Watch Association is located at the Nomura Building, 1-1, Ohte-machi 2-chome, Chiyoda-ku, Tokyo 100. (Telephone: 241-4300). Time-related instruments are usually included in Japan's Precision Instruments statistical classification.

It is essential to write to those people you wish to meet prior to departure. Letters of introduction are extremely valuable and should accompany your request for a meeting. Mail these at least four weeks before you plan to depart. Don't plan on more than two business meetings per day. They will take at least twice as long, if not longer, than they would in the United States. A trip of two to three weeks is recommended for optimum time payoff. You won't accomplish much in less time, and your own efficiency will drop off with a longer stay.

Don't try and arrange specific appointments, it's a waste of time. Say when you will be in the country, where you will be staying, and the purpose of your visit. Call to pin down the appointment time as soon as you arrive. Use the executive lounge in your hotel when telephoning. The Japanese secretary will save you much time and frustration, as telephone operators in Japan are likely to simply pull the plug if they have difficulty understanding you.

It is important to try and understand something of Japanese culture and social structure if you are to have any hope of successfully negotiating a business arrangement with a Japanese firm. However profitable it may appear, a deal will not go through until the firm has thoroughly assessed it in terms of their company's traditions, its impact on their business community and their competitors, and the loss of face they may suffer if it doesn't pan out. The assessment will come primarily from their middle management people (*buchō* and *jōmu*);* the top executives will mostly take care of ceremonial hosting and toasting. Don't expect them to know the details of a complex negotiation; you'll be wasting time if you discuss it with them, and they will be embarrassed. After these *aisatsu* call to pay respects, you may not see them again until the formal contract signing ceremony.

Beware of Westernized Japanese "front men." They are there to buffer the movers and shakers from you, because you're a foreigner. In Japan, close contact with any foreigner brings loss of face; by the same line of thinking, a Westernized Japanese is "tainted" and is usually regarded as a useful greeter with little real status. (This foreign contact custom is so well ingrained that Japanese business executives who are stationed overseas often have difficulty regaining acceptance and status when they are repatriated.) To maintain face, a Japanese executive will feign discomfort in interacting with foreigners and often pretend not to speak the language (but watch them making notes!). The cultural discomfort becomes acute if the foreigner is black or female. Travelers should be aware that women are not welcome at business functions.

The Japanese business culture is bound by four primary elements: face (*kao*), obligations (*on*), duties (*giri*), and patience (*nintai*). Every Japanese is constantly analyzing his interpersonal transactions within this framework and trying to stay ahead of the game. He uses two basic levels of communication to assist his efforts: *tatemae*, that required by good form, and *honne*, what he really means to say. The preservation of form will frequently force him to use subtlety rather than directness. For example, if he doesn't like a member of your group, he will pointedly omit him when inquiring after everyone else's health. The ability to understand these signals will move your business forward faster than any attempt to push things along by force.

Make sure you have a stack of business cards (*meishi*) printed in English and Japanese. Pan-Am or Japan Airlines will, with a three-week lead time, print them for you if you don't have a local source. The ceremonial exchange of meishi is important and should be accompanied with a slight bow. A Japanese can be offended, too, if you don't study his meishi before pocketing it.

Check your visa and immunization requirements.

---

*buchō=department head; jōmu=managing director.

Remember that Japan has more festivals and public holidays than most other countries. You will be wasting your time to do business there during the following times of celebration:

January 1	New Year's Day
January 15	Adults' Day
February 11	National Foundation Day
March 20*	Vernal Equinox Day
April 29	Green Day
May 3	Constitution Memorial Day
May 5	Children's Day
September 15	Respect for the Aged Day
September 23*	Autumnal Equinox Day
October 10	Health and Sports Day
November 3	Culture Day
November 23	Labor Thanksgiving Day
December 23	Emperor's Birthday

Contact the Japan National Tourist Organization Office in Chicago, Dallas, Honolulu, Los Angeles, New York, or San Francisco for current dates on the sixty-seven other festivals that take place each year.

The Japanese are meticulous in preparing for business meetings and will normally field a backup troupe to sit in on meetings. They are there partially for the consensus ritual employed in Japanese decision making and partially to supply any detail that the chief negotiator may have forgotten. If your business trip is to be worth your time, your preparation and briefing must be detailed and intense. You may even want to take your own backup team along. You will lose face by making calls back to the home office. Be prepared.

IN JAPAN

Most travelers enter Japan through Narita International Airport, serving Tokyo. You won't save much time getting a taxi downtown, and it will cost nearly $100. Use the bus; it's fast and convenient.

From the moment you land, hang on to your patience. Things

---

*These holidays may be one day later in some years.

just will not happen in Japan as fast as you may expect. Even the smoothest negotiations will drag along at a snail's pace, while the Japanese take their time in collective decision making. Don't be fooled by lavish entertainment and long visits either; they are *de rigeur* for the Japanese even when they do *not* intend to do business with you.

It's wise to spend your first day in Japan getting your bearings. Visit the U.S. Embassy, MITI, and the American Chamber of Commerce. They can give you a lot of time-saving assistance. Use your hotel executive lounge to plan your taxi trips. They can provide written instructions for the driver that will save a lot of time in dealing with Tokyo's confused street numbering system. Don't make the mistake of tipping the driver.

Punctuality is a must in Japan. If you arrive early to a meeting, you can expect to wait. It will start on time, with small talk and refreshments. You will be considered rude if you attempt to push business topics too quickly. Slow down and wait while your host assembles his troops; they will probably outnumber you ten to one. Usually, they will all understand English, but only the top executive will talk to *you* in English. The others will confer in Japanese.

Some sort of a handout—a business article or sample merchandise—can often get things moving into business channels when all else fails. Once discussion gets under way, insure that it's two-way. Don't ask all the questions, without giving your hosts a chance; when they see that you are responsive, they'll open up too. You can often get better off-the-cuff answers as you progress through the obligatory tour of the premises.

Japanese courtesy demands avoidance of negative answers, so don't ever expect to hear a clear-cut "no." Word your questions so that "yes" or "no" answers are unnecessary. And remember, when a Japanese businessman says "yes," all he means to say is that he heard what you said. Unless you are careful, you will draw incorrect conclusions from your business conversations.

Give a small gift to your host(s) upon departure. This can be a product sample, or some toy that may be passed on to a child. It need not be expensive, but should preferably not be available in Japan.

Making the most of your time in Japan depends on your ability to convince your prospects that your company is in for the long haul, and that their loyalty will not be misplaced if they do business with you. These considerations are as important to the Japanese as technical and price factors. However, with good preplanning and acceptance of the different time attitudes that you will meet in Japan, your

> Time is the school in which we learn
> Time is the fire in which we burn.
> *Delmore Schwartz*

personal visit can produce better results than you would ever get through agents or trading companies.

Use these tips to increase your success in dealing with the Japanese:

DO	DON'T
Exchange business cards ceremonially, and establish credentials.	Use a strong handshake. Make the contact brief.
Maintain formality. (Japanese equate informality with rudeness.)	Use first names, or forget anyone's name. File your *meishi* carefully.
Take the seat of honored guest in meeting rooms, facing the door.	Bring a gift to first visit.
	Dress informally.
Verbalize on your host's merits.	Rush into any business discussion. Wait until your hosts elect to begin. Never interrupt. Avoid any aggressive mannerisms.
Avoid saying anything that may be emotionally wounding.	
Avoid slang and speaking too fast. Repeat yourself frequently.	Get ahead of your interpreter. He has a tough enough time. Give him every opportunity to explicate. (Simul International, Tokyo, employs some of the best, by the way.)
Be punctual and precise.	
Make detailed notes of everything.	
Eat and compliment Japanese food. Find something you like, and order it. Don't take the chance of being served distasteful food. You may offend your hosts if you don't eat it.	Bring up the name of a competitor.
	Expect a Japanese to let on when he doesn't understand.
	Avoid social invitations, or criticize Japanese food.
	Expect to discuss business while playing golf.
Have patience. Never raise your voice or walk about and gesticulate.	Enter an *ofuru* tub without showering first.
Make time for socializing, but don't include your wife unless she's specifically invited.	Attempt to copy Japanese mannerisms.
Let your hosts do the talking. Bite your tongue, and don't try and fill silences with conversation.	

DO

Express discomfort subtly—
never directly.

Give small gifts on leaving
after your first visit. Bring
gift(s) aligned to rank on
second visit.

Trust feelings above words.

See also *TRAVEL TIME, JET LAG.*

JET LAG

How to avoid time-wasting jet lag

Since the advent of jet aircraft, travelers have found it necessary to quickly adjust their bodies' internal clocks to new time zones. Until the mismatch is corrected, they suffer numerous symptoms, from a simple feeling of malaise to more unpleasant internal problems.

The worst effects can be avoided by preparing the body clock for resetting through some simple changes in food intake prior to departure. The recommended procedure is as follows:

Figure out the time in your present location at which your first breakfast in your new location will be eaten. Four days before departure, begin to adjust your eating patterns:

Day 4   Eat heartily. Consume a high-protein breakfast with eggs, meat, cereal, etc. Lunch should include meat and green vegetables. Dinner should be high in carbohydrates to stimulate sleep, but meat should be avoided. Pastas (spaghetti but no meatballs), potatoes and other starch foods, and sweet desserts are suggested. Coffee and strong tea should only be consumed between 3:00 and 5:00 P.M.

Day 3   Eat very little, and prepare the body for time changes by reducing the store of carbohydrates in the liver. Fruit, light salads, and broths are recommended. Avoid bread, fats, and any calorie-laden items as much as possible. Caffeine drinks between only 3:00 and 5:00 P.M., again.

Day 2   Eat all you like, using the foods described in Day 4.

Day 1 (Departure Day)   Most eastbound flights begin in the late afternoon or evening. Eat lightly again during the day, using the foods described in Day 3, and avoid stimulating beverages. Break the fast at destination breakfast time. Drink strong coffee or tea between 10 P.M. and midnight. En route, avoid lights, skip the movie, and rest or sleep until destination breakfast time, *but not later*.

Westbound travelers should only drink beverages with caffeine in the morning.

At destination breakfast time, stay awake and active, and eat high-protein foods *without* caffeinated beverages. A substantial lunch or supper, with starches, should be taken on the day of arrival. Continue eating in accordance with destination time from then on.

See also *BODY TIME, TRAVEL TIME.*

LEISURE TIME

The concept of leisure · Leisure and consumerism · The loss of "free" time · Comparison of recreational time in France, the U.S.S.R., and the U.S. · Analyzing your free time

The concept of leisure was first envisioned by the Greek philosophers. And there are few in the world today who can or do enjoy true leisure, according to their views. Aristotle, for example, held that leisure, man's highest state, can only be reached by the contemplative questioning after truth, totally free from bias or necessity. It required education, mental discipline, affluence, and the Greek average of four slaves per leisured person as support.

Classical thoughts of leisure were buried by those of survival for the next two thousand years, as the Dark Ages swept Greek and Roman culture away, and man fought his territorial and political wars around the globe. The weekend fun of sacking and pillaging occupied the time of the Huns, the Celts, and the Goths. When things began to settle down and the Renaissance brought reason back into popular use, the Calvinists and the Puritans stepped in. They exhorted everyone to work in order to avoid the fires of Hell, and to eschew the very thought of idleness or leisure. They did a good job of brainwashing, for as late as 1619, the Virginia Assembly legislated punishment for any idle person in a quaint statute:

> No person, hawseholder or other, shall spend his tyme idely or unproffably, under such punishment as the court shall thinke meet to inflicte.

The idea of leisure probably reached its nadir in the sweatshops of New York and the mills of Lancashire in the nineteenth century, built upon the work ethic, and adulterated with technocracy and greed. When society's conscience began to question child labor and sixteen-hour workdays, and once we had survived two more wars, thoughts of leisure and its definition arose once more.

Sociologist Sebastian de Grazia[1] said that leisure was self-development built upon meditation in an environment of spiritual and bodily freedom from work.

The *Oxford English Dictionary*, noting that leisure stems from the Latin *licere* (to be permitted), and the English "licence," defined it as freedom to do what one will.

Whatever the definition, sociologists agree that today's society could not embrace the classical leisure concept. People who are not hard at work are regarded as socially and psychologically peculiar. Some time ago, following a lecture, a good friend of mine came forward to say some nice things, and remarked how busy I must be. When I told him I wasn't, he apologized and said, "Well, let's hope things start looking up soon!" I didn't have the heart to tell him that I'd planned it that way. At the same time, those who are refused work—the unemployed and the aged—are those least prepared or educated to utilize their leisure. In spite of being an economic giant, America is not a leisured nation. What is labeled as leisure today is really only "nonwork" time, which we are supposed to be able to apply as we wish, and which we are supposed to have more of than ever before. It is when we delve into the manner in which people use their nonwork, or free, time and try to determine how much they have that we find some remarkable dissonance.

For more than a hundred years, technology has been promising more leisure, due to increased productivity and fewer working hours. It was promised in England when steam power was introduced, and again when electricity became available. American mass-production methods were supposed to create more free time, and now automation and robotics are said to be the magic key. The abuse of statistics hides the truth. We have less free time today than we had fifty years ago.

The reason is that we have become subservient to consumerism, and have given away our free time in order to buy and maintain the material possessions that we are told we need. That is, if we want to be elite, upwardly mobile, and "successful." It seems there is little space for quiet introspection and creative contemplation in our lives today. The glue of civilized society—moral values, family commitment, love, and self-actualization—has become very thin, and much of our recreation today only serves to refresh us for another stint on the treadmill.

---

1. de Grazia, Sebastian. *Of Time, Work and Leisure.* New York: Twentieth Century Fund, 1962.

Toffler notes this dedication to the workplace, rather than having work support our private lives, in his *Future Shock*. He graphically describes the stresses that uncontrolled technocracy is placing on our way of life. De Grazia shows that moonlighting, commuting, working homemakers, and time spent maintaining our toys and gadgets have combined to completely offset the touted improvement in the working week.

In the developed nations, the average amount of active time away from the job is about two hundred minutes per day. How it's used is shown in the chart on the following page. The data come from 2,805 interviews in six French cities; 1,243 interviews in forty-four American cities, and 2,891 interviews in Pskov, U.S.S.R.

The power of our advertisers to build demand and activity-patterns is awesomely demonstrated. It is a fact that, although they give the activity low preference ratings, Americans have been persuaded to buy more TV sets per person than any other culture in the world, and to spend the majority of their free time watching them. The enjoyment level can't be that great, either, for the average viewer changes to a different channel every 3.7 minutes, according to the ratings people. The truth is evident in Thoreau's comment, "Our things own us, and we live lives of quiet desperation."

The activity patterns shown in the chart below have some interesting elements:

- Soviets spend three times the amount of time reading books and magazines, and attend movies five times more than do French or American citizens. These activities are affected by much lower TV ownership, less interesting programming, and limited broadcast time. They don't socialize as much as Americans, they have fewer telephones, and they use them less. Like the French, they spend more time on walks than we do.

- The French seem to put their hobbies ahead of socializing, although their telephone usage is close to that in the United States. They relax and rest much more than Americans or Russians, but spend less time in cultural pursuits.

- With so much time devoted to television, Americans lose much of their advantage in free time. Nonetheless, they spend more than twice as much time in athletic activities than do the French, except for taking walks. They spend more time socializing with families and friends than their contemporaries in other countries.

When the television set is shut off, Americans' free time pursuits are strongly correlated with education level, occupation, and in-

COMPARISON OF TIME USED IN RECREATIONAL ACTIVITIES IN FRANCE, U.S.A., AND U.S.S.R.

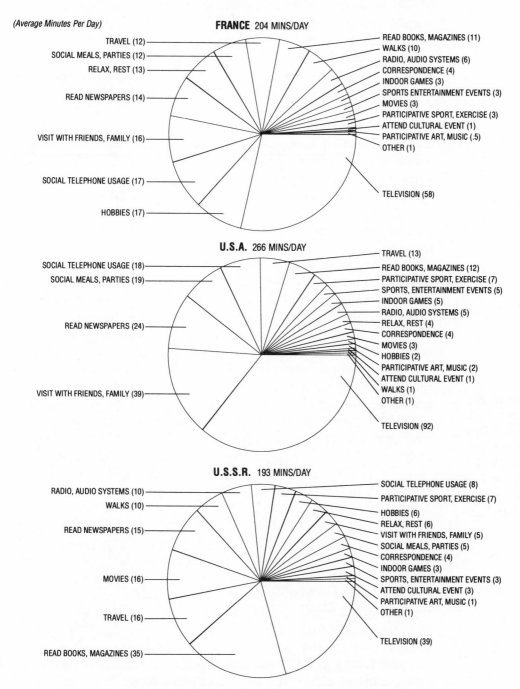

(Average Minutes Per Day)

FRANCE 204 MINS/DAY

TRAVEL (12)
SOCIAL MEALS, PARTIES (12)
RELAX, REST (13)
READ NEWSPAPERS (14)
VISIT WITH FRIENDS, FAMILY (16)
SOCIAL TELEPHONE USAGE (17)
HOBBIES (17)

READ BOOKS, MAGAZINES (11)
WALKS (10)
RADIO, AUDIO SYSTEMS (6)
CORRESPONDENCE (4)
INDOOR GAMES (3)
SPORTS ENTERTAINMENT EVENTS (3)
MOVIES (3)
PARTICIPATIVE SPORT, EXERCISE (3)
ATTEND CULTURAL EVENT (1)
PARTICIPATIVE ART, MUSIC (.5)
OTHER (1)
TELEVISION (58)

U.S.A. 266 MINS/DAY

SOCIAL TELEPHONE USAGE (18)
SOCIAL MEALS, PARTIES (19)
READ NEWSPAPERS (24)
VISIT WITH FRIENDS, FAMILY (39)

TRAVEL (13)
READ BOOKS, MAGAZINES (12)
PARTICIPATIVE SPORT, EXERCISE (7)
SPORTS, ENTERTAINMENT EVENTS (5)
INDOOR GAMES (5)
RADIO, AUDIO SYSTEMS (5)
RELAX, REST (4)
CORRESPONDENCE (4)
MOVIES (3)
HOBBIES (2)
PARTICIPATIVE ART, MUSIC (2)
ATTEND CULTURAL EVENT (1)
WALKS (1)
OTHER (1)
TELEVISION (92)

U.S.S.R. 193 MINS/DAY

RADIO, AUDIO SYSTEMS (10)
WALKS (10)
READ NEWSPAPERS (15)
MOVIES (16)
TRAVEL (16)
READ BOOKS, MAGAZINES (35)

SOCIAL TELEPHONE USAGE (8)
PARTICIPATIVE SPORT, EXERCISE (7)
HOBBIES (6)
RELAX, REST (6)
VISIT WITH FRIENDS, FAMILY (5)
SOCIAL MEALS, PARTIES (5)
CORRESPONDENCE (4)
INDOOR GAMES (3)
SPORTS, ENTERTAINMENT EVENTS (3)
ATTEND CULTURAL EVENT (3)
PARTICIPATIVE ART, MUSIC (1)
OTHER (1)
TELEVISION (39)

Adapted from: *The Use of Time : Daily Activities of Urban and Suburban Populations*. The Hague: Mouton. A. Szalai, Ed.

come. Professionals and business executives attend concerts, the theater, lectures, and museums; they travel, and read for pleasure. Middle managers and white-collar groups do more partying and golf-playing. Skilled tradesmen and unskilled laborers spend more time working on cars, watching TV, and attending sports events. There is no indication, though, that cultural pursuits are becoming more popular, and government support of the arts in America continues to be among the lowest of the developed nations.

Books and the electronic communications media continue to vie for Americans' free time. Print-oriented consumers are found primarily among the higher occupational and socioeconomic groups; watchers and listeners predominate in the blue-collar and lower-income groups. Newspapers, magazines, and broadcasting companies have become amalgamated, with reduced independence and numbers, and most American cities today suffer under monopolistic and propagandistic media reporting, with little intelligent coverage of foreign news.

The American cinema has never recovered, of course, from the impact of television, in spite of offering wide-screen features and stereophonic sound, as well as graphic sex and violence. The forced split of production and distribution operations has resulted in a preponderance of formulaic Hollywood films, presented in poorly maintained, small theaters with bad-mannered audiences. Videotape availability is thus persuading more consumers to forego theater attendance in favor of quiet home-viewing comfort, with large-screen television and surround-sound simulating the theater environment.

According to sociologist Arlie Hochschild, working women have 15 fewer leisure hours per week than their husbands. In a year they work an extra month of 24-hour days.

Sporting activities have been part of man's recreation at least since the Greeks began the Olympic Games in 1300 B.C. The Romans denigrated their purpose by escalating the competition from individual amateur contests to massive, staged spectacles that became such brutal circuses that they were finally banned by Theodosius in 394 A.D. This same process of deterioration appears to be at work today, since the Games' revival in 1896. The Eastern bloc nations use them for political advantage, with government-supported athletes; the Western nations go after the advertising revenues. Although this century has seen the greatest popularity of sports activities in history, the positive enjoyment values are being supplanted by commercialization and professionalism, and winning at all costs, rather than having fun.

In outdoor recreation and travel, the pressure to consume goods has made fancy gear and gadgetry more important than simple enjoyment of our natural resources, as expenditures on motor homes,

148   TIMESOURCE

trailers, power boats, and designer "uniforms" have obediently risen to the advertisers' call. Although on the average Americans spend but 2 percent of their lives outdoors, they spend more than $120 billion on outdoor paraphernalia each year.

Dr. Thomas Kando is bluntly critical of the way in which we use our leisure time.[2] He says, "Our vast affluence and the enormous energy that has been freed over the past decades are diverted into dead-end streets and blind alleys, requiring continued energy expenditure but no imagination. We tax ourselves and our resources to the utmost while maintaining intellectual torpor."

Fortunately, there are increasing numbers of people who agree with him and want to recover some of the values inherent in a modern version of civilized leisure. They want to get off the materialistic carousel without retreating into drug- or TV-induced anesthesia. They want their lives to have more quality and less material quantity and are realizing that too much time at the workplace forces high-consumption time away from it, and perhaps both are excessive.

If you feel you would like to improve your use of time off the job, start by using the Free Time Analysis worksheet at the end of this chapter. It will help you to see what your free time is focused upon. You've worked hard to gain it, and it's the most valuable time you have. What do you really want to do with it? When you have completed the worksheet, you will have an opportunity to do some of the most important thinking you can do, thinking about what you want to do with your life.

To rearrange your recreational and free time activities to fit better with your personal values or schedules, use the worksheet as a road map, and make adjustments to fit with a new plan, which you can fill in on another blank worksheet.

These important personal planning activities will help you to achieve dreams and pleasures that may never be yours while you remain a part of Linder's "harried leisure class."[3]

Now what of the future? America is said to be entering a post-industrial era, wherein most of us will be employed in service and development occupations rather than in manufacturing. There are signs of this already, and sociologists forecast four possible scenarios for leisure in the twenty-first century.

Television set ownership per 1000 people:	
USA	785
Japan	562
Canada	479
Netherlands	449
Australia	429
Italy	404
Sweden	390
France	375
W. Germany	360
E. Germany	357
UK	328
USSR	310

2. Kando, Thomas M. *Leisure and Popular Culture in Transition.* St. Louis: C. V. Mosby Co., 1975.

3. Linder, Staffan. *The Harried Leisure Class.* New York: Columbia University Press, 1970.

1. Technocratic forces will continue to make leisure a materialistic search for luxury, with deepening separation of work and nonwork activities, so long as economic growth is maintained. Within two hundred years, the continuing overproduction and consumption of superficial goods will cause the economic collapse of both socialist and capitalist societies.

2. Multinational organizations will lower living standards in the United States through continuing transfer of profits and capital to foreign shareholders. Consequent deterioration of leisure quality will result in cultureless mass spectacles and television programming, and will gradually eliminate the middle classes whose members will become very rich or very poor (mostly the latter).

3. The world population explosion, coupled with increased pollution, drug usage, and deterioration of natural resources can, according to computer projections, bring about a total collapse of existing economic and leisure patterns by 2100. The resultant social disorganization would practically eliminate leisure and force a return to survivalist activity.

4. There will be a weakening of the line between work and nonwork activities. The separate workplace where most of us now spend forty hours a week will vanish as work becomes integrated with living activities; home offices/workshops and creative pursuits will support both production and leisure.

Numerous indicators of trends towards the above scenarios are obvious today. The most likely trend currently appears to be the expansion of technocratic leisure patterns—at least until environmental plundering and material waste forces a change. Perhaps that crisis will produce leaders who may, before it is too late, guide us in the development of a world of creative pleasure, where work and leisure are intelligently mixed to avoid both boredom and anxiety.

Recommended for further reading, in addition to the sources cited:

Chubb, M. and H. *One Third of Our Time?* New York: John Wiley & Sons, Inc., 1981.

FREE TIME ANALYSIS

My total free time each week is _____ hours.

I SPEND IT LIKE THIS:
Use decimal hours for ease in addition.
15 minutes = .25 hour, etc.

	TIME	% OF TOTAL
Home cleanup/maintenance	_____	_____
Home improvement	_____	_____
Home management (bill paying, etc.)	_____	_____
Auto maintenance	_____	_____
Work at a second job or business	_____	_____
Office "homework"	_____	_____
Spectator activity (sports/movies/shows, etc.)	_____	_____
Watch TV	_____	_____
Read newspapers	_____	_____
Read books, magazines	_____	_____
Creative hobbies	_____	_____
Community or fraternal service	_____	_____
Religious activities	_____	_____
Further education	_____	_____
Entertain family/friends at home	_____	_____
Visit family/friends	_____	_____
Work-related travel, including commuting	_____	_____
Pleasure travel	_____	_____
Engage in physical activities (sports/exercise)	_____	_____
Shopping	_____	_____
Rest, relax	_____	_____
Yard/garden work	_____	_____
Other: _____	_____	_____
_____	_____	_____
TOTAL FREE TIME HOURS:	_____	100%

LISTENING TIME

How much time we spend listening ·
Knowledge transfer by sound · The modes
of communication · Improving listening
habits · Listening skill test

The average person is involved in listening about 45 percent of their waking time, but although it is the first communication skill we learn, it is usually not well developed—perhaps because it is rarely taught or practiced in school. Good listening skills are essential to good communication and people who have learned to listen well save time because they make fewer mistakes and absorb more factual information. They spend less time having to repair damaged relationships, too, as such damage is often caused by poor communication.

Although we spend so much of our time listening—more so students and upper-level managers—most of us concentrate more on what *we* want to say than on what others are saying, so we miss much of the transmission. And because our minds work faster than our tongues, we find it easy to let our attention stray briefly to other thoughts. The trouble is, that's just when the speaker may be saying something important. We tune back in and never know we've missed a beat.

Listening is a complex process of sensing intelligible sounds, evaluating their content, interpreting their meaning, responding appropriately, and storing part of the experience in memory. *Listening* requires total concentration, as distinguished from *hearing*, when sound is permitted to wash over us with little absorption of its content. We usually only hear background music, the hum of voices, and natural sounds. Our response to them is subliminal, and though they may affect our sense of well-being, we don't really think about them because hearing is a passive activity. Listening, on the other hand, is an active process and demands some effort.

Knowledge transfer by sound is as important as reading and is patterned in four ways:

Time takes all and
gives all.
Giordano Bruno, 1582

Informative Communication in which ideas, facts, and needs are transferred.

Social Communication which establishes an interactive atmosphere rather than communicating ideas.

Cathartic Communication which vents feelings and emotions.

Persuasive Communication which reinforces and changes attitudes, or causes a desired action.

Skilled listening requires the recognition of which of these communication forms is in use, even though a speaker may make it difficult by switching from one to another, or using more than one at once. Alert perception is needed to give a sensitive and appropriate response and to save time by not requesting a repetition of the delivery.

Factual or informative communication requires concentration on the voice and skill in ignoring the distractions of poor delivery, hand waving, and surrounding noise. All of these can divert attention, with subsequent loss of information transferred to the listener. At the same time, too much concentration on detail can also distract. It is preferable to listen to overall ideas and themes and to make notes of facts.

Use social communication to learn about the speaker, so that the tendency to second-guess or prejudge is lessened. In a social atmosphere, it is frequently possible to discern the speaker's underlying emotion; this can be very useful if the conversation later turns to business.

Listen for *feelings* as well as facts when it seems that the speaker is cathartically unburdening emotions. Measure the energy that is being put into the speaker's delivery and if it is inappropriate, search for the underlying reason. Feelings hide behind words, and communication is reduced when they are not acknowledged and satisfied. You can jot down facts as they are given, if necessary, to keep your mind free for communication.

Guard against your surface impressions of the speaker, which may be quite wrong. Prejudgment usually produces "tuning out," with consequent loss of important cues and facts.

Tuning out also takes place when one is planning witty responses or cutting counter-arguments, or being introduced to a stranger. Names are not forgotten; they are most often not heard, because the listener is so mentally involved in comparing appearances, sizing up the newcomer, and trying to insure that the social rules are in place. Concentration on the words will help to improve name retention. (See *MEMORY*.)

Time will explain it all. He is a talker and needs no questioning before he speaks.

Euripides

Encourage speakers with your own nonverbal cues. Nod in agreement from time to time, indicate empathy with appropriate sounds, and maintain eye contact and suitable facial expressions. Avoid looking away or adopting the dropped eyelid expressions that indicates boredom. At work, don't try to impress by signing checks, shuffling papers, or doing other tasks while pretending to listen.

Try and avoid emotional involvement by dispassionately observing and interpreting emotionally-laden words, off-color language, and offensive delivery. Emotions are listening blocks. Control any tendency to be contentious, which frequently makes one cut off speakers before they finish, suppressing their thought and expression. When an exciting concept sparks your imagination, resist the temptation to leap ahead with extrapolation. Keep listening, and let your mind take off later.

Use the ability to think (which can be done at eight hundred words per minute) between spoken words, the flow of which rarely exceeds two hundred words per minute. Pinpoint the speaker's themes, store key points for future reference, and tune in to the areas of interest while continuing to listen. These pointers are particularly valuable in a selling environment.

Avoid negative response techniques like "grandstanding"—that is, displaying one's superior knowledge of a subject, or dominating the conversation.

Use response techniques to amplify transfer of knowledge. Ask questions, rephrase ideas in your own words, and answer implied or direct questions leveled by the speaker.

Personal listening skills are critical to avoid the time wasted by communication errors. Even when you have to listen to something you don't like, listen hard. And last, but certainly not least . . . let the other person have the last word!

MEASUREMENT OF TIME

The historical development of time measurement from the earliest recorded time to modern atomic clocks and world time zones

The first human measurement of time was undoubtedly the recording of the passage of the sun and moon, the tides, and the seasons. Primitive markings on bones have been found, made by cave dwellers in 4000 B.C., that recorded the moon's changes and appearance. The historical development of time measurement since then goes like this:

3761 B.C.   The Hebrew calendar is dated from this year, once believed to mark the creation of the world.

3500 B.C.   A stick pushed into the ground, called a *gnomon*, was the first primitive way of measuring time by the length of a shadow.

The gnomons were a part of the worship of the sun god Ra by the Egyptian priests. Sticks were supplanted by large stone obelisks, and by the continuous measurement of the length and angular movement of their shadows, the year, equinoxes, and solstices were found. (See *YEAR*.)

3000 B.C.   The Sumerians developed a calendar with seven-day weeks. They divided the twenty-four-hour day into twelve periods, and their resulting "hours" into thirty parts. Their knowledge was lost as wars destroyed subsequent cultures almost continuously over the next thousand years.

2500 B.C.   In England an enormous stone structure at Stonehenge was aligned to record the sun's rising on Midsummer's Day, thus measuring the passage of a year by the solstice.

2000 B.C.   The first known observations of the stars and planets were made by Babylonian priest-astronomers, with the objective of forecasting future events. They believed that the heavens belonged to the gods, and that by noting the movement of the stars, divine intentions might be predicted. Their calendar was based on the moon's cycle, with a year of twelve "lunations." (See *YEAR* and *CALENDAR*.)

1800 B.C.   The Babylonian star catalogs and mathematical tables were developed with such accuracy that little improvement was made upon them for three thousand years. The planets were associated with gods who controlled time and life on earth, and as their orbits were observed to be circular, the first concepts of time were cyclic rather than linear. It was believed that the world would periodically come to an end, and then life would begin all over again.

1500 B.C.   The oldest sundials we have discovered (unearthed in Egypt) come from about this time. Rudimentary clepsydrae, or water clocks, were first used to measure nighttime hours by a regulated flow from a graduated container.

1500–700 B.C.   The Indian Vedic philosophers embraced the concept of cyclical time. They calculated that life would start over again every four hundred years. The same concept was popular among the Mayans, Chinese, Greeks, and Romans.

1300 B.C.   The Arabian Abu al-Hasan introduced the concept of a day divided into equal hours. Pharaoh Thutmose III had two great gnomons erected at the entrance to the Temple of the Sun at Heliopolis.

776 B.C.   The Olympic Games began. The Olympiad cycle was set alternately at forty-nine and fifty months by the Greeks to correct the thirty-day slippage in their calendar, because they used a 354-day year. (See *CALENDAR*.)

738 B.C.   In Rome, King Romulus instituted a calendar with ten months to a year. Two more months were added in 713 B.C. by Numa Pompilius, and this was the origin of our present calendar.

689 B.C.   A solar eclipse occurred, visible in the Middle East, which coincides with a statement about Isaiah in the Bible: ". . . and he brought the shadow ten degrees backward, by which it had gone down in the dial of Ahaz" (2 Kings 20.11). Ahaz was the king who introduced the sundial to Judah.

650 B.C.   An improved sundial was developed which did not require turning to show the afternoon hours.

600 B.C.   Astrology became an important social force in Chaldean society.

500 B.C.   The nineteen-year repetitive relationship between the sun and the moon, now called the Metonic cycle, was discovered by Babylonian priest-astronomers.

400 B.C.   The Greek philosopher Anaxagoras first explained the eclipses of the sun and moon.

336 B.C.   Alexander the Great conquered the Babylonian Empire and encouraged continued study of visible stars and planets. The Babylonian astronomer Kidinnu's later calculations of the sun's motion were improved upon only in the twentieth century. The trade routes began to spread this Babylonian science throughout Mediterranean lands.

330 B.C.   A portable sundial, or "hemicycle," was developed by the Babylonian priest-astronomer Berossos. (See *SUNDIALS*.)

300 B.C.   In Greece, Euclid developed the first principles of geometry.

275 B.C.   The Great Year Doctrine was preached by Berossos, who still believed that the world would end periodically, but at the conjunction of certain stars, every 36,000 years. Plato and Seneca supported the concept in their writings.

160 B.C.   The Romans divided the day into five marked periods.

47 B.C.   The 365.5-day Julian calendar was introduced by Julius Caesar.

12 B.C.   The Egyptian gnomons at Heliopolis were moved on the orders of Caesar Augustus to the Temple of the Caesars at Alexandria. They became known as Cleopatra's Needles, as she ruled Egypt at the time.

7 B.C.   According to many theologians, Jesus Christ was born in Jerusalem, initiating the Christian religion. Both Christians and Jews rejected the cyclical time theory.

50 A.D.   Pole star alignment of sundials was discovered, so that they remained accurate throughout the year. As late as the Middle Ages,

The oldest city in the world is probably Gaziantep, Turkey. It was founded around 3650 B.C.

few people knew the time of day or even the year. Their lives were simply geared to sunrise and sunset.

500 A.D.   The abacus was invented in China and Europe.

532 A.D.   The abbot of Rome set the date of the birth of Christ as December 25, and established the B.C. and A.D. numeration.

570 A.D.   Birth of Muhammad, founder of the Islamic religion, whose calendar recognized twelve lunar months, beginning with each new moon.

590 A.D.   Pope Sabinianus added two more periods to the Roman day divisions, creating the seven canonical hours for services: matins (morning), lauds (praise), prime (first), tierce (third), sext (sixth), nones (ninth), vespers (evening), and complin (complete).

683 A.D.   The first use of zero in figures took place in the Far East.

860 A.D.   Candle lantern "clocks" were used by the Anglo-Saxon king, Alfred of Wessex, England. The Saxons later divided the day into periods called "tides" which were equal to three modern hours. (See *ETYMOLOGY.*)

900 A.D.   Sand began to replace water in time-measuring devices, heralding the development of sandglasses.

977 A.D.   In China, Chang Ssu-Hsun constructed what was probably the first astronomical water clock.

1094 A.D.   Building on Ssu-Hsun's work, Su Sung directed the construction of a massive, forty-foot high water clock with a rudimentary escapement. It displayed hours and *k'o*, or quarters (1 k'o = 14.4 minutes). (See *CLOCKS.*)

1275 A.D.   The Great Year Doctrine was condemned as heresy by the bishop of Paris.

1280 A.D.   The invention of the clock escapement in Europe (see *CLOCKS*), brought improved accuracy to timekeeping devices, primarily used at that time for the ringing of bells to summon the faithful to their prayers. The ancient French song . . .

> Frère Jacques, Frère Jacques
> Dormez-vous? Dormez-vous?
> Sonnent les matines. Sonnent les matines.
> Din, din, don, din, din, don.

was probably composed around this time.

1300 A.D. The first clock which struck the hours was erected in Milan, Italy. The oldest surviving striking clock, built about 1305, is in Salisbury Cathedral in England. It is one of the first to have been used for nonreligious purposes; the strike of one bell signaled the opening of the food markets.

1350 A.D. Public clocks were built, showing minutes for the first time. Their appearance began to change time attitudes from an experiential base to a visible base. People could now "see" time.

1360 A.D. The Italian scholar and poet, Petrarch, was one of the first writers to treat time as a commodity that could be wasted or saved; Father Time appeared as an illustration in his *Trionfi* (*Triumphs*).

1380 A.D. A group of Oxford scholars led by William Heytesbury became the first to study time and motion in order to quantify acceleration.

1495 A.D. A German locksmith, Peter Heinlein, introduced the first spring-powered clocks.

1520 A.D. Clocks were made with the capability to show hours, minutes, and seconds. Martin Luther determined that the world was about four thousand years old. Swivelling sand- or hourglasses were still in wide use.

1530 A.D. The accuracy of spring-driven clocks was improved by the invention of the fusee in Prague by Jacob the Czech.

1543 A.D. Copernicus determined that the sun lay at the center of the solar system and produced new astronomical tables.

1572 A.D. A visible supernova was interpreted as a sign that the end of the world was at hand. A repeat performance occurred in 1604.

1580 A.D. Tycho Brahe, the Danish astronomer, corrected the Copernican astronomical tables and provided the basis for Kepler's later work.

Bells and automatic chimes were used to signal the start and end of work periods for laborers and merchants. Galileo began experimenting with pendulums.

1582 A.D. Pope Gregory XIII established the Gregorian calendar in Europe. It was not adopted by England (or later, Colonial America) until 1752.

Time has laid his hand
Upon my heart, gently,
  not smiting it
But as a harper lays his
  open palm
Upon his harp to
  deaden its vibrations.
  Henry Wadsworth
  Longfellow,
  The Golden Legend

1604 A.D. Galileo began to relate motion and time, with his studies on falling bodies. Contrary to popular belief, he did not experiment with weights dropped from the Tower of Pisa, although another scholar did in 1612. Unfortunately, Galileo was unaware of Heytesbury's work, and his first postulations were incorrect, because he related velocity with distance instead of time. He later realized his error and corrected it, establishing the important distance/time equation: $d = \frac{1}{2}at^2$.

1609 A.D. The principles of planetary motion were established by Johannes Kepler (Germany).

1641 A.D. Galileo adapted the pendulum to clock mechanisms.

1656 A.D. Christian Huygens substituted the pendulum for the foliot bar to regulate clocks.

1658 A.D. In England, Robert Hooke invented the anchor, or recoil, escapement, providing greater accuracy for less power.

1675 A.D. In Denmark, Olaus Romer determined the speed of light. In England, Charles II established the Royal Observatory at Greenwich.

1687 A.D. Isaac Newton published his *Philosophiae Naturalis Principia Mathematica*, which correctly related the laws of motion/time and gravity through the use of calculus.

1692 A.D. The Swiss watch-making industry was begun by Daniel Jean-Richard; a commemorative statue is located in Locle, Switzerland.

1714 A.D. The marine chronometer was invented in England by John Harrison, in a competition sponsored by the government.

1715 A.D. The deadbeat escapement was invented by George Graham. It was not improved upon for two hundred years.

1759 A.D. Thomas Mudge of Exeter, England, invented the detached lever escapement that is still used in watches today.

1783 A.D. The first watch manufacturing firm, Vacheron & Constantin, was founded in Switzerland.

1785 A.D. The Scottish geologist, James Hutton, proposed that the earth's formation took place gradually, over a long period of time, rather than by a series of catastrophic events. He challenged traditionalists by saying, "There is no vestige of a beginning, and no prospect of an end."

1795 A.D.   The French Revolutionary Convention introduced a decimal calendar with a ten-day week. Thirteen years later Napoleon, under religious pressure, returned the country to using the Gregorian calendar.

1816 A.D.   The first metronome was constructed in Germany by Johann Malzel.

1803 A.D.   The atomic structure of matter was determined by John Dalton (England).

1809 A.D.   The first wristwatch was made by order of the Empress Josephine by M. Nitot in Paris.

1827 A.D.   Karl Gauss began to retest Euclidian geometry to determine whether it would work in space.

1829 A.D.   The first time ball, invented by Captain Robert Wauchope of the British Royal Navy, was installed at Plymouth, England. It was dropped each day at 1 P.M. and used by ships' navigators to correct their chronometers, with which they established longitude when at sea.

The United States National Observatory in Washington, D.C., completed in 1844. The time ball, used by navigators to calibrate their chronometers, may be seen at the top of the mast.

1830 A.D.   Charles Lyell's *Principles of Geology* forced scientists to recognize that the earth must have existed for millions, not thousands, of years. He was later a strong supporter of Charles Darwin's evolutionary theories.

1843 A.D.   The first electric pendulum clock was invented by Alexander Bain.

1844 A.D.   The United States National Observatory was completed in Washington, D.C. A time ball, using Wauchope's design, was dropped from a mast at noon each day.

1848 A.D.   The time at the Royal Observatory, Greenwich, was established as a standard throughout Britain, and its position designated as the world prime meridian.

1853 A.D.   The first American-made watches were manufactured in Roxbury, Massachusetts, by Aaron Dennison and Edward Howard.

1859 A.D.   In England the great clock in Westminster Tower, now called Big Ben, was designed and installed by Edmund Beckett.

1865 A.D.   The German mathematical physicist Rudolf Clausius developed the principle of entropy, or the natural equilibration of energy.

1880 A.D.   The Khedive of Egypt gave Cleopatra's Needles to London and New York to commemorate the opening of the Suez Canal.

1883 A.D.   The U.S. time zones were established.

1884 A.D.   The Mean Solar Day was established as a worldwide standard at the International Prime Meridian Conference in Washington, D.C.

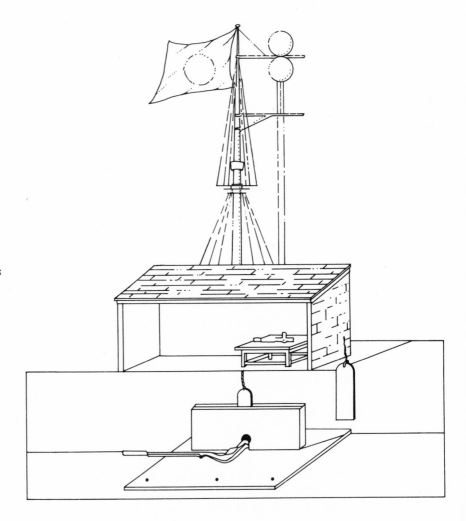

Captain Robert Wauchope's design for a time ball, first used at Plymouth, England in 1829.

1896 A.D.   The French scientist Henri Becquerel discovered that uranium emits radiation. The phenomenon was further investigated by the Curies and Ernest Rutherford.

1897 A.D.   Kelvin calculated the probable age of the earth at twenty-four million years, based on his laws of thermodynamics. He later revised this to one hundred million years, which became the orthodox belief of the period.

1905 A.D.   Albert Einstein published his special theory of relativity: $E = mc^2$. It showed that time dilation is real, and increases as motion approaches 186,300 miles per second. Travel into the future (but not the past) was thus shown to be theoretically possible.

1906 A.D.   The first self-contained battery-driven clock was developed.

1907 A.D.   The first attempt to establish the age of the earth using radioactive dating methods was completed by the American physicist Bertram Boltwood. He calculated that the earth had to be at least 2.2 billion years old. In the same year, Herman Minkowski developed the space-time concept to satisfy the differences in event-times that observers will make when in different states of motion.

1908 A.D.   J. E. McTaggart, the English philosopher, defined two different time concepts. He called the description of time that covers past, present, and future *A-series time*, and the simpler "earlier and later" description *B-series time*. The idea of "now" does not appear in B-series time.

1915 A.D.   Einstein established his general theory of relativity, showing the existence of four-dimensional space-time. The inapplicability of Euclidian geometry to the cosmos is confirmed by Lobatchevsky, Bolyai, and Reimann.

1918 A.D.   The accuracy of domestic clocks was improved through the use of synchronous electric motors.

1922 A.D.   The Shortt electric pendulum clock was installed at the Royal Observatory, Greenwich, as the primary world time standard. It was accurate to one part in four million, or seven seconds per year.

1927 A.D.   The principles of quantum mechanics, dealing with the behavior of atomic matter, were established by the German physicist Werner Heisenberg and the Danish physicist Niels Bohr.

Half our life is spent trying to find something to do with the time we have rushed through life trying to save.

Will Rogers,
American humorist

1928 A.D.   The first quartz crystal clock was constructed by W. A. Marrison at Bell Laboratories, with an accuracy of one second in ten years.

1929 A.D.   The American astronomer Edwin Hubble showed that the universe is expanding. The Soviet Union unsuccessfully attempted to replace the Gregorian calendar with one of its own. It was abandoned in 1940.

1930 A.D.   A World calendar was devised by Elizabeth Achelis. It is supported by the United Nations but has been opposed by certain religious groups. (See *CALENDAR TIME.*)

1939 A.D.   English astronomer H. S. Jones determined that the earth is not spinning regularly and, therefore, not maintaining accurate time relationships. The first quartz crystal resonator clock was installed at the Royal Observatory, accurate to .002 seconds per day.

1949 A.D.   The first atomic clock, using the ammonia molecule, was constructed by the U.S. National Bureau of Standards, with an accuracy of three parts per billion, or three seconds in 31.7 years.

1949 A.D.   Richard Feynman, an American physicist, showed the possibility of reverse time/motion at the subatomic level of matter. He demonstrated that a positron moving forward in time and an electron moving backward in time have the same properties. He and John Wheeler had earlier pointed out that, as time-reversed radiation theory satisfies electrodynamic laws, it should also exist in nature.

The photographic zenith tube was installed at the U.S. Naval Observatory, through which star images are captured to synchronize Earth time with the universe for time determination.

1953 A.D.   The first electronic wristwatch was developed with a tuning fork controller, and later, in 1959, was introduced to the American market as the Accutron by Bulova. The device was remarkable for the accuracy of its mass-produced parts. The 300-tooth beryllium-copper ratchet wheel was only .09 inch in diameter, and successfully withstood thirty-eight million revolutions per year without excessive wear. Timekeeping accuracy was guaranteed within two seconds per day.

1955 A.D.   The first cesium atomic clock was constructed at the National Physical Laboratory in Teddington, England.

1956 A.D.   Ephemeris time (ET) was first measured as the change in the moon's relationship to a group of stars, and used by scientists

As if you could kill time without injuring eternity.
Henry David Thoreau,
Walden

for correlation with time measured on the surface of the earth (Universal time or UT) in 1900 A.D. Due to the earth's gradual slowing, ET and UT differed by about thirty seconds in 1956.

1958 A.D. A joint experiment by the British National Physical Laboratory and the U.S. Naval Observatory established the frequency of cesium at 9,192,631,770 cycles per second of ephemeris time. With this new accuracy of time measurement, definition of a second again became necessary. The "rubber second" was introduced, which scientists agreed would be adjusted annually to correlate Universal time (UT) with atomic time. The system was abandoned in 1967. The new compromise time scale was christened Coordinated Universal time (UTC).

1961 A.D. Marine chronometers, using quartz resonators, were first submitted to the Swiss Observatory at Neuchâtel, with better accuracy than the best mechanical chronometers. They improved their lead in subsequent years, causing the abandonment of the Swiss annual wristwatch chronometer competition in April of 1968.

1964 A.D. An atomic particle called the K meson was identified, whose decay was found to be time-reversed in certain circumstances. No explanation has yet been found.
   Radiocarbon dating was pioneered by W. F. Libby, who established that the half-life of radiocarbon was 5,720 years.

1965 A.D. Fission track dating of volcanic rock set the minimum age of the earth's crust at 3.7 billion years. The first black hole was discovered in the constellation Cygnus.

1967 A.D. The second was defined and officially adopted by international agreement as the elapsed time of 9,192,631,770 oscillations of the cesium atom.

1968 A.D. Molecular dating was discovered, using cytochrome C, which appears to "tick" at about four unit differences per hundred million years. The Hamilton Watch Company introduced the first Pulsar watch. The first Seiko watches, made in Japan, were introduced, then withdrawn due to quality problems. Later reintroduced, they have now captured a major segment of the U.S. market.

1970 A.D. The moon rock samples from the Apollo mission were dated at 4.2 billion years. Spectroscopic analysis of starlight indicated that the universe is approximately fifteen billion years old.

Texas Instruments Inc. and Ebauches S.A. began producing liquid crystal displays for watches.

1972 A.D.   The "leap second" was introduced, to be added or subtracted from atomic time whenever it differs 0.9 seconds from Coordinated Universal time. The adjustment is made in the last minute of the year or in the last minute of June, and is regulated by the Bureau International de l'Heure (BIH) in Paris, France.

1974 A.D.   Orbital dating was developed, based on cyclical changes in the earth's spatial attitude and attendant climatic changes. Power consumption in digital watches was reduced by 60 percent as liquid crystal displays (LCDs) became freely available.

1976 A.D.   Time dilation theories were proven through the use of an atomic clock installed in a jet aircraft. On landing, the aircraft clock showed a different time than the one which had remained earthbound.

1980 A.D.   MIT physicist Alan Guth proposed the inflationary universe theory that presents the possibility that the universe was created from an element of space-time devoid of matter. The Guth inflationary universe theory is supported with entropic reasoning by the British scientist Paul Davies.

The cesium atomic clock is currently the most accurate time-measuring device in general scientific use. Cesium (used because it

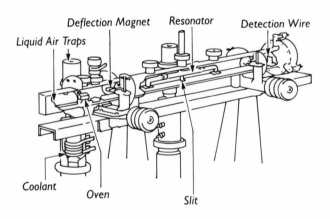

Cesium Beam Atomic Clock

has a low melting point) is heated in an vacuum tube, causing a stream of electrons to flow off through a magnetic field to a resonator. Cesium electrons, like all others, constantly change from a high-energy state to a low-energy state as they switch back and forth in their orbits around the atom nucleus. The frequency at which these changes occur is the most constant physical phenomenon known, and is unaffected by gravity, temperature, pressure, or any other known force. Through feedback loops, the frequency of the magnetic field is matched to the maximum change-of-state frequency of the cesium electrons, and to a quartz clock operating at five million cycles per second. Any change in the operating frequency of the quartz clock results in an immediate correction through a signal received from the frequency detection wire. The cesium clock is now used internationally for time standards, and is accurate to one second in three thousand years. A new hydrogen atomic clock has been developed recently, however, from which even greater accuracy is expected.

As a result of our modern ability to measure time, scientists have learned that the earth's rotational speed varies. Three types of variation have been determined. A *secular* variation, caused by tidal friction, is increasing the length of a day by .001 second per 100 years. *Periodic* variations at fixed periods throughout the year cause annual differences of 0.3 seconds. *Irregular* variations from unknown causes can amount to .005 seconds at any one time, and have added to a total of 30 seconds since 1790.

From a scientific standpoint, time measurement is described in two ways—*epochal time*, which determines the instant at which an event occurs, and *interval time*, which specifies the elapsed time between two instants.

Our attempts to relate Earth time to the rest of the observable universe (epochal time) and define a second (interval time) by its rotational movement were both, until 1956, based on *mean solar time*. The discovery of the rotational variations then caused scientists to use *ephemeris time* or *atomic time* for improved accuracy.

The constantly shifting positions of the sun, the earth, and the moon have caused confusion around the world as to the time of day since biblical times, when most Middle Eastern countries *began* their day at sunset. This observance still exists among Israelis who cling to the Hebrew calendar.

In 1884, an international conference brought agreement from most nations to divide the world into twenty-four time zones, or meridians. The prime meridian passes vertically through the Royal

HOW THE ACCURACY OF TIME MEASUREMENT HAS DEVELOPED

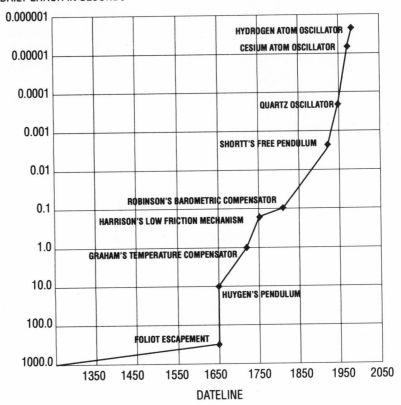

DAILY ERROR IN SECONDS

In the fourteenth century, one could never be sure of the exact time—even the best timepieces were only accurate to within fifteen minutes. Accuracy improved remarkably when Huygens introduced his pendulum and continued at an increasingly faster rate over the next two centuries. Today, atomic clocks are accurate to better than one-millionth of a second per day.

Greenwich Observatory in London, England, continues around the South Pole and up through the Pacific Ocean (where it becomes the international date line), over the North Pole and back to Greenwich.

Unfortunately, some nations refused to accept the international conference plan. Mongolia, Afghanistan, and Saudi Arabia continue to set their own time, so visitors to Mecca may be surprised to find that the sun is setting at noon!

Time zone lines do not always follow the meridians exactly. In the United States, the Interstate Commerce Commission bent some of the boundaries to avoid heavily populated areas.

Currently, within the United States, the United States Naval Observatory (USNO) maintains astronomical time standards, and the National Bureau of Standards (NBS) is responsible for atomic time accuracy. Both agencies contribute data to the Bureau International de l'Heure in France, which is now the international headquarters for world timekeeping.

See also *CALENDAR, CLOCKS, DAY, WEEK, MONTH, YEAR.*

MEETING TIME

*When meetings waste time · Analyzing
meeting costs · Preparing for effective meetings ·
Making interactive meetings work · The interactive
process · Group development phases · Making
small group meetings pay off · Large group
meetings and presentations · Question and
answer periods · Board meetings*

Interaction between people, either in pairs or in greater numbers, constitutes one of management's most vital tools . . . the business meeting. Yet millions of man-hours are wasted monthly because the meetings people attend are worthless; that is, they achieve no measurable result. Some even have a negative effect, because they create dissension where none existed before. Most managers report that they spend about ten hours each week in group meetings, but that only about 50 percent of the time is well spent, so meetings obviously present wonderful opportunities to throw away time and money.

The average Frenchman's business lunch is 124 minutes, compared with the American's 67.

Under the veneer of management efficiency, the time-wasting business meeting brings together as many people as possible on a regular basis. It doesn't matter what for. After all, the benefits of getting the whole team together are well known, aren't they? Look for all the meeting opportunities you can, and send your staff to every one you know about in the organization. They'll learn *something*, even if the subject doesn't concern them, and it's nice to have a finger in everything that's going on.

The unexpected meeting is probably the most exciting. Everybody enjoys the surprise, and it gives a welcome break to their routine activities. Besides, they can't come prepared to argue with you, so things run more smoothly. Spend some time, too, in personal chitchat before anything else; it helps to make everyone feel more at home, and heightens the sense of anticipation.

If these scenarios sound familiar, and you would like to avoid them, read on.

Productive, down-to-earth business meetings can only be created by mixing the right blend of people skills and organizing skills. When this occurs, meeting time becomes some of the most valuable that executives can contribute to their organization.

There are three steps in managing meetings. First, preparation; second, knowledge and management of process; and third, effective follow-up.

MEETING PREPARATION

Before you call a meeting, be sure that it is the best way to deal with a situation. Meetings consume a lot of time and money, yet are rarely evaluated in terms of their true value. The meeting cost/results evaluation sheet (*see* Appendix D) can be a useful control tool. Its preparation should be mandatory for any meeting costing more than $500—or less, in small organizations. It doesn't take long to figure out the per hour cost of the people involved. Are the results worth it? The number of meetings will often decline as much as 50 percent when managers are brought face to face with their real costs.

Meetings should only be called:

- to gain multilevel involvement in the definition of organizational goals.

- to define, analyze, and solve problems. (Group solutions are proven to be better, on the average, than individual solutions.)

- to receive reports on which immediate discussion will add value.

- to gain consensus in decision making, or acceptance of innovation and change.

- for educational purposes, to improve job skills, or to develop awareness of organizational policies and procedures.

- to gain immediate, multilevel response to a situation or proposition.

- to handle "people problems," reconcile conflicting views, relieve tensions and insecurities, and expedite action . . . those items generally called "running the business."

Don't call meetings if any other form of communication will suffice. Avoid them, too, when any key participant is unavailable, when there is inadequate time for preparation, when the timing is not right, or when it is likely that clashing opinions will prevent useful results.

Consider written communication, individual or conference telephone calls, or personal executive action before ever convening a meeting.

Take care that your meetings are not padded with noncontributing individuals. Anyone who is asked to attend will feel obligated to say *something*, even if he has nothing to say. That's exactly the sort of thing that slows things down and wastes everybody's time.

Before inviting people to a meeting, check that each one will be required to execute a decision made during the meeting, has some unique contributory information, has managerial responsibility for the discussion subject, or will add some strategic value.

MAKING INTERACTIVE MEETINGS WORK

Meetings need not be boring. Keep them interesting and valuable by avoiding fixed schedules and routines. Let their frequency be dictated by need, rather than habit. Insure that preparation is adequate and makes the fullest possible use of visual aids.

Two-way communication must be achieved for meetings to be of real value. Synergistic decision making, where minds build on others' thoughts and ideas, is a complex process which must be understood to be successful. If they understand the process, managers or discussion leaders can use group synergy to solve many problems.

A typical business meeting operates at more than one level. The overt agenda is there for all to see, but underlying this is the hidden agenda which develops as the meeting participants engage in the inevitable vying for position that goes on between human beings. The web of business and personal relationships is an added complexity. That's why managers must develop their own and others' skills in running meetings, if they are to be of use. A supportive climate should be developed by:

Active Listening and Clarifying   paying attention and responding to others' feelings and ideas, not interrupting, making open-ended inquiries, not judging others, and summarizing and reflecting back others' ideas and feelings.

Supporting and Building   accepting what others have to say; not debating, persuading, controlling, or manipulating others; speaking in friendly, warm terms; creating opportunities for others to make their thoughts and feelings known; building on others' ideas; responding in an open, spontaneous way; encouraging divergent points of view; and freely offering new ideas at appropriate times.

Differing and Confronting continually focusing attention on the problem-solving process, questioning your own and others' assumptions in a nonthreatening way, dealing directly and specifically with apparent discrepancies, and mentally reflecting on how the team is doing with regard to progress, personal relations, and time.

In this climate, individuals can begin to deal honestly with conflicts, individual feelings, and hidden motivations. From time to time, it may be beneficial to stop dealing with content and start dealing with process—just what it is that seems to be impeding progress.

Problems can surface as individuals adopt various roles in group situations, some of which are constructive while others are not. For a group to function well, the positive roles must be filled, and the group leader should be prepared to step into them whenever their absence is noted. They include:

The detective who asks questions, probes for clarification, and continually seeks information.

The spark who initiates action, suggests procedures, and proposes solutions.

The professor who has most knowledge of the subject and can be counted upon to provide information and facts.

The pollster who keeps score as to how group members stand on issues and can provide a consensus.

The editor who clears up points of confusion and insures understanding among group members.

The collector who summarizes group feelings as movement toward a decision is made.

Some individuals who are out to satisfy their ego needs at the expense of the group will adopt negative roles. They are frequently unaware that their supposedly task-oriented behavior is actually self-oriented. It's important to explore underlying feelings to try and determine just how severely ego needs are affecting attitudes. These are the roles which tend to block group progress:

The joker who uses comic antics or expressions to gain attention, to avoid having to deal with a sensitive issue or with an underlying attitude.

The star who attempts to dominate the group and hogs the limelight at the group's expense.

The immortal
Gods alone have
  neither age nor death!
All other things
  almighty Time
  disquiets.

Sophocles,
Oedipus at Colonus

The invisible man who protects his ego by never exposing it and withdraws from the group activity by saying nothing.

The lamb who always defers to stronger group members in case his ego is attacked.

The sadist who enjoys undercutting group members and takes pleasure in snide criticism.

Coping with these roles demands that two corrective roles be used to preserve group integrity:

The conductor who silences the Star, strengthens the Lamb's voice, and calls upon the Invisible Man to establish his presence. The Conductor attempts to have every member of the orchestra make a contribution.

The buffer who assists in resolving interpersonal troubles by creating a warm, open atmosphere of understanding and concern. He makes it possible for the group to attack deeper issues, instead of avoiding them.

To see some of these roles in action, let's eavesdrop on a typical staff meeting.

John Spark: Would you mind if we stop for a minute to straighten something out? It seems to me that we haven't accomplished much in the last ten minutes. There are probably some hang-ups in people's minds that need airing.

Bill Detective: I agree. Just why are we bogged down? What do you think, Joe?

Joe Professor: Well, I've noticed that Jack has been pretty quiet since Carl criticized him a few minutes ago. Perhaps . . .

Carl Sadist (interrupting): I just figure it's about time we laid the blame where it belongs! That's all.

Karen Collector: Okay, then let me quickly outline the points on which we've agreed and perhaps Jack can then restate his position.

Jack Pollster: Before I get involved, do you all agree that we've been floundering? If you do, is it really my fault? (The group agrees that they've been floundering, but they do not feel it's his fault.)

Bill Detective: Then what is the real problem?

Joe Professor: Frankly, I think that Carl was out of line. Why do you think Jack is to blame for our problem, Carl?

The group is now focusing directly on an issue which has been hidden but smoldering. By dealing with it, rather than permitting it to remain hidden, they can recover their effectiveness.

As they begin working together like this, groups go through a series of development steps. These are the functions, common behavior patterns, and rules that occur in the various phases:

Phase 1: The *Polite Stage*, when individuals focus on getting acquainted, sharing values, and establishing the usual foundations for group structure.

Common behavior will include light conversation and initial information-sharing as well as stereotyping (to help categorize other members) and clique formation.

During this phase:

- Hidden agendas stay hidden.
- The need for group approval is strong.
- Group identity is low or completely absent.
- Group members participate actively, though unevenly.
- Conflict is usually avoided.

The implicit rules at this stage are to keep ideas simple and acceptable to avoid serious, controversial topics, and to give as little feedback as possible in order to avoid self-disclosure.

Phase 2: The *Discovery Stage*, wherein the objectives and goals of the group are defined.

Some members of the group will demand an agenda, cliques will grow and merge, and the beginning of power bases will take shape. Group identity will still be low, but hidden agenda items will begin to be sensed. Usually there is more active participation from all members as the need for group approval declines; people take more risks and show more commitment.

As structure evolves, participants may look to the leader to provide a push in one direction or another. Even when purpose has been established by outside edict, group members may still discuss it in order to gain understanding and to build commitment.

The amount of time spent in this phase varies widely. Some groups will omit it completely, while others will give it most of the available time. The easier it is to define objectives, the faster a group will agree on them. A task-oriented group needs to spend more time in this phase than a team-building group.

Phase 3: The *Power Play Phase*, when attempts to influence one another's ideas, values, or opinions take place, together with competition for attention, recognition, and influence.

Some individuals will try to rationalize their own position and convince the group to take whatever action they feel is best. Other members, relishing the opportunity to compete, will attempt to dominate the group. Those who remain closed-minded may be accused of not listening, etc. Conflict in the group increases, and a struggle for leadership occurs. Stinging exchanges can take place. Typical attempts to resolve this struggle may include voting, compromise, or seeking arbitration from an outside resource. Because there is no strong team spirit yet, some members may feel uncomfortable when latent hostility begins to show. Others may retreat into a silent posture. Cliques take on the greatest importance at this point. Hidden agenda items cause behavioral change as disclosure is cautiously attempted.

Wednesday comes from Woden's day—named for the most powerful of the Norse gods (later known as Odin). This drawing is derived from a tenth-century helmet decoration.

While the group still has not built an identity, the need for group approval declines. Some members may be willing to go out on a limb and risk group censure. Creative ideas will not succeed yet though, because the group will still feel that the originator wants credit (power) for his suggestion.

The range of participation by group members is the widest in this phase, but the need for structure remains strong. The issues of selecting a leader, a recording secretary, and so on are, in reality, bids for power. The tendency for men to ignore or underrate input from women group members should be avoided.

Group-building and maintenance roles are most important in this phase. Positive steps to build harmony and balance are necessary to keep conflict within bounds.

Phase 4: The *Win-Win Stage* arrives when group identity overcomes individualism and, working as a team, the group begins to interact cooperatively and constructively.

When this occurs, group members give up their attempts to control and substitute an attitude of active listening. They develop a willingness to change preconceived ideas or opinions, on the basis of facts presented by others. They actively ask questions of each other; a team spirit starts to build and cliques begin to dissolve.

Real progress toward the group's goal becomes evident as temporary leadership is shared. Group identity starts to become important, and when conflict arises it is dealt with as a mutual problem rather than a win-lose battle.

There is more group willingness to use the talents of any individual who can contribute effectively. Practical creativity can be high because the group is now amenable to creative suggestions; they will be solicited, listened to, questioned, responded to, and, if appropriate, acted upon. At this point it may be difficult to bring in a new member without losing group cohesion.

Depending on the talents of the group members and the problem to be solved, an optimum solution or decision—almost always better than any offered by a single member—can result from fourth-phase interaction.

Managers can be most effective in this phase by asking constructive questions, summarizing and clarifying the group's thinking, trusting the group to achieve its maximum potential, trying to blend in as much as possible, and avoiding any comments that appear to reward or punish participants.

Phase 5: The *Gold Medal Phase* comes when there is a high level of group morale and loyalty. Empathy replaces the need for group approval because each group member supports his peers and accepts them as individuals.

Both individuality and creativity are high and cliques are absent, as a nonpossessive warmth and freedom of expression takes over. The group may even create its own identity symbol or name. The group is now closed. If a new member is introduced, the feelings of camaraderie and esprit will be destroyed, and the group must regress to an earlier stage and then grow again, carrying the new member along in the process.

A group in this phase will be at its most constructive and productive, and usually achieves more than is expected or than can be explained by the apparent talents of the group members.

Transitions Between Phases

From Phase 1 (Polite) to Phase 2 (Discovery).

This transition can occur when any single group member desires it. He can simply say, "Well, what's on the agenda today?" and the group will usually move to Phase 2. But for this progress to occur, each member must relinquish the comfort of nonthreatening topics and accept the possibility of conflict.

Phase 2 (Discovery) to Phase 3 (Power Play).

This transition requires each group member to put aside a continued discussion of the group's purpose and commit himself to a purpose with which he may not completely agree. Further, he must risk personal attacks, which he can anticipate in Phase 3.

Phase 3 (Power Play) to Phase 4 (Win-Win).

The ability to listen has been found to be the most important human trait in helping groups move from the third to the fourth phase. Moving from Phase 3 to Phase 4 requires individuals to stop defending their own views and to risk the possibility of being wrong. Phase 4 thus demands some humility. When the group as a whole wants to relate at the fourth phase, yet one or more members stay rooted in the third phase, the group may reject these members.

Phase 4 (Win-Win) to Phase 5 (Gold Medal).

This final step demands that each group member trusts himself and other group members. Because to trust is to risk a breach of trust, this transition seems to require unanimous agreement among group members.

Making Meeting Time Pay Off

The model for effective small group development brings the following practical suggestions from meeting experts.

Before the meeting:

Develop a meeting agenda days, not hours, ahead of time. Expect people to be ready. If they aren't, adjourn immediately and set a new date if their presence is essential. If not, proceed on time. The practice will become accepted.

When scheduling meetings, set the time for the meeting to end as well as for its start. Try and keep meetings to an hour or less.

Insure that meetings are held for a real purpose—not just because a week has elapsed since the last one. Weekly staff meetings, used for fast information transfer, should not be prolonged by discussion. When a problem surfaces, let those involved get back to each other afterwards. Go round the table with a quick one-minute limit roundup to start. Then give each person a chance to ask clarifying questions. Keep it moving. Keep it short. Start and end on the dot. Circulate minutes the same day.

Don't invite people who really have nothing to contribute. If they are there, they'll feel they must say something, and thus waste everybody's time.

If a decision has already been made, don't meet on it. You won't fool many people into thinking they have participated when they have not.

At the meeting:

The person in charge of a meeting should know how to run it. Ask for specific reports, or ask direct questions of noncontributors.

If you're the senior person in a meeting, don't use it as a forum for your own ideas, or the discussion of trivia. Give others a chance to contribute; in fact, see that they do.

Be aware of the common tendency to avoid speaking up for fear of recrimination. Ask yourself if coworkers have reason for their fears. Try to resolve them.

Use meetings to maintain a sense of urgency through review of established priorities and the dates for their achievement.

Use informal settings for "let it all hang out" sessions.

Balance agenda with performance reporting and information dissemination.

After the meeting:

Insure that the meeting is a real link in the action system. Get minutes circulated fast, with a highlighted "Action" column. When decisions are made, act on them.

Use feedback techniques to check whether the meeting was as good as you thought it was. A rating sheet for this purpose will be found in Appendix D.

Time is money.
Benjamin Franklin

LARGE GROUP MEETINGS AND PRESENTATIONS

Most of the informational flow in large meetings is one-way. (See *COMMUNICATIONS*.) There are, however, some time-wasting situations that can occur at even the best organized mass meetings, so let's talk about them.

The Environment

You may not have much control over seating layout and sight-lines when your meeting is in a hotel or conference facility, but you owe it to your speakers to support them with an adequate public address system. This is not to be taken for granted, unfortunately. Service staff frequently install the PA system and check it out before the meeting, but then vanish. When excessive volume, feedback squeal, or other problems show up, nobody knows where the controls are or how to adjust them.

Avoid the problem by insisting that somebody in your own group is always made familiar with the system and knows where spares are too. The same care should be exercised to insure the smooth operation of audiovisual equipment. *Never* be without spare bulbs and a fifty-foot extension cord.

Sound levels set in empty halls are useless; the audience will soak up a much greater volume. Arrange a signal procedure with somebody at the rear of the room to indicate when volume levels should be adjusted. If you plan to use multiple microphones, remember that any placed in front of a speaker will produce feedback. If you speak frequently, consider investing in your own portable backup system to cope with impossible situations.

Plan ahead to control other environmental problems like outside noise, temperature, and ventilation. Assign somebody to quiet loud talking and hooting in adjacent corridors.

The Presentation

A good presentation requires about eight times as long to prepare as it does to deliver. Give yourself adequate time for preparation. Sort your material into "must say," "should say," and "can say" groups, arrange topics in logical sequence, and trim to fit the time available.

Use numbered file cards for cue notes, but talk spontaneously. If you want to hold your audience, never read a speech. Use a tape recorder to rehearse, and work on eliminating the too fast, nervous delivery that plagues us all. Watch for other mannerisms that break the pace.

Plan on a "kicker" about ten minutes into your presentation. Research has shown that there is a decline in attention at this point.

Don't try and cram too much into a presentation. Experienced speakers use a 3 × 3 rule: Three main points, said three times—one each in the opening, middle, and closing words.

Humorous material needs lots of practice to get the timing and accent right—and it should never be off-color. Practice your jokes as well as your other material.

If possible, determine the material that will be used by the speaker(s) ahead of you. It will avoid the problem of having to cut a part of your own talk to avoid duplication, or boring your audience with repetition.

Unless you can see a clock, put your watch on the podium and keep track of the time. Running over your time will not be appreciated by anybody. If necessary, be prepared to cut your speech.

Prepare your audience for the conclusion of your presentation. Don't stop abruptly or unexpectedly, or fizzle out. Work hard to make your closing sentence a stunner.

Here's a summary of do's and dont's used by professional speakers. Use it as a checklist to improve your own presentations:

Come what may
Time and the hour runs
  through the roughest
day.
  William Shakespeare,
  Macbeth, Act I

DO	DON'T
Arrive early.	Think you are the only
Dress appropriately.	nervous one.
Stand still and erect.	Ever read a speech.
Exude enthusiasm, smile.	Use nonwords.
Adjust the microphone if	Try and hide your notes.
necessary.	Walk around, fiddle, or clutch
Pause frequently.	the lectern.
Control humor.	Talk down to your audience.
Talk directly to the audience.	Argue with a questioner.
Use handouts if possible.	Fizzle out.
Finish on time.	

Question & Answer Periods

It's wise to plan for a Q & A session, as well as your presentation. Put down as many questions as you can think of on separate file cards, and compose brief answers. Ask others for questions, too. Do your homework ahead of time, and you won't be caught offguard.

Hand out cards for the audience to write out questions, or place one on each seat before your speech. Designate gatherers, and identify them in your opening remarks. If possible, have an aide screen the cards and rank them for you before handing them over.

If you don't have question cards, work up one or two questions with easy answers that *you* can ask a member of the audience to get the ball rolling if no questions are brought up spontaneously. Audiences often need a few moments to think about what they've heard before raising questions, so don't sweat if the response is slow.

Concentrate on hearing questions correctly. Don't start thinking about your reply while the questioner is still talking.

Always repeat a question briefly before answering it. This way, the audience will hear it and you will have a moment to formulate your answer. It also returns control of the presentation to you. This is especially useful when any sort of snide question is tendered.

Don't answer a question when you don't know the answer. Say so, and offer to find the answer and send it on.

Always break visual contact with a questioner and give your answer to the audience as a whole. This way, you'll discourage a string of questions from the same person, or the appearance of a public argument. As soon as you have given your answer, pick a new questioner.

BOARD MEETINGS

Current trends in management thinking, backed by the courts, are making boards of directors more responsible to stockholders. Their meetings should thus be planned to be as useful as possible, without becoming time-wasting nuisances for the operating people. The pace of business change is usually such that more than four board meetings a year are a waste of time. Monthly meetings are nonsensical. Such frequency may well be based on outdated tradition rather than practical need.

Good boards of directors need members with a real interest in the company. They should be prepared to pry into all corners of the operation, ask tough questions, and personally invest in the firm. The fewer operating people on the board, the better.

Board meetings can accomplish more in less time if directors are briefed with financial reports and other essential information ahead of time. They should be expected to do their homework, and to commit one day each quarter year to looking after the stockholders' interests. Their two most important functions are to continually assess the chief operating executive's performance (and get rid of him if it's lacking), and to declare corporate dividends. If the CEO needs more frequent input from a director, he can be invited to meet with key people more frequently on an ad hoc basis without wasting the time of the other directors.

Effectively planned and managed, meetings can become an effective management tool instead of an excuse for management. Constantly review their necessity and their conduct, and you will eliminate one of the biggest time drains mankind has invented.

See also *COMMUNICATION TIME.*

Recommended for further reading:

Doyle, M. *How to Make Meetings Work.* New York: Jove Publications, 1986.

Kirkpatrick, D. L. *How to Plan and Conduct Productive Meetings.* 2d ed. New York: AMACOM, 1986.

Mosvick, R. K., and R. B. Nelson. *We've Got to Start Meeting Like This.* Glenview, Ill.: Scott Foresman, 1986.

Seekings, D. *How to Organize Effective Conferences and Meetings.* New York: Nichols Publishers, 1987.

MEMORY

How memory works in the brain ·
The engram · Short-term and permanent
memory · Effective storage
of information

We usually suffer a frustrating loss of time when memory fails us. Forgetfulness causes missed appointments, retraced steps, and sometimes embarrassment. Fortunately, with some understanding of the memory process and some reinforcement routines, it is possible to reduce forgetfulness to a minimum. There is a great deal of published literature describing various systems for memory improvement, and for those who would like to explore the subject further, a bibliography is provided at the end of this chapter. Many of the systematic approaches utilize mnemonic,* or associative, techniques with various degrees of evangelistic fervor, and the search for nuggets of value in the rivers of exhortation can be, in itself, a waste of time. Many of the techniques are well known, and some were actually invented by the ancient Greeks. Those regarded as most useful will be found under *MNEMONICS.* Their application is improved by some understanding of how memory is believed to work.

In 1950, Karl Lashley published an important paper, "In Search of the Engram," after many years of neurological research. An engram is a durable mark "engraved" on protoplasm, and Lashley coined the word in his work on the mystery of memory. He wanted to know how memory is retained in the brain over a period of time. He was intrigued by previous research by the German physiologist Emil du Bois-Reymond, who had proved that minute electrical impulses flow through the nervous system.

After twenty-five years of study, Kandel and his colleagues at Columbia University, using a primitive sea snail, were able to show how experience leaves its mark on the nervous system. Kandel demonstrated that when the snail's snout is tapped, it draws in its gill.

---

*Mnemonics (*nem 'oniks*): the art of improving or assisting memory.

But continue tapping, and the snail begins to ignore the stimulus. Its neural response has changed.

Neural response may be understood by considering the brain as a biological computer with a massive network of tens of billions of neurons that communicate through a "language" of electrical impulses. It has an internal connective capability greater than all of the world's telephone networks combined. Each neuron receives information from sensory organs or from other neurons through a dendrite, a spiky structure that acts as a conduit.

When a neuron collects signals from a dendrite it acts like a spark plug, firing an electrical impulse through a stalk called an axon. The axon may be composed of thousands of branches, all of which receive the signal. Or, the impulse may jump across a synaptic gap to another dendrite, triggering a new "spark" and communication to yet other cells. But while this flow of communication is known, the method of data storage in the brain is still at the theoretical stage.

Neuroscientists think that when a new experience is encountered (such as a new sound, image, or smell), a unique neuron pattern is created and fired through the dendritic system into the brain cells. If it matches a previous pattern, it is reinforced through a kind of overlay; if not, it establishes a new engram.

Recognition occurs when we experience something that is similar to a stored neural pattern. The image of an automobile, for example, may be a neural circuit that partially overlaps the already stored features of many automobiles. We would then be able to identify the object as an automobile, but perhaps not its manufacturer. An exact match might identify the vehicle as a Ford. The ability to make partial matches or to associate a recall with partial information is an outstanding feature of man's mental capability, and appears to be linked to the number of dendritic spines contained within the brain. Einstein's brain, which was preserved for analysis, disclosed a much higher number of dendrites than normal.

More recent research by Lynch and his associates at the California Center of Neurobiology indicated that the engram may be implanted electrochemically. They believed that the neural impulses spark a chain of chemical reactions in the enzyme *calpain* to create biological engram structures. This, of course, meant that Lynch had to show that the brain actually *changes* in response to neural information input, and that the changes could happen very quickly.

They implanted electrodes in tissue removed from a rat's brain, stimulated the neural paths, and examined the results with an electron microscope. The synapses had increased *by more than a third.* Their work added to evidence produced in 1979 showing that when brain tissue is electrically stimulated, more receptors appear, and that calcium is the agent which causes the reaction.

Calcium has a number of important functions in the body's chemistry. Among other positive effects, it assists in the healing of body tissue by changing the shape of blood cells from smooth to rough and spiky, enabling them to hook together and clot. The change in cell structure occurs very rapidly when the level of calcium is increased.

Lynch has theorized that memory formation begins when an electrical signal allows calcium to flood into a selected dendrite. Then, assisted by calpain, it breaks down almost instantaneously and reconstructs the cellular skeleton to form a new memory engram. Groups of receptors may even cluster in new locations, creating new synapse structures, and the two processes—strengthening existing synapses and adding new ones—may account for short-term and long-term memory. These theories have been challenged by other neuroscientists, however, who believe that memory is contained in a series of distributed patterns with associative nuclei. Our knowledge of molecular computers is advancing but is not yet able to clinch the argument.

Scientific analysis has shown that there are actually three types of memory, usually called *immediate memory*, *short-term memory*, and *long-term memory*. Each of these memory systems operates in a different manner.

Immediate memory is easily overlooked because it operates automatically, yet it is an essential part of our brain. It provides the immediate linking of sensory input to response and, among other things, is permitting you to read this book. Without immediate memory, each word would be forgotten as your eyes moved along, and you would be unable to make sense of the string of words. Immediate memory goes to work when, for example, you select an ingredient in response to a recipe instruction, or copy a telephone number from a directory. But immediate memory doesn't last long and can only handle a small amount of information. The retention time is usually no more than a few seconds, after which the entire memory vanishes to make room for new inputs. Only one input will be remembered, others will rapidly decay. Conscious attention is required to select and move sensory information from immediate to short-term memory.

Short-term memory is different from immediate memory in that

My mind is like a tape recorder with one button—ERASE!
Andy Warhol

it permits retention for some minutes of more than one item. Most of us use it to remember an unfamiliar telephone number as we go through the dialing process, and we often repeat the number under our breath to make sure that we keep our attention focused upon it. We know that if someone calls out to us, or we are distracted even for a moment, we can easily forget it. Most peoples' short-term memory is limited to no more than ten items; try and force more in and a total wipeout can result.

Students who try and read textbooks while the television is on or converse with others as they study frequently waste much of their time, for one cannot switch attention between arenas without quickly forgetting input from one or the other.

Fortunately, there is a method to improve short-term memory. It's called "chunking," and it means organizing a list of random items into a smaller number of chunks containing related items. This reduces the number of items requiring rehearsal to a small enough number for short-term memory to handle. (See MNEMONICS.)

Long-term memory has the capacity to store as much information as we want, for as long as we live. Its efficiency depends, however, on how we organized informaiton on the way in, as well as the method by which we store it. Scientists believe that the more information one has stored in memory, the easier it is to add to it, because the brain has more prepared receptacles available. Some of them can absorb new information through the overlay process, described earlier, which simply strengthens existing memory cell structures; others benefit from the more extensive cataloging that is created.

Storing information with as much associative data as possible significantly improves one's ability to recover the information at a later date. The brain can and will use associated "data bits" to help locate a desired engram. Try an experiment: ask yourself where you were on Friday, November 22, 1963. It is doubtful that you can remember your whereabouts so long ago. But ask yourself where you were the day President Kennedy was assassinated, and your mind may well use the solid engram that recorded that event to assist in supplying the other information through association.

Recommended for further reading:

Baddeley, Allen D. *The Psychology of Memory*. New York: Basic Books, 1976.

> Memories may escape the action of will, may sleep a long time, but when stirred by the right influence . . . they flash into full stature and life with everything in place.
>
> *John Muir*

Bartlett, F. C. *Remembering*. Cambridge: Cambridge University Press, 1932.

Bugelski, B. R. *Principles of Learning and Memory*. New York: Praeger, 1979.

Gruneberg and Morris. *Aspects of Memory*. London: Methuen & Co., 1978.

Halacy, D. S. *Man and Memory*. New York: Harper & Row, 1970.

Herold, Mort. *You Can Have a Near-Perfect Memory*. Chicago: Contemporary Books, 1982. An exposition of various mnemonic memory aids, based on the three-stage principle of registration, retention, and retrieval. Employs Henry James' associative techniques.

Hilton, Hermine. *The Executive Memory Guide*. New York: Simon & Schuster, 1986. A business-oriented guide to the application of mnemonic techniques, coupled with a positive thinking approach to absorbing and remembering information.

James, William. *Principles of Psychology, Volume 1*. Reprint of 1890 edition. New York: Dover Books.

Yates, F. A. *The Art of Memory*. Chicago: University of Chicago Press, 1966.

MNEMONICS

*Techniques for improved memory ·
Attention factors · Visualization ·
Association · Acronyms and rhymes ·
Phonetic association · Organizing data*

Techniques for improving the memory function were used and described more than two thousand years ago by Greek orators and philosophers. Refined and expanded over the centuries, today they form a valuable group of time-saving procedures. This chapter contains descriptions of all of the viable methods for memory training, condensed for faster reading. Their effective application, however, requires an understanding of the seven primary factors that contribute toward memory retention: *attention, visualization, association, interest, understanding, organization,* and *feedback.* One or more of these elements may be used whenever effective retention and retrieval of information is desired. In each stage of the memorization process, they can significantly improve and speed the transfer of information from ephemeral immediate memory to long-term memory, which will last a lifetime. (Read *MEMORY* for a functional description of immediate, short-term, and long-term memory.) Anyone can avoid time-wasting forgetfulness and absentmindedness by applying the following principles for gathering, storing, and retrieval of information in the brain. Essentially, they support the use of more than one sensory input to solidify the memory engrams* and make them easier to locate when information retrieval is required.

Attention. Most people bring insufficiently focused attention to bear in any particular situation. For example, on being introduced to a stranger they will simultaneously try to check their own appearance and posture, determine if they like the newcomer, check out any handshake signals, guess whether the stranger's jewelry is fake,

---

* A memory engram is a mark caused by a stimulus placed on brain protoplasm. See *MEMORY* for a complete description of the process.

and so on. Among this welter of signals comes the stranger's name, and if it's even heard, it's almost immediately discarded. It never got into the memory because it was given no *attention*. Would you say that you've handled enough pennies to remember what they look like? Only in a general way, if you're like most people. Can you say whether, on the U.S. penny, Lincoln wears a tie? And have you observed which letters are missing from your telephone dial? Most of us give the minimum amount of attention to things, and consequently our memory engrams suffer from poor definition. Input must be clear if we expect later retrieval to be effective.

Visualization is a technique built upon scientific proof that we can remember pictures better than anything else. Use your visual senses to the utmost. Look around when you're meeting someone for the first time; note some details of the room, look into their face and ask yourself if they look trustworthy, and see whether they have any noteworthy bodily features. Go a step further and try to make a picture from their name. Using these procedures, and the associative techniques described later, it has been demonstrated that hundreds of names can be successfully memorized.

Visualization can help you avoid the time loss and frustration caused by misplaced articles. By taking a moment to *visualize* the spot where you are laying your keys, for example, and saying to yourself, "I'm putting keys on the _____," you will create a solid memory engram of the incident that will simplify later recall. Visualization can also assist in encoding verbal and written material, as part of an associative recall process.

Association is probably the most powerful tool in memory training, and the oldest. It depends upon our ability to interrelate material to be memorized with familiar items that are already strongly impressed in our minds. For example, you could mentally place, one at a time, a series of items that you need to remember in each of the rooms of your house, or on a piece of furniture within them. Once your items are placed in a well-known setting, they become "organized" as they are stored in memory, and are easily retrieved later by a mental browse through the house. It helps to always use the same series of familiar places when using this "location" method which was, by the way, used by Socrates.

Rhyming or acronymic associations are frequently useful. Here are some:

> Thirty days hath September,
> April, June and November.

All the rest have thirty-one
Except February alone,
Which hath twenty-eight in fine,
'Til leap year gives it twenty-nine.

To set clocks for daylight savings time:

Spring forward, Fall back.

To remember π(3.1415265358979), using the number of letters in each word:

How I want a drink, of course, after the eight
chapters involving quantum mechanics.

Trigonometric functions may be remembered using the Indian chief SOH-CAH-TOA:

SOH = Opposite over Hypotenuse (sine)
CAH = Adjacent over Hypotenuse (cosine)
TOA = Opposite over Adjacent (tangent)

The five Great Lakes (Huron, Ontario, Michigan, Erie, Superior):

HOMES

The seven hills of Rome (Palatine, Quirinal, Viminal, Esquiline, Capitoline, Aventine, Caelian):

Poor Queen Victoria Eats Carp At Christmas

The cranial nerves (olfactory, optic, oculomotor, trochlear, tregiminal, abducens, facial, acoustic, glossopharyngeal, vagus, accessory, hypoglossal):

On Old Olympus' Towering Top, A Famous Aged German Viewed A Hop

The wristbones (navicular, lunate, triangular, pisiform, multangular greater, multangular lesser, capitate, hamate):

Never Lower Tillie's Pants, Mama Might Come Home

To spell: Accommodation for *two* children and *two* mothers.
Principles . . . belong to peo*ple*.

Principal . . . is a *pal* of my father.

Balloons . . . are used at a *ball*.

The international electrical color code (black, brown, red, orange, yellow, green, blue, violet, gray, white):

Bad Boys Ruin Our Young Girls, But Violet Gives Willingly

The forms of energy (mechanical, chemical, solar, heat, atomic, light, electrical):

Mother Can Soon Have A Large Egg

Another effective associative procedure is to mentally link the items from a group that must be remembered, using an invented ladder or chaining relationship. Focus on two items at a time. Link A to B, then B to C, and so on. Recalling the first item will bring the second vividly to mind, this in turn will give you the third, and so on. One can become quite good at this with a little practice. For example, if you needed honey, eggs, potatoes, bacon, and milk from the grocery store, "eggs and bacon, are small potatoes in the land of milk and honey" would probably lock them all into your mind. Alternatively, you can weave the item list into a brief story, and if you do it out loud, so much the better. Every maneuver helps to anchor the memory engrams more strongly. Remembering a list of items *in sequence* is more difficult, as the average person can only handle up to seven sequenced units without mnemonic help. The bureaucrats who are trying to impose ten-digit zip codes upon us might consider this. Fortunately, with a little more effort, the mind's ability to associate can be applied here too. But first, you must relate a number list with a series of objects, and learn it. It helps if the objects chosen have some relationship to each number, as shown in the first column of the following table. (This particular list of phonetic associatives was devised by a European. Americans may find "Nought" and "Severn" a bit hard to remember. Feel free to make up your own list.)

Each item to be remembered sequentially is associated phonetically or mentally with one from the previously learned code list. The association will allow you to recall the items in sequence. The efficiency of this system is such that some individuals have created a stage performance around their use of it to remember long, complex lists correctly.

In 1844, Fauvel-Gouraud published his *Phreno-mnemonotech-*

nic Dictionary in Paris. It used a system of randomly chosen letters or phonetic particles to aid in memorizing up to 10,000 numbers. His system is still in use today. While you may not need this capability, the system is worth knowing; the digits are phonetically coded in column 4 of the table.

PHONETIC AND VISUAL ASSOCIATIVES

NO.	PHONETIC ASSOCIATIVES	MENTAL ASSOCIATIVES	PHONETIC ALPHABET
0	Nought	Egg	Z, S or C
1	Won	Me	T, D or TH
2	Too	Company, Tango	N
3	Free	Bird, Easy	M
4	Fore	Golf, Ship	R
5	Thrive	Nickel	L
6	Sex, sax	Pistol	J, G, Sh, Ch
7	Severn (river)	Dice, Seas	C, K, Q
8	Ate	Spider, Ball	F, V, PH
9	Nein	Pins, Cloud	B, P
10	Tin	Dime, Indians	. . . . .

Substitution of the arbitrary letter sounds for numbers permits the construction of words or sentences that translate into number strings. Vowels are ignored in the translation. For example, the number 943 may be translated as "brim" or "broom"; any word could be used that keeps the letters B-R-M in sequence. Although some effort is required to learn the phonetic code, it can be a great help in remembering important number sequences.

Once the phonetic code is learned, it may be used in many other valuable ways, particularly if you take the time to learn a phonetic code word for, say, a hundred numbers. Following is a list of suggested words. If you take the time to do this once, you will have added a skill that will be useful for the rest of your life. You will be able, for example, to remember all of the cards played in a game or what appears on each page of a magazine, in addition to telephone numbers, financial data, and identification numbers.

10	TIS	51	LET	84	FARE
11	TOT	52	LANE	85	FAIL
12	TON	53	LAM	86	FIG
13	TOM	54	LORE	87	FAKE
14	TOR	55	LIL	88	FIFE
15	TALE	56	LAG	89	VIBE
16	TAG	57	LAKE	90	PACE
17	TIC	58	LOVE	91	PATH
18	DOVE	59	LOPE	92	PAN
19	TAB	60	GAS	93	POME
20	NOSE	61	GAD	94	PAR
21	NOD	62	GIN	95	PAL
22	NON	63	GAM	96	POSH
23	NAME	64	GAR	97	PAK
24	NOR	65	GAL	98	PAVE
25	NIL	66	GAG	99	PIPE
26	NOG	67	JAKE	100	TOSS
27	NIK	68	GAVE	110	TATS
28	NAVE	69	GAPE	115	TOTAL
29	NAB	70	CASE	120	TANS
30	MAZE	71	COTE	125	TONAL
31	MAT	72	CANE	130	TAMES
32	MAN	73	CAME	140	TARS
35	MALE	74	CARE	145	TRAIL
36	MASH	75	CAUL	150	TALES
40	ROZ	76	CASH	200	NOSES
41	RAT	77	CAKE	250	NAILS
45	RAIL	78	CAVE	300	MASS
47	RAK	80	FEZI	350	MILES
48	RAVE	81	FAD	400	RAZZ
49	RAP	82	FAN	450	ROLES
50	LAZE	83	FAME	500	LASS

Interest. Our ability to remember is strongly assisted when we develop some interest in a subject. My mother always claimed she had a bad memory, but she never forgot family birthdays or anniversaries. Interest helps the memory process because it helps us to pay attention and stimulates an effort to attach meaning to the material we want to absorb.

Developing such an interest is not always easy, of course. The best approach is to search for ways in which apparently uninteresting material can be usefully applied. My son became much more interested in geometry when shown how it could save time in planning model railroad layouts. Many homemakers have developed an interest in mathematics or basic electrical principles because it helped them run their homes more effectively. And the mnemonic routines described above can add interest to sometimes boring material by adding imagery and meaning.

Understanding. Throughout this chapter, the importance of linkage and association to memory becomes evident. By the same token, material that doesn't make sense is hard to learn. Meaningfulness will improve memory at all levels. Experiments have shown that nonsense syllables take three times longer to memorize than meaningful prose, and prose takes three times longer than poetry. The reason, of course, is that when rote memorization has to substitute for meaningful association, learning time is vastly increased.

Organization. William Filwood, writing about memory in 1562, said:

> The first is well to understand
> The thing that he doth take in hand.
> The second is, the same to place
> In order good, and formed race . . .

He well understood, even then, what psychologists have since proved: the better that material is consciously organized when it is learned, the easier it is to retrieve from memory. We can quickly recall the alphabet, for example, because we have organized its storage; to try and recite the twenty-six letters at random would be quite difficult. Organization should not be limited to words and letters, but applied to everything that we want to memorize.

The process of "chunking" is basic to organization. It means organizing a mixed bag of items into related chunks. For example, suppose you wish to remember the following items: apples, toothpaste, milk, nails, aspirin, potatoes, sandpaper, fertilizer, lettuce, eggs, and lipstick. Instead of trying to remember them all individually, group them mentally in some manner—perhaps the different stores in which they may be purchased: drugstore, supermarket, and hardware store. This reduces the number of items requiring rehearsal to three, which is no problem for short-term memory. When you want to recall the individual items, you will find that simply recalling the store types will also bring each of the various items back to your conscious mind. We frequently perform chunking almost automatically, because we've found that it works. To organize your memory better, practice it deliberately.

Feedback in the learning process helps to sustain interest in the subject, and also provides the opportunity to correct any gaps while

The butterfly counts not months but moments, and has time enough.
Rabindrath Tagore,
Stray Birds

the raw material is still available. The simplest form of feedback is recitation, particularly useful when learning speeches and scripts. They can be learned most quickly by only looking at the original when you blank out. Both self- and interactive testing (where two people test each other) are valuable. When learning from textbooks, half the time should be spent in recitation, more if the material is not easily integrated or has weak connections between sentences.

With these techniques and a little practice, you will discover that your memory can be improved tremendously. Research has shown that there is little difference, if any, between individuals' capacity for memory, so you may be confident of success.

MONTH

The origin of the month ·
Cultural comparison

The Babylonian priest-astronomers were the first men to note that about thirty days passed between new moons, and this became the second ancient measure of time (the day being the first) about 5,000 B.C. The name *month* stems from moon-measure, or "moonth." The period was originally multiplied by twelve to yield a year of 360 days. The error of 5.25 days became noticeable after a few years, so an extra month was added every sixth year as a temporary solution.

Farmers soon found this was unworkable, as their planting times were moving out of phase with the seasons. To find a solution, astronomers watched the moon more closely. Their observation paid off. A new moon, the ancient scientists discovered, came close to every 29.5 days, not 30 days. Nobody was able to fit the odd half-day into the calendar, however, so they compromised by making one month of twenty-nine days followed by another of thirty days. By the end of the first year, they recognized that they were worse off—this time by 11.25 days—so, in desperation, they plugged in holidays throughout the year to balance things out.

Incredibly, this awkward arrangement persisted for centuries, since ancient men were ideologically locked in to the moon rather than the sun as the key to time, as were the Persians, Greeks, and Chinese who followed them. In fact, the lunar calendar is still used in parts of the Middle East today, and by the Christian church to establish the dates of important festivals such as Easter.

We can thank the ancient Egyptians for getting us out of the rut. Ptolemy III, in 238 B.C., proposed the leap year cycle which we use today, although it did not catch on for some time because (a) the priests didn't think of it first and (b) nobody else cared (see *CALENDAR*). They found the annual Nile flooding a much more reliable marker for the seasons. Years later Julius Caesar, who had been hav-

Man is the longest-lived mammal, with a potential life span of up to 113 years—maybe more. Galápagos Island tortoises frequently live to be 190 years old.

ing problems with Romulus' ten-month year, adopted Ptolemy's idea. The plan finally gained respectability in 47 B.C.

The Romans managed to keep their months complicated by counting their dates backwards from three special days: the *Kalends*, always the first day of the month, the *Nones*, and the *Ides*. In March, May, July, and October, the nones fell on the seventh day of the month, but on the fifth day in all of the other months. In March, May, July, and October, the ides fell on the fifteenth day of the month, but on the thirteenth day in other months. For example, instead of Maius XIV, or May 14, they would call the day the second of the ides. January 26th would be the seventh day of the kalends of February, and so on. In leap years, there was an added gimmick. They would add the extra day in March, six days before kalends, and count *both* days as the sixth of kalends of Aprilus. The leap years thus became known as "bisextile," meaning twice sixth. At least the Romans had a ready excuse for forgotten birthdays. We should not be too critical, though, for modern man has yet to resolve the problems of Easter dates and a World calendar.

While all these Mediterranean attempts to link the days, months, and years with the sun and the moon were going on, other cultures, such as the Mayans, had other ideas. (See table of months in this chapter.)

Over the last two thousand years, scientific knowledge has improved to the point that we have a better idea of what constitutes a month, or lunar cycle. It is not as simple as it appears because it is subject to the relative measurement that affects everything in the universe. From a star far out in space, one revolution of our moon around the earth would be measured at 27.32166 days. When we measure the time between one full moon and the next from Earth, we get a mean value of 29.53059 days. Why the difference? Because the earth has also moved in relation to the sun; therefore so has the moon, and that movement delays the planetary relationships that cause a "full moon."

Then, for our months to fit accurately into our years, we are forced to consider solar time. The solar month is 30.4368 days, with twelve making 365.2416 days. That's why we have to add in an extra day every fourth year, to make up for the .2416 of a day that we are short. Obviously, at some time in the future, another small adjustment will have to be made to correct the .0084 of a day that is still missing from our calendar and accumulating from year to year.

THE BASIS OF OUR CALENDAR MONTH

MAYAN MONTHS	ROMAN MONTHS UNDER ROMULUS	ROMAN MONTHS UNDER POMPILIUS	ROMAN MONTHS UNDER JULIUS CAESAR	ROMAN MONTHS UNDER AUGUSTUS CAESAR	MODERN CALENDAR MONTHS	JEWISH CALENDAR MONTHS
POP	UNRECKONED PERIOD	JANUARIUS GOD OF THE GATES 27 DAYS	JANUARIUS	JANUARIUS	JANUARY 31 DAYS	TISHRI 30 DAYS
UO						
ZIP		FEBRUARIUS FEAST OF PURIFICATION 27 DAYS	FEBRUARIUS	FEBRUARIUS	FEBRUARY 28 OR 29 DAYS	MARHESHVAN 29 OR 30 DAYS
ZOTZ	SPRING MOONRISE MARTIUS GOD OF WAR 30 DAYS	MARTIUS	MARTIUS	MARTIUS	MARCH 31 DAYS	KISLEV 29 OR 30 DAYS
TZEC						
XUL	APRILIS EARTH'S AWAKENING 30 DAYS	APRILIS	APRILIS	APRILIS	APRIL 30 DAYS	TEVET 29 DAYS
YAXKIN	MAIUS GODDESS OF GROWTH	MAIUS	MAIUS	MAIUS	MAY 31 DAYS	SHEBAT 30 DAYS
MOL						
CHEN	JUNIUS AFTER JUNO, QUEEN OF THE GODS	JUNIUS	JUNIUS	JUNIUS	JUNE 30 DAYS	ADAR *** 29 DAYS

*   *BER* is a contraction for measure.

**   The Pompilius months added to a 354 - day year. Even numbers were considered unlucky, so an extra day was added in December to make a 355-day year.

***   In the Jewish monthly calendar, Adar II is added seven times over a period of nineteen years to correct the discrepancy between the solar and lunar cycles.

MAYAN MONTHS	ROMAN MONTHS UNDER ROMULUS	ROMAN MONTHS UNDER POMPILIUS	ROMAN MONTHS UNDER JULIUS CAESAR	ROMAN MONTHS UNDER AUGUSTUS CAESAR	MODERN CALENDAR MONTHS	JEWISH CALENDAR MONTHS
YAX / ZAC	QUINTILUS FIFTH MONTH	QUINTILUS	JULIUS	JULIUS	JULY 31 DAYS	NISAN 30 DAYS
CEH	SEXTILIS SIXTH MONTH	SEXTILIS	SEXTILIS	AUGUSTUS	AUGUST 31 DAYS	IYAR 29 DAYS
MAC / KANKIN	SEPTEM-BER* SEVENTH MONTH	SEPTEM-BER	SEPTEM-BER	SEPTEM-BER	SEPTEMBER 30 DAYS	SIVAN 30 DAYS
MUAN	OCTO-BER* EIGHTH MONTH	OCTO-BER	OCTO-BER	OCTO-BER	OCTOBER 31 DAYS	TAMMUZ 29 DAYS
PAX / KAYAB	NOUE-BER* NINTH MONTH	NOUE-BER	NOUE-BER	NOUE-BER	NOVEMBER 30 DAYS	AB 30 DAYS
CUMHU	DECEM-BER* TENTH MONTH 30 DAYS	DECEM-BER** 31 DAYS	DECEM-BER	DECEM-BER	DECEMBER 31 DAYS	ELUL 29 DAYS

UAYEB (5 DAYS)   300 - DAY YEAR   365 1/4 - DAY YEAR

MOVIE TIME

Time-related educational and
entertainment films

For those who enjoy motion pictures with time themes, here are some selections from publicity material on various films which employed the theme. Most are now available on videotape.

Time After Time

As Jack the Ripper terrorizes women in Victorian London, H. G. Wells introduces a group of close friends to his newly invented time machine. One of the friends, Dr. Stevenson, is suspected of being the Ripper, but he escapes from the police in Wells' time machine, which returns empty. Wells boards his machine to travel forward to the twentieth century and arrives in San Francisco, where Stevenson has begun to kill again. Wells is instrumental in dealing with him in a novel manner, and then returns home with the modern woman who befriended him, and with whom he has fallen in love.

(1979, Brit.) 112m WB-Orion c
Malcolm McDowell (*Herbert G. Wells*), David Warner (*Dr. John Lesley Stevenson*), Mary Steenburgen (*Amy Robbins*), Charles Cioffi (*Lt. Mitchell*), Laurie Main (*Inspector Gregson*), Andonia Katsaros (*Mrs. Turner*), Patti D'Arbanville (*Shirley*), Keith McConnell (*Harding*), Geraldine Baron (*Carol*), James Garrett (*Edwards*), Byron Webster (*McKay*).

Time Bandits

The mixture of Monty Python-like comedy with a time travel adventure undertaken by a gang of dwarfs and a small boy may not be everyone's cup of tea, but the special effects and lighthearted wit are amusing. Under the comedic theme, a warning of the negative effect of television on spontaneous imagination is delivered.

(1981, Brit.) 110m Handmade Films/AE c
John Cleese (*Robin Hood*), Sean Connery (*King Agamemnon*), Shelley Duvall

(*Pansy*), Katherine Helmond (*Mrs. Ogre*), Ian Holm *(Napoleon)*, Michael Palin (*Vincent*), Ralph Richardson (*Supreme Being*), Peter Vaughan (*Ogre*), David Warner (*Evil Genius*), David Rappaport (*Randall*), Kenny Baker (*Fidget*), Jack Purvis (*Wally*), Mike Edmunds (*Og*), Malcolm Dixon (*Strutter*), Tiny Rose (*Vermin*), Craig Warnock (*Kevin*), David Baker.

p&d, Terry Gilliam; w, Michael Palin, Gilliam; ph, Peter Biziou (Technicolor); m, Mike Moran; ed, Julian Doyle; prod d, Millie Burns; art d, Norman Garwood; m/l, George Harrison.

Time Flies

A crazy inventor and his valet are thrust into Elizabethan England when their time machine, to everyone's surprise, really works.

(1944, Brit.) 88m Gainsborough/GFD bw
Tommy Handley (*Tommy*), Evelyn Dall (*Susie Barton*), George Moon (*Bill Barton*), Felix Aylmer (*Professor*), Moore Marriott (*Soothsayer*), Graham Moffatt (*his Nephew*), John Salew (*William Shakespeare*), Leslie Bradley (*Walter Raleigh*), Olga Lindo (*Queen Elizabeth*), Roy Emerton (*Capt. John Smith*), Iris Lang (*Princess Pocahontas*), Stephane Grappelly (*Troubadour*).

The Time Machine

A well-conceived action film about a Victorian inventor who creates a successful time machine to explore the future. Most of his friends doubt his account of his test run, through two world wars and an atomic holocaust, so he sets off again, this time further afield. Arriving aeons in the future, he finds the earth peopled by two tribes, the Eloi, and the Morlocks who dominate them. He falls in love with an Eloi maiden and persuades her people to revolt.

George Pal, who produced and directed the film, received an Oscar for his work on this and other science fiction films.

(1960, Brit./U.S.) 103m Galaxy/MGM c
Rod Taylor (*George*), Alan Young (*David Filby/James Filby*), Yvette Mimieux (*Weena*), Sebastian Cabot (*Dr. Philip Hilyer*), Tom Helmore (*Anthony Bridewell*), Whit Bissell (*Walter Kemp*), Doris Lloyd (*Mrs. Watchell*), Paul Frees (*Voice of the History Machine*), Bob Barran (*Eloi Man*).

p&d, George Pal; w, David Duncan (based on the novel by H. G. Wells); ph, Paul C. Vogel (Metrocolor); m, Russell Garcia; ed, George Tomasini; art d, George W. Davis, William Ferrari; set d, Henry Grace, Keogh Gleason; spec eff, Gene Warren, Tim Baer, Wah Chang; makeup, William Tuttle.

Timerider

A gang of old west desperadoes are confronted by a young motorcyclist who strays into their lives via a time warp. The outlaw leader determines that the biker may be an asset to the gang.

(1983, U.S.) 93m Jensen-Farley c (aka: *The Adventures of Lyle Swann*)
Fred Ward (*Lyle Swann*), Belinda Bauer (*Clair Cygne*), Peter Coyote (*Porter Reese*), Ed Lauter (*Padre*), Richard Masur (*Claude Dorsett*), Tracey Walter (*Carl Dorsett*), L. Q. Jones (*Ben Potter*), Chris Mulkey (*Daniels*), Macon McCalman (*Dr. Sam*), Jonathan Bahnks (*Jesse*), Laurie O'Brien (*Terry*), William Dear, Susan Dear (*Technicians*), Bruce Gordon (*Earl*), Ben Zeller (*Jack Peoples*), Tommy Leyba (*Manuel*), Ernie Quintana (*Zapata*), Miguel Sandoval (*Emil*), Reginald Johnson (*George*), Philip L. Mead (*Wally*), Manny Smither (*Devil Man*), Ray Valdez (*Man in Crowd*), Bob Dunbar (*Pilot*), Sam Chadwyck, Rusty Dillen, Joseph V. DiPrima, Audie Edmundson, Buddy Edmundson, Raleigh Gardenhire, Christopher Garrett, Steven Hartley, Luke Jones, Curtis Plagge (*Outlaws*).

Time of Roses

A twenty-first century historian decides to make a film about the effect of twentieth century mass media on his society. His impressions are distorted by his own politics and the accidental(?) death of his girl friend. His radical employees violently disagree with his views.

(1970, Fin.) 90m Filminor/Cinema Dimensions bw (aka: *Ruusujen Aika*)
Ritva Vespa (*Saara*), Arto Tuominen (*Raimo*), Tarja Markus (*Anu*), Eero Keskitalo, Kalle Holmberg, Eila Pelikonen, Unto Salminen.

Time Slip

Modern Japanese soldiers are caught in a time slip that forces them to confront ancient Samurai warriors. They attempt to return to their own time by changing history. Some remarkable battle scenes and an unusual ending.

(1981, Jap.) 139m Toei c (aka: *Sengoku Jieitai*)
Sonny Chiba (*Lt. Iba*), Isao Natsuki (*Samurai Leader*), Miyuki Ono (*Village Girl*), Nana Okada (*Modern Girl*).

The Time Travelers

A group of scientists, experimenting with time portals, accidentally enter the future. They find the vestiges of civilization attempting to construct a spaceship to leave the polluted planet. Attacked repeatedly by mutants, they fail in spite of help from the scientists, and the survivors find themselves in an eternal time warp.

(1964) 83m Dobil Productions/AIP c (aka: *Time Trap* and *Journey to the Center of Time*)
Preston Foster (*Dr. Erik von Steiner*), Philip Carey (*Steve Connors*), Merry Anders (*Carol White*), John Hoyt (*Varno*), Dennis Patrick (*Councilman Willard*), Joan Woodbury (*Gadra*), Dolores Wells (*Reena*), Steve Franken (*Danny McKee*), Gloria Leslie (*Councilwoman*), Peter Strudwick (*Deviant*), Margaret Seldeen, Forrest J. Ackerman (*Technicians*).

Time Walker

An archeologist brings an alien creature to life by applying an over-
dose of radiation to Tutankhamen's sarcophagus. The alien, who had
killed the Pharaoh, and needs special crystals to escape from Earth,
begins another killing rampage.

(1982, U.S.) 83m Villard-Wescom/New World c
Ben Murphy (*Doug McCadden*), Nina Axelrod (*Susy Fuller*), Kevin Brophy (*Peter*),
James Karen (*Wendell Rossmore*), Robert Random (*Parker*), Austin Stoker (*Dr. Ken
Melrose*), Clint Young (*Willoughby*), Shari Belafonte-Harper (*Linda*), Antoinette
Bower (*Dr. Hayworth*), Jason Williams (*Jeff*), Jack Olson (*Ankh Venaris, Mummy*),
Melissa Prophet, Sam Chew, Gerard Prendergast.

2001: A Space Odyssey

Astronauts investigating a monolith which may explain the origin
of mankind are forced to deal with a computer which takes over their
spaceship. Escaping in a small exploration module, a survivor becomes entangled in a web of confused time elements and symbols
of birth and age. The film is notable for its spectacular special effects,
and received Academy Award nominations for direction and
screenplay.

d, Stanley Kubrick; w, Arthur C. Clarke (1968, Brit./U.S.) 141m MGM c
Keir Dullea (*Dave Bowman*), William Sylvester, Gary Lockwood (*Astronauts*).

MUSIC TIME

*The elements of musical rhythm and
their development · Expression
marks · The metronome*

Musical rhythm is composed of four elements. The *meter*, or beat, which usually stays unchanged throughout; the *tempo*, or pace; the length of a *note*; and the *phrasing*, such as syncopation. To remember the meaning of syncopation, you may like the story of the doctor who diagnosed his alcoholic patient's problem as syncopation—an irregular movement from bar to bar.

The development of modern musical time notation has not been easy or fast. The ancient Greeks used the same rhythmic notation for both music and poetry. But music-making became more complex as new instruments were invented and musicians began to play in concert, and a more precise system was needed. That is, if everyone was to finish at the same time.

The first signs, or *neumes*, used to guide vocal and instrumental sounds were usually related to the words rather than the notes, and date from the sixth century. Over the next six hundred years, their form was changed many times. Different colors and shapes were used, making a medieval hepcat's life quite confusing.

The situation was improved when, in 1260 A.D., Franco of Cologne proposed four basic note values, which he called *long, duplex long, breve,* and *semibreve*. His system worked for a while, until the French and Italians began to add colored notes for certain rhythms and differently shaped notes for others, so that by the end of the fourteenth century, musical notation had once more become a complicated mess. It got worse in the fifteenth century when the black notes were changed to white, and the red notes became black, to make transcription easier as paper began to replace parchment. A color-blind piper was out of luck in those days.

The invention of the bar line by lute players of the sixteenth century finally brought sanity to the music world. Over the next two hundred years usage reduced the number of anomalies to practical limits, and the basis of our modern metrical notation (shown in the table below) was established.

METER	POETRY	MUSIC
Iambic	˘ ‑ | ˘ ‑	
Trochaic	‑ ˘ | ‑ ˘	
Dactylic	‑ ˘ ˘ | ‑ ˘ ˘	
Amphibrachic	˘ ‑ ˘ | ˘ ‑ ˘	
Anapestic	˘ ˘ ‑ | ˘ ˘ ‑	
Spondaic	‑ ‑ | ‑ ‑	
Tribrachic	˘ ˘ ˘ | ˘ ˘ ˘	

Bar lines divide music into measures, which contain notes and beats. The note (and rest) symbols each designate a time value:

Whole	Half	Quarter	Eighth	Sixteenth
SEMI BREVE	MINIM	CROCHET	QUAVER	SEMI QUAVER

The number of beats and notes allocated to a measure by the composer is spelled out by the *time signature*, written at the start of the score. The bottom figure establishes the value of each note in relation to the semibreve, which is valued as 1. The top number indicates the number of beats in the bar.

Seconds: 2   1   1/2   1/2   1   1   1   1

Two quarter time was popular with the ragtime composers in the early part of this century, three quarter time established the waltz craze, and four quarter time is used for rock and disco music. Other beats are used for special effects. Gustav Holst used 5/4 time in part of *The Planets*, for example, and 6/8 time is used for very fast rhythms.

The adoption of Italian expression marks to help musicians interpret the composer's rhythmic intent began in the seventeenth century. They have proliferated over the years, and sometimes produce peculiar results when interpreted by those who don't speak Italian. Here are the time-related expression marks found in music today:

accelerando	quickening
acciaccatura	of the shortest possible duration
adagio	"at ease," or slowly
adagietto	slightly faster than adagio
alla breve	twice as fast as the notation (because the breve replaces the semibreve as the metrical standard)
allargando	becoming broader, or slower
alla tedesca	in the German triple time dance-style
alla zoppa	syncopated
allegretto	moderately quick
allegro	lively
allentando	slowing down
andante	moderate tempo
con animo	with spirit
animato	animated
a piacere	the time is at the performer's discretion
arioso	in a lyrical style
arpeggio	in rapid succession
a tempo	in time
con brio	vigorously
comodo	at a convenient speed
doppio movimento	twice as fast
con fuoco	with fire
giocoso	merrily
grave	solemn and slow
largo, larghetto	slowly
legato	smoothly
lento	slow
l'istesso tempo, medesimo tempo	keep the same time
meno mosso	less quickly
molto allegro	very fast

mosso	lively
pesante	ponderous
portato	staccato
presto	brisk
rallentando, ritardando	becoming slower
risvegliato	animated
ritenuto, stentando	held back
rubato	slight quickening
scherzando	playfully
sciolto	free and easy
slentando	becoming slower
soave	smoothly
sostenuto	sustaining, slowing
spiritoso	spiritedly
staccato	short, detached
stringendo	becoming faster
tardo	slow
tempo di ballo	in dance time
vivace, vivo	quick and lively

The metronome, used for setting and maintaining tempo, was introduced by the Frenchman Loulie in 1696. His apparatus was somewhat different from the models found on students' pianos today. It was more than six feet high, and weighed nearly half a ton. Piano teachers were not known to take one along when visiting their pupils. A friend of Beethoven, one Johann Maelzel, about a hundred years later, developed the small, pyramidical instrument with an oscillating rod on its face still used today.

In 1945, a pocket metronome was introduced in Switzerland, and ingenious devices to maintain irregular beats like 5/4 time are also available. In the past, the audible ticking of a clock or watch was often used to keep time. William Turner wrote, in 1724, that "crotchets are to be counted as fast as the regular motions of a watch." Perhaps they all ticked alike in those days.

The metronome has even found its way onto the concert stage. Ligeti wrote a symphonic poem for one hundred metronomes in 1962, and Crosse included the instrument in his *Play Ground* in 1977. It has not developed a popular following.

The fundamental importance of rhythm and note duration, versus pitch, has been argued for many years among music theorists. Schoenberg always held that time or rhythm was the determining factor in shaping a musical phrase. And of course, most of us who have grown up with exposure to classical and romantic music have become used to its somewhat inflexible conventions.

Modern composers are seeking new relationships between tonal structure and rhythm. In some of Boulez's orchestral works, for example, the conductor does not keep time at all, but concentrates on shaping the overall tonal values and texture. For some composers, the computer had added a new dimension for more precise time control; for others, a return to the ancient freedom from precise musical time would seem preferable.

To the degree that these divergent approaches are resolved, there will undoubtedly be an exciting period of rediscovery ahead, with the promise of new kinds of rhythmic invention.

ORGANIZING TIME

*Diary-style organizing systems for
personal and business use*

The medieval monks probably should be given credit for developing the world's first time organizing systems. Their "books of hours" carefully spelled out the time of day at which various devotions were to be conducted, and a few beautifully illuminated examples have survived as a record of well-ordered monastic lives. One, created in 1326 by Jean Pucelle and given by Charles IV of France to his wife Jeanne d'Evreux, is owned by the Cloisters in New York.

Samuel Pepys, who was born in London in 1633, is famous for his skill as a diarist. He is probably best known for his graphic description of the disastrous London fire which destroyed much of the city in 1688, and for his oft-quoted sign-off, "and so to bed."

A hundred years later, those who could read and write often used the page margins of the family Bible to note their important dates—in many cases because it was the only book they possessed.

Our lives today are not so simple, and neither are the many personal time organizers available. The British Filofax* people claim to have been the first to introduce a modern organizer, developed in 1921 from an American engineers' notebook by Grace Scurr, who at that time was employed as a temporary secretary. The success of the product was instrumental in her eventually becoming board chairman of Filofax before she retired.

In recent years, Filofax has developed a strong international following by expanding the range of loose-leaf pages and ring binders beyond that of a diary, to include many special purpose page inserts and exotic leathers. Filofax is expensive, but offers everything from

---

* Filofax is the registered trademark of Filofax Limited.

technical data pages to birdwatchers' checklists. If money is not an issue, the wide choice of special purpose inserts may make you a Filophiliac.

Filofax desk and pocket agendas are available in exotic leathers, calfskin, canvas, rubber, and vinyl and come in a wide variety of colors. The 7/8-inch metal ring closures are top quality and operate smoothly and accurately. Insert forms and data sheets are printed on blank bond paper.

Manufacturer: Filofax PLC, Filofax House, Forest Road, Ilford, Essex IG6 3HP, England. Distributed in the United States by Filofax Inc., 2216 Federal Avenue, Los Angeles, CA 90064 (213-312-1140). Available through major department stores and stationers.

A sample of the versatile Filofax personal organizing system.

The Time/Design* organizer system comes from Denmark. It's a medium-priced basic system, with a detachable pocket appointment diary and a limited but adequate range of insert materials. They include various ruled sheets which one can use to design one's own forms, and printed forms for financial, sales, communications, and general business applications.

A valuable feature of the Time/Design system is NameBank—a database program for IBM and compatible personal computers. NameBank stores all contact information and relevant notes. The

---

*Time/Design and Time/system are registered trademarks owned by Time/system AS, Denmark. All rights reserved.

database may be customized, cross-referenced, and searched by any field criterion, then printed out on continuous-form computer paper that will fit the Time/Design binders. The program requires a minimum 256K RAM, PC-DOS 2.0 or MS-DOS 2.11, and a dot matrix printer.

For those who like to be totally coordinated, and have the money to prove it, Time/Design also offers a completely fitted leather attaché case, with storage for their binder, writing instruments, and cards in the lid.

Manufacturer: Time/system AS, Gydevang 25, P.O. Box 19, DK-3450 Alleroed, Denmark. In the United States: 11835 Olympic Boulevard, Suite 450, Los Angeles, CA 90064-5005 (1-800-637-9942).

The extensive range of Day-Timer organizers and productivity tools has been continuously expanded as their direct mail customers have made the company one of the largest in the field. One of the first to offer individually bound monthly pocket book inserts, Day-Timers are popular with businesspeople who want a practical, business-oriented system at medium cost. Day-Timer, Inc. offers both pocket and desk organizer systems, in a wide range of quality leather and vinyl binders, wallets, and portfolios. Their catalog is a cornucopia of time-saving products, and it may be obtained by calling their twenty-four-hour customer service number.

The Day-Timer system is supported with computer database programs for both IBM compatible and MacIntosh PCs. The programs provide name, address, and telephone number storage; and printout formats to fit the Day-Timer products; plus mailing labels and rotary indexes. They require a 512K MacIntosh or 256K IBM or compatible PC plus dot matrix or Imagewriter compatible printer.

Manufacturer: Day-Timers, Inc., 1 Day-Timer Plaza, Allentown, PA 18195-1551 (215-395-5884).

Day Runner, Inc. was founded in 1982 by a Hollywood, California, husband and wife team who had begun designing time planning systems two years previously. Sold extensively through retail outlets, the system is available in three loose-leaf formats in leather or vinyl ring binders. Insert pages measure 3¾"×6¾", 5½"×8½", or letter size, and the broad selection includes child-oriented sheets that fit their Dinky Diary.*

The Day Runner Executive Weekly, new in 1989, uses ultrathin

---

*Dinky Diary is a registered trademark of Day Runner, Inc.

paper to put a four-year planning calendar, telephone directory, task planning pages, a weekly dated calendar, and a pop-out ruler into a ³⁄₁₆"-thick pocket agenda, which also has pockets for money and cards. In the medium to low price range, the Day Runner products are good value for your money.

Manufacturer: Day Runner, Inc./Harper House, 3562 Eastham Drive, Culver City, CA 90232 (1-800-223-9786).

Another international product, Time Manager, originated in Denmark in 1975, and is supported with training courses in fifteen countries. It is available with or without the training course. The loose-leaf system is offered in a limited range of portable and desk portfolios, with locks if required, and manufactured in leather and vinyl. The insert pages are geared to the Time Manager approach, but most lend themselves to customization.

The Time Manager Key Keeper is a useful accessory product that brings duplicate keys under control, and a zippered money pouch that may be separated from the portfolio for safekeeping may be valuable for those who travel extensively.

Manufacturer: Time Manager International, Huginsweg 8, DK-3400 Hillerod, Denmark. Telephone: (02) 26 23 39.

An inexpensive wirebound collegiate organizer is produced by Academic Advantage, available through selected retail outlets. The nonremovable pages provide space for keeping track of course information, roommates, addresses and telephone numbers, clubs and activities, financial planning, class planning and grade records, and resume planning in addition to monthly and weekly calendar pages. It's a well-designed product for budget-conscious college students.

Manufacturer: Academic Advantage, 15455 Blackberry Hill Road, Los Gatos, CA 95032.

For those who like to organize their activities and projects with a simple card system, Executive ScanCard Systems provides leather, corduroy, and vinyl portfolios and pocket agendas containing panels to accommodate data cards for up to 120 concurrent topics or tasks. The modestly priced binders are designed with a three-ring loose-leaf section and also contain wirebound calendars, telephone/address directories, and calculators. Available through selected retailers or direct from the company.

Manufacturer: Executive ScanCard Systems, 6480 Busch Boulevard, Suite 200, Columbus, OH 43229 (1-800-848-2618).

For business organizations who would like to help their customers become organized, the Per Annum series of well-designed slim pocket organizers may fit the bill. They contain extensive information on twelve major American cities, plus a schedule calendar. Street maps, transit maps, restaurants, stores, and emergency services and numbers are included. The Metropolitan diary covers all twelve cities; other diaries cover specific cities in greater depth. Custom printing of names and logos is available on covers and endpapers.

Manufacturer: Per Annum, Inc., 114 East 32nd Street, Suite 1200, New York, NY 10016 (1-800-548-1108).

See *ELECTRONIC TIME* for electronic organizers.

PAPERWORK TIME

*The paper avalanche · Categorizing
paperwork · Action paper, info paper, and
waste paper-handling skills*

The avalanche of paper that continues to stream through American businesses represents one of the costliest elements of overhead. It clogs a business with cost because, in general, there is a 90 percent input versus 10 percent output ratio. That means that, unless rigorous cleaning occurs, file cabinets multiply, file maintenance cost increases, and file access becomes more difficult.

Most organizations have their quota of people with squirrel complexes—the urge to store everything—that keep them busy every day. They open the mail, file the advertising literature (new folders for those that don't fit), copy and distribute everything possible . . . and probably staple the envelopes to the letters, too. Recognize them by their bulging pockets and pens poised to note everything discussed; their constant reorganization of paperwork, with complex forms in all colors of the rainbow; and their permanent collection of logarithmic grid paper, multicolumn analysis paper, ruled, unruled, side-punched, top-punched, in green, white, gray, and buff. Their file cabinets are expensive garbage cans.

There are three basic types of paper: *action* paper, *info* paper, and *waste* paper. For each, there are four possible actions: toss it, file it, pass it on, or act on it. If possible, start to cut your paperwork time by training an assistant or secretary to screen and sort incoming paperwork before it hits your desk. Have it put into separate folders so that you can deal with the action items first.

If necessary, make a record of everything that crosses your desk for two weeks, then categorize it by source and type. Check how these relate to your own objectives. Then work with your secretary to control it, providing him or her with guidelines to handle as much of it as possible. Delegate to others, too, wherever it makes sense.

Sharpen your skills in dealing with the essential paperwork (see

WRITING TIME and *READING TIME*), and don't let it sit around. (See *PROCRASTINATION*.) Use these ideas to speed things up:

Action Paper   Simplify it. Insist on one-page summaries of long reports. Have all of the figures checked before signing disbursement approvals. Have previous correspondence clipped to letters needing a reply or some other action on your part.

Save everybody's time by replying to correspondence on the back of memos and letters. Consider using a simple rubber stamp to outline and formalize your reply.

Handwritten interoffice memos are good time-savers. My experience is that they are often unavailable because their initial cost is higher than blank paper and it may require executive action to break the habit of typing everything. Both of these are unacceptable blocks and should be removed.

Avoid the pending file like the plague. Try and handle everything only once. If you find yourself putting things aside, ask yourself why. Could be that what you're really doing is avoiding an unpleasant issue; if so, it's better to deal with it sooner than later.

Avoid overcorrection. The Declaration of Independence had two handwritten corrections, so why retype your flawed works?

Handle requests for charity by setting up a charity committee, with an appropriate budget, and funnel everything to them. Get yourself out of the loop.

Info Paper   Highlight key sentences with a yellow marker as you read, to avoid having to read the whole thing over to find the important items. Make marginal notes of your thoughts and ideas. Keep asking yourself if there is a message *behind* the text.

Set up an alphanumeric code for subject filing to save your assistant from having to reread material and decide how to file it. Use a desk telephone index, and organize filing codes with it. Start by writing down all of your A file names with a unique number suffix: A1, A2, A3, A4, etc. You can add up to twenty-six subcodes under each one: A1A, A1B, A1C, A1D, etc. If you ever need to, you can add sub-subcodes (A1A1, A1A2, etc.), although none of the executives that I know who use the system have ever found them necessary.

A typical subject file set might look like this:

A   Miscellaneous
A1   Accounts
    A1A   Accounts Receivable
    A1B   Accounts Payable

Junk mail occupies us for eight months of our lives.

            A2   Associations
                    A2A   Associations, National
                    A2B   Associations, Regional
                    A2C   Convention Planning
                    A2D   Speeches
            A3   Administration

            . . . and so on.

When you want to file a document, hit the A button on your desk index, and your subcodes will display. Write the appropriate one at the top of the document, and your assistant will know exactly where to file it.

When you want to retrieve a file, the fact that *you* determined the file code will help you to recover the document, even when your assistant is not there.

Copies of others' correspondence kept for information purposes should not be filed. Instead, set up the policy that only the originator makes a file copy. Others can reference it, if and when necessary. The high cost of file maintenance demands this sort of shared responsibility. (See *FILING TIME.*)

Printed matter is another ball game. Avoid having periodicals placed directly on your desk, if possible. Have somebody copy the index page of magazines that come in, and send a copy to all those likely to be interested. A check-off area should be added to the page, to determine whether the recipient would or would not like to see the entire magazine or a specific article. Those who don't want the magazine will avoid a pile stacking up that they "hope to get to." Those who want it will get it. Your subscription expense can often be drastically cut by using this system. Reading is essential to avoid "knowledge obsolescence," but be very selective.

Waste Paper   Keep your paperwork bulk down by practicing these five basic habits: don't ask for it, discontinue it, don't record it, throw it away, and use the telephone.

Maintain an effective records management program. Insure that your records retention policies are up to date and followed actively.

Check out every possible way to avoid hard-copy files. It can cost more than $4,000 per year to maintain a five-drawer file cabinet. Can you afford it? Check alternative information storage systems, microforms, or electronic storage. Separate active files from historical records, and keep the system clean with flow-process analyses and forms control. An organization that has a good records

But at my back I always hear
Time's winged chariot hurrying near. . .
Andrew Marvell,
To His Coy Mistress

READING TIME

Reading habits and skills measurement ·
Reading speed and comprehension
test · Controlling the reading pile ·
Improving reading skills

Managers spend an average of about twelve hours each week reading business correspondence and trade literature, and perhaps technical books. Like most of us, they learned to read in grade school and many have never sharpened their skills since. We are often inefficient and inflexible in our reading habits, and waste a great deal of time, money, and energy. Fortunately, it is easy to improve the situation with a little self-training and discipline. In a research project that I conducted involving nearly two hundred executives, 83 percent claimed that they didn't have enough time to keep up with their reading; help is clearly needed.

Good readers gear their reading speed to the material. Concentrated study is accomplished at about 200 words per minute (WPM), normal reading between 250–350 WPM, rapid reading from 350–500 WPM, and skim-reading at speeds up to 2,000 WPM.

How fast do you read? Check it out with the reading test that follows, then you'll know whether you should skip the rest of this section or read on. Either way, you'll save time.

Record your starting time, then read the text. As soon as you finish, note your ending time, then subtract one from the other to find your reading time. Use the graph on page 230 to convert that to reading speed in words per minute. The areas between the dotted lines reflect the general population's performance, which frankly isn't that great. With some training, most people can increase their reading speed to well over six hundred words per minute.

Check your comprehension level by answering the questionnaire.

THE QUALITY OF MAINTENANCE
(1,000 words)

START TIME: END TIME: READING TIME:

Changes in the average maintenance cost per product will be determined by the sector in which productivity is increasing most rapidly. If the productivity increase is higher in the production of goods than in services, then maintenance will become increasingly expensive in relation to goods. In this situation it will pay to reduce the maintenance per product and instead devote a corresponding amount of time to highly productive work that will offer income to replace the goods that needed service. This is the "use-and-throw-away" system. The maintenance per item is reduced to a level where we only perform service when the yield on the effort corresponds with the level of hourly earnings in specialized work. If productivity were instead to increase more rapidly in the service sector than in production, we should get the converse result. It will then pay to reduce our work time and prolong the maintenance time per commodity.

The case we have most cause to interest ourselves in is a reduction in service time per item as the result of a slower productivity increase in the service sector. This will mean a deterioration in the quality of maintenance provided. Is such a deterioration possible from the technical point of view? In ordinary production there exist, without doubt, situations on which it seems impossible to cut down the service per goods. We cannot, for instance, reduce the maintenance given to aircraft, without regrettable consequences. It is probable, however, that maintenance time varies more in consumption than in production. One reason for this is that a lot of maintenance serves only to increase the pleasure in using goods, not to ensure their technical performance. We wash the car to make it look nice, not to keep it in working order. It is entirely possible to cut down on this sort of maintenance if we like.

Even when the object of maintenance is to get consumption goods to function technically—as with greasing a car—there are still wide margins in the amount of possible service per product. There are two reasons for this. To begin with, the amount of service required often depends on how old the goods are. Service increases with the age of the goods. If, therefore, we discard goods earlier, they will need less service. This must apply even to such sensitive objects as aircraft. Secondly, we can choose to cut down on maintenance, if this will only mean that the goods in question wear out more quickly and have to be replaced sooner. When service costs show a relative increase, one can draw up a new maintenance plan with less service in the initial phase and earlier reprocurement.

Thus openings definitely exist for reducing the quality of maintenance. Such reductions, however, will have a very different effect on the pleasure derived from different goods. The reduced maintenance of certain goods will render them less enjoyable, while with other goods, the amount of pleasure they give will not be affected. It is, therefore, probable that the servicing requirements of different goods will influence the structure of consumption as incomes rise. The man about to buy a large house may hesitate at the thought of the relative rise that will later occur in cleaning costs. When we calculate how the demand for different goods is dependent on the level of income, we must bear in mind that the relative prices of the goods, owing the discrepancies in the service they require, will necessarily change as incomes rise. (This must be borne in mind in economic theory, in which it is customary, when investigating the correlation between income and demand, to assume that the relative prices of goods are constant.)

Products are also designed with a view to the shifts occurring in the price of maintenance. It is interesting to note that this occurs in two diametrically opposed ways. Either one can make very cheap, simple goods which can be discarded before they require any service, or else one can make especially high quality products that need no service. Both methods are designed to save maintenance time.

If it becomes relatively more expensive to provide maintenance services, then one reduces the maintenance per product. Will the same thing also apply in the case of human servicing? This is doubtful. The reason for cutting down on the maintenance of goods is, after all, that one can, to some extent, substitute reprocurement for maintenance. No such possibility exists in the case of the human body. For this reason, people may want to devote a higher proportion of their growing incomes to increased physical care, the better to enjoy possession of their own, more or less irreplaceable bodies. The scope of this type of service may thus actually increase. Such an income effect, however, could never assert itself with respect to the maintenance of goods, since there it both pays, and is technically possible, to substitute goods for services.

That development has been faster in production proper than in services does not, of course, mean that productivity in the services sector has not increased. Technical advances make it possible to maintain and service a given item in a shorter time than previously. Plastic boats, for instance, save the boat owner a great deal of work and worry in the spring and autumn. The maintenance work of the housewife has been simplified by dishwashers and vacuum cleaners. Motor-powered lawn mowers make a noise, but undoubtedly reduce the time it takes to keep a lawn trim. Electric shavers perhaps reduce the time spent on our morning toilet. And who, in this context, will not think immediately of the electric beater as an aid in the mixing of dry martinis? Speed reading is another interesting phenomenon. Many of us have felt the urge to develop our reading power by answering one of the advertisements and signing up for a course. As the skeptics realize, however, comprehension depends on intelligence and motivation, qualities that are not easily procured. Even so, our initial positive reaction to such an idea reveals what we would like to achieve.

SELF-RATING COMPREHENSION TEST
The Quality of Maintenance

Select the answer you believe is correct, based only on the information contained in the reading passage. Circle the corresponding letter. Check your answers with the score key at the end of the chapter.

1. The amount of service required on a product is dependent on
   a. the cost of manufacture
   b. how old it is
   c. a maintenance plan
   d. the amount of pleasure it provides

2. Product maintenance may be reduced when
   a. different goods are available
   b. the goods become less enjoyable
   c. we want the goods to wear out more quickly
   d. service costs increase

3. Cheap products result in
   a. more maintenance time
   b. less pleasure
   c. less maintenance time
   d. a service sector productivity increase

4. High-quality products and cheap products are similar in that they save
   a. maintenance time
   b. money
   c. worry
   d. productive time

5. Technical advances in the production sector
   a. reduce product maintenance time
   b. increase expenditures on health care
   c. increase product maintenance
   d. make goods less expensive

6. Housewives
   a. don't like cleaning large houses
   b. don't like repairing appliances
   c. have more maintenance work
   d. have simplified maintenance work

7. Increased health care
   a. requires more income
   b. is related to maintenance of goods
   c. affects the relative price of goods
   d. increases physical enjoyment

8. Speed-reading may increase
   a. productivity in the service sector
   b. the ability to read advertisements quickly
   c. intelligence
   d. the need for motivation

9. A slower productivity increase in the service sector of the economy affects goods by
   a. reducing the amount of service they get
   b. improving the quality of maintenance
   c. reducing aircraft maintenance
   d. reducing consumer enjoyment of them

10. Maintenance becomes more expensive when
    a. production productivity increases
    b. technical performance is at stake
    c. cheap products are purchased
    d. yield on the maintenance effort is not calculated

From Linder, Staffan B. *The Harried Leisure Class*. New York: Columbia University Press, 1970.

Absorb what you read by *understanding* rather than memorizing. Think as you read, and don't let diversion reduce your attention. Do not read at a constant pace; learn to adjust your speed to the material.

Practice by reading a daily newspaper feature which usually has the same amount of copy. Time yourself, reading at your normal speed on the first day, then consciously trying to read faster on subsequent days. Make brief notes of the important points and then check back to see how well you comprehended the material. You can double your reading speed and comprehension in about a month with this simple exercise.

READING SPEED ASSESSMENT CHART

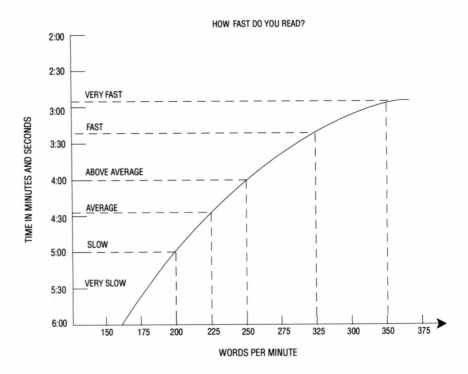

HOW FAST DO YOU READ?

Use this conversion scale to translate your reading time into reading speed. The dotted lines indicate the comparative boundaries of U.S. high school-educated adults.

CONTROLLING YOUR READING PILE

Cancel magazines and newsletters that you don't look forward to receiving, particularly the free ones. If you're not getting anything out of them, they're stealing your valuable time.

Check magazine indexes and mark those items you want to read. Slice them out, and then treat them as part of your incoming mail, or put them all in a binder that you can take with you to read on business flights, or as a waiting-time filler. In a small business organization, arrange for a secretary to photocopy the index pages of trade magazines and circulate them. Those who want to see a specific article can check it off, and return the sheet. Copies of needed articles can then be sent to the interested persons. This avoids the problem of magazines slowly making their way through an organization, or one person holding on to them. If certain articles should be retained, mark them for subject filing and have the secretary do that too.

Always have a highlighter handy so you can mark and reference important sections, because you will forget 50 percent of what you read within two months, and your reading time is too valuable to lose 50 percent of it. Don't hesitate to write in books unless they are valuable first editions or borrowed. Then use a card or computer reference file, such as the one below, so you can obtain the material again when necessary.

DATE _____ DATA FILE SUBJECT: _____

SOURCE/TITLE: _____ PAGE _____

AUTHOR _____

PUBLISHER _____ YEAR _____

LIBRARY/CALL NUMBER _____

NOTES:

Insist that internal correspondence that runs four pages or more be headed with a summary not to exceed one page.

Business reading is usually done to gather information. Read with a purpose and learn to pull the meat from text without letting the fat slow you down.

Don't let nonessential material that you want to read "when you have time" sit on your desk. Keep it in a drawer. When you can't stuff any more in, you'll have to do somthing with it or throw it out, and that may help to keep your squirrel complex under control.

If you would like to improve your reading skills, there are some techniques that can help. Many of them are built upon pioneering work by my friend James Duncan and his colleagues Joseph Quick and James Malcolm in understanding and measuring the reading function.[1] Other books to read for self-improvement are listed at the end of this chapter. Experts agree that whatever course you adopt, the first essential for improved reading is a positive attitude. To succeed, you must be *convinced* that you should improve your reading ability. Once convinced, try these approaches:

Capture as broad a span of words as possible when you read. This will reduce the slowing effect that physical eye movement has on overall speed and comprehension. A slow reader scans like this:

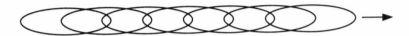

A fast reader scans like this:

Rapid improvement will come by reducing your scanning overlap.

Skim-reading will help you to break free of a habitual scan pattern. Move your eyes rapidly down a page, slowing briefly when you spot key facts. Mark those that warrant more study. Even though you will not use this technique all the time, it's a quick and useful way to gain an initial feel for a document or book. If this previewing persuades you that the material is worth reading fully, you can do it more quickly with the partial grasp you've already gained. If it's not worth reading, you've saved yourself wasted time and effort.

Training in speed-reading can increase reading speed to eight hundred words a minute and more without loss of comprehension. If your work demands a lot of reading, you should consider taking a course. Most courses use pacing techniques to increase reading speed, and you can apply some of these yourself. Start with a newspaper, because it has a narrow column. Draw your finger or a pencil down the center of the column, and *keep your eyes on it*. You will find that you are able to read entire lines without horizontal eye movement. Then try wider columns and faster vertical movement. Push yourself; you will probably be surprised at how much faster you can go.

> The universe is not only queerer than we imagine, but it is queerer than we *can* imagine.
>
> *J. S. Haldane*

---

1. Quick, Duncan, and Malcolm. *Work-Factor Mental Work Standards.* New York: McGraw-Hill, 1962. Chapter on concept reading and action reading.

Orient your mind to unfamiliar reading matter before you dive into it. Always read the index to learn the scope of the text. If there's no index, subheadings can often give you the picture. The preliminary scan may convince you that you don't need to read the whole thing. Never feel that you *have* to read every word.

In lengthy materials, look for summary paragraphs. Try and spot the author's style; the first or last sentence in a paragraph will often disclose its entire content.

Look for markers that may flag the need to read carefully—words like "first," "second," "finally," and so on. Every paragraph has an "idea peg" or topic sentence. Once you've grabbed it, you can skip forward faster.

Effective reading will not only save your time, but also bring added pleasure. The quality of comprehension is unaffected by gradual increases in reading speeds, and may even be improved. Purposeful reading should be an essential component of your communication skills. By learning to get through your business reading faster, you may even recover enough time to enjoy the luxury of savoring the thoughts and craftsmanship of the world's great authors, when you can read again and again those moving passages in literature that make reading really worthwhile.

Sir Richard Steele, the famous English essayist, said back in 1720, "Reading is to the mind what exercise is to the body." He was right.

> Time is a circus, always packing up and moving away.
>
> *Ben Hecht, writer*

For further help, the following books are recommended:

Bray, Jane, et al. *Read to Succeed*. 2d ed. New York: McGraw-Hill, 1980.

Cutler, W. *Triple Your Reading Speed*. New York: Prentice-Hall, 1987.

Lewis, N. *How to Read Better and Faster*. New York: Harper & Row, 1987.

COMPREHENSION TEST SCORING KEY

1.(b) 2.(d) 3.(c) 4.(a) 5.(a) 6.(d) 7.(d) 8.(d) 9.(a) 10.(a)
7–10 above average   5–7 average   3–4 below average   1–2 poor

RECORDING TIME

Activity recording methods and tips ·
Electronic data collection · Task
distribution reports

S cientists have long known that in order to understand any-thing one has to be able to measure it. The same principle can be applied to time use. For those truly determined to improve managerial effectiveness, or to get more out of life in general, a pe-riod of activity measurement is recommended. It is superior to guesswork, because we tend to have an "elasticized" impression of time when thinking about our own activities. If a task was boring or unpleasant we imagine that it took longer to complete than it ac-tually did. Conversely, the time given to absorbing or exciting tasks is usually underestimated, as is that taken up by a series of small diversions like drop-in visitors.

Peter Drucker claimed that he was constantly surprised to find executives deceiving themselves about the way that they budgeted their time. He held that the first step for an effective executive is to begin tracking time use accurately, and to do a close analysis of the record periodically.[1]

So, since both behavioral scientists and basic logic confirm the value of personal time recording, perhaps you should try it. You may well be surprised at what you really do in a day. You will, at least, have advanced beyond guesswork and will have something solid on which to base a plan to improve the quality of your time allocation.

There are numerous ways of making a time record, and this chapter deals exclusively with the methodology. You can pick any system which appeals to you. When you have completed a few days' record-keeping and have some accurate information in front of you, it may then be analyzed. The procedures will be found in *TIME QUALITY CONTROL*. First, though, some consideration of how

---

1. Drucker, Peter F. *The Effective Executive.* New York: Harper & Row, 1966.

you are going to go about recording your time is in order, so that it may be accomplished as quickly and effectively as possible.

A shorthand code can help you identify and analyze your activities. I have developed this one, which has found favor with many executives.

ACTIVITY CODES
FOR RECORDING TIME USE

C Creative
   Analytic, creative, and decision-making activities performed alone.

E Elective
   Personal errands, etc.
   EM Meals (*Nonbusiness*).

I Instruction/Training

M Meeting

   MP Planned Meeting
       MP1, 2, 10, etc. = Number of people involved
       MPC Conference Meeting
       MPCA Attendee
       MPCL Leader
       MPT Exposition/Trade Show

   MU Unplanned Meeting
       Unplanned interruption or visitation by individuals as well as unplanned group meetings.

O Organizing, Planning, and Scheduling

P Phone
   PI Telephone in
       PIU *Unexpected and interruptive incoming calls.*
   PO Telephone out

R Reading
   RE Editing
   RI Information

S Supervision
   Overseeing and inspection.

T Travel
   TC Commuting
   TB Business

W   Writing
   WD   Dictation
   WC   Correspondence/Memos
             Electronic or handwritten communication.
   WR   Record Keeping

X   Idle, Waiting

This activity-coding system has the advantage that it may be expanded or contracted as required. For example, planned meetings with one other person (MP1) may be further detailed by adding suffix letters, like this:

MP1E	Engineering
MP1F	Finance
MP1S	Sales

Any modification that will allow you to define your daily time allocation more clearly can be accommodated. As a first step, then, look over this basic coding system and modify or expand it to suit your needs. With a little use, the codes are quickly memorized.

Personal computers can help in recording time use, even without a dedicated software program. For example, most word processing programs have a "date" and "time" macro. (A macro is a built-in automatic routine triggered by a single keystroke.) It will put those data on the screen, using an internal clock chip to keep track of the hours and days. Those who have a computer at their workplace can dedicate a window to the time recording function, run the time macro, and then add the appropriate activity code.

For manual time recording, two types of chart have been found valuable. (Blank versions will be found in Appendix E.) The Time Analysis Chart is a general purpose form for managerial use. The tasks and activities normally performed during a business day are entered in the TASK LIST column. Use the descriptive elements from the activity code list or any others you prefer.

Choose days for analysis that are as typical as possible, and insure that all time is accounted for. From the beginning of your workday, indicate the time spent on each activity by drawing a horizontal line across the corresponding time span.

Don't lump brief activities together; it is important to record each one. Activities triggered by unplanned interruptions should also be recorded carefully, as these frequently add up to be big time-wasters, even though each one may be of short duration.

We are condemned
to kill time
thus we die
bit by bit.
Octavio Paz,
Cuento de los Jardines

Maintain your recording activity for a week, or until you are satisfied that you have a good record of your work patterns. Summarize each chart daily by calculating and entering the time spent on each activity in the TOTAL TIME column.

Some poor time utilization patterns may become obvious from the first day. Most managers, for example, are surprised by the number of unplanned activities in which they become involved. Studies show that they are interrupted, on the average, every seven minutes by some unexpected occurrence. Make whatever immediate corrections are possible, based on the evidence that develops, before getting into an in-depth analysis of your activity patterns. Your chart should look better at the end of the week than at the start. Comprehensive analysis will improve it even more.

The Time Utilization Record chart uses a more condensed, but flexible, format. The left column provides a time line marked in fifteen-minute increments, which translate easily into decimal fractions of an hour (15 minutes = 0.25 hours). Bars are drawn to mark the time allocated to functions identified at the head of each column. The functions are identified with the shorthand code. Analysis may be completed on the *TIME PAYOFF ANALYSIS* chart in Appendix G.

Ring sundial.

The column headers may be changed to indicate the person or group with whom interaction is taking place (manager, secretary, sales, engineering, customer service, etc.), roles (counseling, expediting, investigating, etc.), or activity values, based upon a set of predetermined priorities or levels of stress and/or gratification.

When the chart is used with these extradimension column headers, the activity codes are written adjacent to the time bars. The information is a little more difficult to read, but the method works quite well.

More sophisticated activity/time recording may be accomplished with random sampling techniques. Random sampling avoids the need for continuous time recording. It employs a series of random observations made only at times determined by a random numbers table. In a seven-hour work period, 280 random observations would produce an 80 percent confidence level of accuracy, provided that all observational patterns are truly random.

For executives who decide to attack their time problems as a group, which is highly recommended, statistical sampling recorders may be used. In effect, they are random impulse generators coupled with data input devices. One such system is provided by the Extensor Corporation of Minneapolis (612-933-2044). Desk units are provided, permitting the direct entry of individual time use data in machine-readable form.

A matrix chart is prepared, typically divided into "activity," "function," and "interaction" components. Charts may also be created to include value judgments or other determinants. It is then slipped into a visible panel on the desk unit.

The matrix chart is easily visible, and an alphanumeric code simplifies the task of recording individual activities. The coding also provides confidentiality in later statistical analysis of the respondent's time. A computer program has been developed to analyze the data.

Whatever form of time record you use, it may be necessary to get more detailed information on specific activities. Interruptions and diversions, for example, may be so frequent that they demand an in-depth investigation. In this case you should keep file cards on hand and note each interruption or diversion, one to a card. Later, the cards may be sorted and organized to identify the primary source(s) and/or basis of the interruptions.

It is later than you think.
Robert Service, Songs of a Sourdough

ROAD TIME

Controlling traffic · Saving time
while on the road

Americans spend nearly two billion hours annually in traffic jams. By 2005, the Federal Highway Administration expects the figure to climb above eight billion hours.

Authorities do not believe that new highways can be built to correct the problem, which is primarily caused by unexpected collisions and spills. Traffic experts feel that roads and highways can be used more efficiently if drivers know what conditions are like before they reach the access ramp. So, in late 1988, the Pathfinder Project was initiated in Los Angeles on one of the worst stretches of the Santa Monica Freeway. Implanted road sensors and remote TV cameras feed information on traffic conditions into a central traffic operations computer. The computer controls stoplights at all entrance ramps, which regulate the flow of vehicles on to the highway. In addition, the computer provides up-to-the-minute traffic information to drivers in cars equipped with telephones or radios. Experiments are also underway with dash-mounted videoscreen maps. The maps will indicate preferred routes and estimated travel times. The Los Angeles experiment has provided a test group of drivers with these navigational aids, to determine whether they can help in spreading the traffic load more intelligently and reducing highway overloads.

Fully automated highways, on which the driver gives up control of his vehicle to a computer, are not likely before 2020 according to the Federal Highway Administration. They are included in the department's plans for selected major highways.

The ultimate in road navigation, eliminating time lost finding one's way around unfamiliar (and familiar) areas, is now available in the United States, although still quite expensive. The Etak Navigator (Etak Inc., 1430 O'Brien Street, Menlo Park, CA 94025, 415-328-3825) is a dash-mounted electronic screen that displays a road map, and pinpoints your position on it with a flashing star. As you drive, your vehicle's position on the screen remains constant and the map automatically scrolls as you travel. Your destination's address may be entered into the system with a small keyboard, and its position then appears on the map as a second flashing star. The screen also displays the distance between the two stars. If the destination is far enough away to be offscreen, an arrow appears at the appropriate edge of the screen.

This system requires no training to operate, and its accuracy depends on a self-regulating distance sensor that is keyed on installation to your particular vehicle. The position indicator is claimed to be accurate to within fifty feet. The system is available with either a four-inch or a seven-inch screen with zoom capability for a close-up map of your current location, or an area overview. The system has been licensed to Bosch in Europe and GM in the United States, but don't expect to see it in automobiles before 1993.

Whether or not you install this sophisticated gadgetry depends upon how much time you spend on the road, and for what purpose. But it makes sense to equip your vehicle with some time-saving accessories, even for the easy commute.

While driving try listening to cassettes for self-improvement. A broad range of materials are available, from foreign language instruction to business education.

Use a hand-held dictation unit (Olympus makes one of the best) to dictate letters and memos, and to capture ideas en route.

Get someone else to drive whenever you can and make use of a traveling work kit, or catch up on your reading.

Get into the habit of leaving early for appointments whenever you're going by road. Arriving a few extra minutes to find the building you want, find a parking place, and gather your thoughts is a great stress-reliever.

Make a note of the color and make of your rental car if you park it in a lot without numbered spaces. It's easy to forget what they look like. If the car breaks down, leave it in the safest spot possible and carry on. Call the rental company later. They'll pick it up.

If you habitually waste time trying to find your *own* vehicle in crowded lots, check out an electronic car-locator (Hammacher Schlemmer & Co. New York, NY 212-421-9000) which will flash your headlights or sound a one-second signal when the pocket transmitter is activated.

From the day they start driving until they give it up, motorists spend six months waiting at stoplights.

SHORT-INTERVAL SCHEDULING

*A shortcut method of developing
work-time relationships*

Short-interval scheduling (SIS) is a technique used to get a grasp of work-time relationships without using stopwatches or detailed work-study standards. It can improve pacing and on-schedule completion of tasks by overcoming some basic but unproductive time attitudes, particularly when lengthy tasks are encountered.

A person required to produce a report in three months tends, typically, to adopt a vigorous pace only a few days before the deadline. This leisurely start and frantic finish usually lowers the quality of work and increases errors.

Two friends of mine recently took a week off to drive from New York to San Francisco, each in his own car. They agreed to meet on the following Sunday at Fisherman's Wharf. One, knowing that he had plenty of time to complete the trip, didn't hesitate to stop and explore anything that interested him along the way. But as the days passed he realized how much farther he had to go, so he began to increase his speed. On his last day, he collected a speeding ticket as he roared along a western highway, trying to arrive on time. The other man broke the trip into seven segments and established a mileage goal for each day, with an allowance for sight-seeing. He arrived in good time, unstressed and unticketed. He was using short-interval scheduling.

In the work environment, SIS also helps by detecting errors or problems at the earliest opportunity, saving time and money by reducing the number of things that have to be redone. An error made in the early stages of a task may lie undetected until the end of the work, with disastrous results. A foreman may start a machinist on a three-hour job, only to find that half of the parts are out of tolerance because a die shifted, or that the job took five hours because the machinist was constantly resetting the die. Had the foreman used SIS, he would have checked the job within fifteen or thirty minutes and been able to take corrective action, with significant savings in time and materials. Being at the right place at the right time soon adds up to success in business management.

Most of the success of SIS is in its psychological time impact, however. People simply pace their work better when they have a realizable, short-term task schedule. So the three important rules for applying SIS are:

1. The "control interval" time must be short enough to correct unacceptable conditions before they offset the job objective.

2. The interval time, though short, must be flexible and rational. For example, a twenty-minute control time would be inappropriate on a construction job expected to last a month, but not on a fast, repetitious order-processing task.

3. The primary objective is to create a sense of time and productivity in supervisors without the need for industrial engineering work standards—the goal is to develop a feel for the reasonable expectancy of work output.

To determine a reasonable time expectancy for preparing invoices, for example, the invoices would first be divided into similar types. For instance, those with under ten line items might represent the first category. Tests can then establish the usual completion time for preparing them—say forty per hour. Then, instead of providing an invoicing clerk with a daily pile to process, his or her output would be determined at the end of each hour. If the output deviates from expectancy, later joint cooperative review can quickly pinpoint problems. Frequent computer downtime, missing price information, or procedural misunderstanding may surface as the cause, and can be corrected immediately before the whole day's work is affected.

An underlying value of SIS is the skill which supervisors gradually develop in accurately measuring and scheduling work loads. The intelligent "rules of thumb" that result produce better results and more confidence in projected completion dates and output quantities.

The basic simplicity of the SIS technique does not mean that it is easy to grasp. Grasping the concept that the *management* of time is more important than the *measurement* of time is the key issue. SIS is a useful way of providing it.

In developing an SIS program, care should be taken to avoid emphasis on individual productivity issues. Productivity and schedule attainment may certainly rise, but that improvement will come from the improved mindset of individual workers *and* their supervisors, working in concert. An imposed SIS system without multilateral understanding and acceptance of the principles involved is likely to fail.

Immediate results should not be expected either. Supervisors must have sufficient time to apply the mechanics of the program, develop their individual short-interval planning skills, and educate their subordinates. Team recognition of SIS benefits will come as more and more predetermined goals are attained.

Studies have shown repeatedly that most clerical and production functions have a great deal of lost time hidden within them, entirely beyond the control or desires of the individual worker. In many cases, this loss has been shown to exceed 40 percent of the total job time. Intelligently installed short-interval scheduling can cut this waste by half.

SLEEP TIME

What happens during sleep cycles ·
Optimizing sleep habits · Sleep therapy ·
Sleep learning · Daytime fatigue ·
Combatting insomnia

W hy we sleep as much as we do remains a mystery. There is actually a decrease in protein production during sleep, so it does not restore the body. The brain does not rest much either, but in fact stays quite busy. Yet lack of sleep brings severe trauma, including paranoia and hallucination. Dreaming apparently permits each and every one of us to be quietly and safely insane every night of our lives, as psychiatrist William Dement has pointed out.

The longest that a human has ever been able to stay awake without mental damage is 288 hours. Yet even if one goes without sleep for days, it requires only about ten hours of good sleep to make it up. The giraffe gets by with only two hours of sleep daily. So the question remains; why must the brain sleep so long each day to debug itself?

Sleep cycles are controlled by the pineal gland, which produces a hormone called *melatonin*. Melatonin is a potent sleep inducer, and will make one sleep at any time it is administered. The body clock[1] which triggers its release at nighttime is directly connected to the retina and uses the presence of light for daily synchronization. This timing mechanism is so sensitive that it actually begins two months before birth, started by an as yet unknown link with the mother's circadian rhythms.

The fascinating sequence of events that occur when we go to sleep begins with body temperature and blood pressure. They both drop within minutes, followed by a slowing in breathing and heartbeat as we enter the first sleep stage. For about three minutes, the

Time is a Test of
  Trouble—
But not a Remedy—
If such it prove, it prove
  too
There was no Malady.
  Emily Dickinson

---

1. The sleep body clock is located in nerve cells in the hypothalamus, known as the suprachiasmatic nucleus, or SCN.

brain's electrical patterns lose their alpha rhythms[2] and become irregular, while our eyes move slowly around behind our closed lids.

The second sleep stage, which usually lasts about fifteen minutes, is characterized by greater amplitude in the irregular brain pulses, interrupted by occasional spurts and waves of activity, and cessation of eye movement.

The third sleep stage lasts ten minutes. As it begins, 1.5 cycles-per-second delta waves are generated in the brain and the pituitary gland releases growth and sex hormones.

Time eases all things.
Sophocles, Oedipus Rex

Finally, we reach deep sleep, stage four, where for about thirty minutes we lie with our eyes and muscles inert, thereafter alternating between stages two, three, and four for approximately ninety minutes in all.

Then, without warning, the curtain goes up and our dreams begin. We follow the action with our closed eyes, and this rapid eye movement (REM) stage is accompanied by quickened breathing and pulse, higher blood pressure, and genital arousal. We alternate back and forth for hours through the five sleep stages, although stages three and four are skipped after about five hours of sleep.

Studies have shown that, no matter how old we are, the REM stage remains the same length, although our sleep patterns change in other respects as we age. Older people may even sleep more during the day than at night, and rest through a series of catnaps rather than continuous deep slumber.

Those who have trouble sleeping may or may not have insomnia. It's possible to dream that you are awake, or simply to imagine that you should be sleeping more. Most people tend to sleep too long, according to studies done at the University of Virginia and at Dartmouth Medical School. Too much time in the sack actually produces daytime tiredness.

To optimize your own sleeping habits, start by setting your clock to wake you up thirty minutes earlier than usual and do something pleasant as soon as you get out of bed. If there's no problem, keep it up for some days, until it's routine. Then go to bed thirty minutes later than is your habit, and stick with that for about ten days. You can probably trim still another half hour from each end of your sleep cycle before you feel any daytime drowsiness. Although the norm of eight hours sleep is well established, individual needs vary widely. Determine your own personal requirements, and gain all of the effective waking hours you can.

---

2. See *BODY TIME*, footnote 3, for an explanation of brain rhythms.

Some people feel daytime fatigue no matter how long they sleep. The sleeping environment may be the problem. Room temperature should be no higher than sixty-five degrees Fahrenheit. Aches or stiffness can point to the need for a new or different mattress. External noise can be smothered by turning on a radio, finding a spot between stations, and letting the gentle white noise assist deep slumber.

True insomniacs take more than thirty minutes to drift into sleep, wake frequently throughout the night, and as a result have great difficulty in getting up. Insomnia can be a transient, one- or two-night condition, triggered perhaps by a job-related problem, or a longer-lasting temporary condition caused by a divorce or death. Doctors can usually offer sedatives to help out in these circumstances, and 10 percent of adult Americans are said to use them.

Over the past twenty years doctors have prescribed a number of drugs from the benzodiazepine family to treat sleep disorders. Current favorites are Halcion, Restoril, Dalmane, and Xanax. Halcion, produced by Upjohn, has the largest market share, and was used by nearly ten million people last year. But any of these drugs can be extremely addictive. Habitual users may suffer memory loss and light-headedness while those who try to quit often experience severe nervousness. And those are just the known dangers. Doctors are not required to report suspected side effects of FDA-approved drugs, so the best policy is to avoid medication and attempt to work out the physical or mental problems that produce most insomnia without drugs. Certainly avoid medication in cases of chronic or long-term insomnia until a thorough medical diagnosis establishes the basic cause. If you *must* sleep in order to function, use the minimum dosage for as short a time as possible. New York State has recently limited benzodiazepine prescription to thirty days, and other states are expected to draft similar laws.

Remember, too, that an addiction to sleeping pills can actually prevent good sleep over the long term. Clinics report, in fact, that many insomniacs sleep longer and better when they *stop* taking drugs.

The ten best strategies for attacking insomnia are simple, and often the most effective:

1. Avoid any form of alcohol before retiring. Nightcaps can disrupt sleep patterns and even cause nightmares.

2. Don't eat anything within two hours of going to bed. Warm milk can even be a problem for some.

3. Get some good exercise within the first six hours of your waking day.

4. Don't ingest caffeine or nicotine after 3 P.M.

5. Don't nap during the day. If you feel drowsy, move around, stretch, inhale fresh air deeply, or exercise briefly.

6. Improve your sleep environment. Use earplugs and/or eyeshades if necessary. Use white noise to block external sounds.

7. Develop a preparatory routine. Take a warm bath, turn on soft music, do relaxing things before going to bed. Make the routine a habit. If you wake up at night, repeat the routine.

8. When you lie down, practice blocking all thoughts from your mind. Imagine you are staring at an empty chalkboard. As thoughts try and creep in, push them away. This is a learned skill but can be quite effective.

9. Relax every part of your body deliberately. Start with the toes and work upwards. Imagine you are going to sink right through the mattress.

10. Don't worry about your sleeping habits. Linking your bed with failure to sleep can even create a problem.

We haven't the time to take our time.

Eugène Ionesco

If insomnia persists, medical help is available. Call the Better Sleep Council (800-52-SLEEP). Attend a sleep clinic. (The American Sleep Disorders Association, 604 Second Street S.W., Rochester, MN 55902 can find one for you.) See your physician.

The latest sleep therapy focuses on natural sleep-promoting substances, rather than drugs which produce negative side effects. Research laboratories have recently isolated peptides which cause rats to fall rapidly asleep, and Harvard Medical School's Dr. James Kreuger has developed a muramyl peptide from urine which induces sleep quickly when injected into the bloodstream.

Can you learn while sleeping? Hypnopedia, or sleep learning, was first attempted at the U.S. Naval School in Pensacola, Florida, in 1922. The practice gained adherents in the U.S.S.R. and France over the next five decades, and was actively promoted by the British Sleep Learning Association. Results were intriguing but inconclusive, because sleep learning demands the use of language, and the brain appears able to assimilate only pictures during sleep cycles. No doubt experimentation will continue.

SPACE-TIME

Time elasticity · Speed, distance, and time · The basis of Einstein's relativity theories · The expanding universe

Only in the last century have scientists come to understand the elasticity of time, through their comparatively recent discoveries of the nature of the universe. But perhaps it all started in 300 B.C. when Aristarchus of Alexandria first had the temerity to suggest that the sun, rather than the earth, was the center of our planetary system. He was promptly condemned and punished as a heretic, and religious bodies managed to suppress the idea for twelve hundred years. The mounting weight of evidence finally forced Copernicus, in 1514 A.D., to come to the same conclusion. He had to publish his theory anonymously, out of fear for his life. His writings were placed in the Catholic Index as not fit for public consumption, and another hundred years were lost. Were it not for Galileo's telescope and Kepler's calculations which led both scientists to support Copernicus in 1609, we might still be struggling to understand the mysteries of space.

With the door to logical thinking open a crack, Sir Isaac Newton, in 1687, produced the most important scientific document in man's history. His *Philosophiae Naturalis Principia Mathematica* explained the movement of bodies in space brilliantly and delineated his law of gravity. Based on Newton's work, and that of Maxwell, Einstein, Hubble, and other great scientists, we know now that time as established by the stars is far from the simple linear yardstick that we use in our own limited environment. Clock time, solar time, and sidereal time are sufficient for our daily lives. To understand space-time, however, one must abandon these local time structures and delve into the very nature of the universe and all the matter it contains.

Maxwell led the way to understanding by explaining that all of the various waves we can sense (microwaves, ultraviolet, radio, light, etc.) are rhythmic disturbances, or waves, in electromagnetic fields.

These electromagnetic forces form the fabric of space into which all the physical bodies are woven. The waves are measured by the distance between their peaks. Those that travel slowly, like radio waves, can measure more than a meter; visible light has a wavelength of about 60/1,000,000 centimeters, depending on its color. Nothing in the known universe can move faster, because light has no mass. For this reason, scientists now use the speed of light, multiplied by cesium clock time units, to measure distance. If you travel one meter at the speed of light it takes you 0.000000003335640952 seconds. That's about 186,000 miles per second. If our sun were extinguished, it would take us about eight minutes to find out about it.

In the nineteenth century, when scientists could at last measure the movement of heavenly bodies more accurately, some disturbing inconsistencies became evident. Some planets, such as Mercury, were not performing *exactly* as Newton had predicted. Albert Einstein, between 1908 and 1915, provided the answers.[1] He knew from Newton's work that everything in the universe is in motion, so the problem was: If we attempted to pin down the speed of light, to what should it be relative? A tough question. He began to realize as he thought about it that an event observed by two people in different places is not seen at the same time *or* place. For example, an air traveler who stands up briefly and then sits down again will not feel that his seat has moved. It hasn't, relative to the plane in which he is flying. Relative to a person on the ground, though, his seat has probably moved a mile across the sky. In addition, of course, all of the action is taking place on a planet spinning at half a kilometer per second at its equator, and moving at 29.8 kilometers per second relative to its sun. So, if he could see it, an observer on Mars would put the passenger's seat someplace else again in space and time.

Einstein felt that all of the physical laws should work for *any* observer of an event, whether he was flying above the earth, standing on the ground, or on Mars. A common denominator was needed to cancel out the apparent differences caused by the observational positions. He knew that, of all the physical phenomena, light-speed was the most constant, so he built his theories of relativity upon it. One ($E=mc^2$) describes the increase in energy (E) and mass (m) that an object accrues as it approaches the speed of light (c). Just as important was his observation that, using the basic equation:

---

1. A high school dropout, Einstein was wandering at leisure through Italy in 1880, contemplating a recently published book of popular science, when he developed his revolutionary theories. Creativity has frequently been linked to true leisure, as long ago as ancient Greece. (See *LEISURE TIME.*)

$$\text{SPEED} = \frac{\text{DISTANCE}}{\text{TIME}}$$

a. If the speed of light is the same for all observers of an event, wherever they may be,

b. and as the observers will not agree as to the exact *place* of the event,

c. then time, also, cannot be absolute, and can only be associated with, or related to a particular observer.

In other words, for any specific event to which the speed-distance-time equation is applied, one cannot have a variation in the distance value without a corresponding difference in the time value, if the speed is to remain constant.

This means that if three astronauts lifted off in different directions from Cape Canaveral with synchronized watches guaranteed for accuracy, they would never agree while in space as to the time each observed the same event. What Einstein did was establish the method by which they could accurately correlate their space-time differences.

He wasn't satisfied with that remarkable achievement. He knew his theories worked for objects with mass, but they didn't fit the gravitational forces that followed Newton's laws. Without getting into the mathematics involved, if one had applied Einstein's special theory of relativity to gravitational effects, the waves have been shown to travel at infinite velocity, and that is not allowed because it would be faster than light. So Albert scratched his shaggy head and came up with yet another blockbuster. Space-time, he reasoned, cannot be *linear*.

The space-time environment that contains the universe, said Einstein, is warped by the mass and energy of matter within it. The shortest path between two points will not be a straight line. It only *seems* to be straight to us because the light waves are bent by gravitational fields, and we interpret what we see in three-dimensional terms instead of four-dimensional space-time. When his theories were applied to the apparent movement of bodies in space, they clicked perfectly into place with Newton's laws. Unfortunately, the civilized world was then engaged in something more important—world war—so tests to prove Einstein's incredible breakthrough were postponed.

With both space and time acting as dynamic rather than static elements in the universe, both affected by gravitation, some odd effects that had scientists puzzled for decades could now be explained. As light tries to move within Earth's field of gravity, it loses energy

Time goes, you say? Ah, no!
Alas, Time stays, we go.
Austin Dobson

and slows down. Thus, to a person high in an orbiting spacecraft, events on the planet's surface appear to occur a little slower than they do to someone on the ground. The effect increases as one moves further into space, and our navigational satellites would be useless without correction for this general relativity effect. It also means that those who live in mountain regions, further from Earth's core, will age slightly faster than those who live in the valleys.

The opposite effect would be caused by traveling away from Earth, at speeds approaching that of light. The energy and space-time relationships would slow time for such a space traveler and he would not age as fast as a person left on Earth. Time is elastic, and is different for each person, according to his position and movement.

Building upon Albert Einstein's work, Edwin Hubble, in 1929, proved that our universe is expanding, and that all observable bodies are moving out and away from one another. This effect provides a time direction which, eons in the future, may be reversed if our universe begins to contract when the momentum of the "big bang" is finally overcome by gravity—time as we know it would begin to run backward. This expansion and contraction comprise "cosmos time." However, it is doubtful that humans could truly perceive this. We have a very linear mental or psychological perception of time; when we remember, we look back in time, and some parapsychologists suggest that certain individuals can look forward in time.

The flow of time within these perceptual parameters is critical to our very existence, and to that of the universe. Any unified theory that will effectively link *all* of the forces that shape our world must incorporate an understanding of how cosmos time and human time coexist. This problem is occupying many of our leading scientists today. Perhaps foremost among them is Stephen Hawking. In his recent book, *A Brief History of Time*, he points out that the general theory of relativity forces us to accept that there must have been a state of infinite density in the past, and that the big bang therefore gave a beginning to time.[2] The big crunch may end it. In the meantime, the striving for understanding must sustain us.

Let us alone. Time driveth onward fast, And in a little while our lips are dumb. Let us alone. What is it that will last? All things are taken from us, and become Portions and parcels of the dreadful past.
Lord Alfred Tennyson, Choric Song of the Lotus-Eaters

---

2. Hawking, Stephen W. *A Brief History of Time*. New York: Bantam Books, 1988.

STRESS

Positive and negative stress · The Life Event
Stress chart · Stress symptoms—
coping with stress

W hen deadlines are rushing up, or when we feel that there are just too many things to do, we experience time-related stress. For some it's a debilitating pressure; for others, an exciting race against time.

Hans Selye, one of the world's foremost stress researchers, defined stress as wear and tear on the body which can produce an exhilarating *eustress*, or an unpleasant and disease-inducing *distress*. It has three stages: reaction to an alarm, protective action, and exhaustion. It works in the same way today as it did when our ancestors huddled in caves, alert to the slightest noise that might signal a predator. The hypothalamus triggers the pituitary gland to speed the hormone ACTH to the adrenal glands, and as adrenaline floods into our nervous system, an incredible series of rapid changes occur. All nonessential systems, such as digestion, disease fighting, and growth are closed down. Pain receptors are dulled. Blood sugar surges into the muscles, our pupils dilate, our senses and our mind sharpen. We feel great, ready to conquer the world. The people who make carnival rides learned this long ago, and if the condition is transient, the effect is beneficial.

Problems begin when the period of stress is extended, and our bodies are kept in an overalert state. We remain hypersensitive, yet many of our normal-state systems are suppressed, notably the immune system. In short order, invading cells create havoc with our bodies. The skin, our first line of defense, erupts with acne and rashes; we suffer aching muscles, heads, and backs as well as colds and other viral infections. These are but the early warning signs. Unless the stress is relieved and our protective systems reactivated, peptic ulcers, mouth infections, impotence, and infertility beset us, followed by atherosclerosis and cancer. And while this carnage is taking place, our mental balance is disturbed, resulting in with-

> The strongest of all warriors are these two: Time and Patience.
>
> *Leo Tolstoi*

drawal, defensiveness, subservience, and lack of creativity. That's why learning to cope with negative stress is absolutely essential or it will exhaust and kill you.

How do you know if you are undergoing stress? Doctors Holmes and Rahe developed a simple questionnaire to measure stress level and susceptibility to disease which has shown remarkable accuracy since it was constructed in 1967. Check everything that has happened to you over the last two years, or longer if the event still worries you. Then add the figures adjacent to each event checked. Adjust any individual event value 10 percent up or down if you feel that it was more or less stressful than usual. If your total score is over 300, you should regard the situation as serious; you are in jeopardy, and most likely to succumb to a major health problem within the next few months. If your score is between 150 and 300, you still have moderate risk and should take some corrective action. A score below 150 means that your health is not at risk.

SOCIAL READJUSTMENT RATING SCALE

RANK	LIFE EVENT	MEAN VALUE
1	Death of spouse	100
2	Divorce	73
3	Marital separation	65
4	Jail term	63
5	Death of close family member	63
6	Personal injury or illness	53
7	Marriage	50
8	Fired at work	47
9	Marital reconciliation	45
10	Retirement	45
11	Change in health of family member	44
12	Pregnancy	40
13	Sex difficulties	39
14	Gain of new family member	39
15	Business readjustment	39
16	Change in financial state	38
17	Death of close friend	37
18	Change to different line of work	36
19	Change in number of arguments with spouse	35
20	Mortgage over $10,000	31
21	Foreclosure of mortgage or loan	30
22	Change in responsibilities at work	29
23	Son or daughter leaving home	29
24	Trouble with in-laws	29
25	Outstanding personal achievement	28

26	Wife begin or stop work	26
27	Begin or end school	26
28	Change in living conditions	25
29	Revision of personal habits	24
30	Trouble with boss	23
31	Change in work hours or conditions	20
32	Change in residence	20
33	Change in schools	20
34	Change in recreation	19
35	Change in church activities	19
36	Change in social activities	18
37	Mortage or loan less than $10,000	17
38	Change in sleeping habits	16
39	Change in number of family get-togethers	15
40	Change in eating habits	15
41	Vacation	13
42	Christmas	12
43	Minor violations of the law	11

Originally published in *Journal of Psychosomatic Research*, Vol. 2, pp. 213–218, by Holmes and Rahe as "The Social Readjustment Rating Scale," 1967. Used by permission of Pergamon Press.

Some of us, of course, are hardier than others and don't worry as much about life's problems. Others are worry-prone. Evidence has built a picture over the years of the individual who is reacting to stress, for whatever reason, or is psychologically a candidate for stress-related disease. The profile of a stressed person may include these traits:

- Driving ambition, aggression, competitiveness, and inflexibility.
- A crisis-driven activity level, to the point that they may frequently invent an emergency to rationalize their hurry or short temper.
- A habit of overtaking other vehicles on the road, even when not pushed for time.
- Feeling guilty about taking holidays or vacations.
- Self-centeredness, and few friends.
- Inappropriate, quick-tempered, hostile reactions to minor annoyances.
- Fidgeting and foot-wagging.
- A habit of finishing other people's sentences and pushing the speed of conversation.
- Antisocial behavior, such as shoplifting.

Those businessmen most likely to be stressed are in middle management, over forty, and concerned about job security. They fear that they cannot keep pace with new technologies. They are suspicious that the newly-hired MBA will displace them. They suffer from conglomerate psychosis, having heard horror stories of what happens in the rush of corporate takeovers. These are real fears, and often well founded. They underlay the grim statistics that show the life expectancy of businessmen in America to be lower than in twenty-four other industrialized nations. Add the time-related stress of trying to pack too many appointments into the day, jet travel, the disruption of body rhythms (see *BODY TIME*), and the domestic problems caused by absences, and you have a total picture of the short-lived executive.

Time does not become sacred to us until we have lived it.
John Burroughs

If you are a hard driving, aggressive businessperson, you have a three times greater chance of becoming an angina casualty than the individual who takes enough time to relax and resists taking his job home with him. Take stock; ask yourself if it is *really* so important to maintain the pace? Then consider using some of the techniques discussed elsewhere in this book (*TIME PAYOFF ANALYSIS*, *PLANNING TIME, TRAVEL TIME*, etc.) to dig out from under. If your job is psychologically demanding but lacks any opportunity for independence or creativity, it would probably be in your best interest to work very hard at finding another.

If you can't escape stress, the only alternative is to cope with it more effectively. Dr. Eric Berne, a pioneer in transactional analysis, defined an activity as "a method of structuring time to deal with external reality."[1] What you consider to be external reality may warrant examination and revision if you are to rid your mind of tension. For example, the emotional positions or beliefs that one picks up early in life are usually those which one retreats to automatically in later years. This frequently produces a conflict between the childhood position and the adult stance demanded by logic and reality. The resulting tension will probably remain until the root cause is recognized and dealt with. Make a point to read more on transactional analysis; it may have some answers for you.

Remember that hostility and aggressiveness will produce feelings of guilt and separate you from others. Compete if you must, but set reasonable limits. On the other hand, you can build a bulwark of strength if you develop a truly meaningful relationship with one or

---

1. Berne, E., *Transactional Analysis in Psychotherapy*. New York: Grove Press, 1961.

two people, based on kindness and concern for their well-being. As Emerson said, "For every sixty seconds that you are angry, you lose a minute of happiness."

Look for help in professional stress workshops and seminars. Stress-related problems are often almost impossible to solve without guidance.

Use the power of physical exercise to unravel the knots. It works because it causes the brain to release endorphins which are natural opiates. If you can, learn to temporarily escape your cares by making your mind blank for a quarter of an hour now and then. You may be surprised how refreshed you will feel.

Vent your grievances rather than trying to suppress them. Getting them out on the table may solve them, as well as gaining you respect.

Use the reality of black and white. Write about how you feel. List your problems. Rank them in importance. Think up ways of dealing with them. Then schedule them for action.

The tragedy of life is not what humans attain, but what they miss. Think about that, and slow down—or you may stop sooner than you expect.

SUNDIALS

Origins and development ·
Making and aligning a sundial

As the last great ice age ended about 13,000 years ago, primitive man began to settle in communities in the Middle East where warmth and water were most readily available. As static communities took the place of nomadic hunting groups, the need to mark time became clear. To grow food, for example, the Sumerians had to know when to plant, so the calendar was developed to mark the seasons (see *CALENDAR*). As the tribal communities developed, a period was needed when all could come together for barter. The sun provided the obvious marker, and the position of shadows cast by rocks and trees were first used for the purpose. Appointments were made for a time when a man's shadow was an agreed number of times the length of his foot.

By 3500 B.C. the thriving city of Catal Huyuk in Turkey was bustling with more than five thousand citizens. Its rapid growth, and that of other towns, led to the erection of public sundials, or obelisks. Knowledge of them spread throughout the Middle East, and they got bigger and better as each community tried to outdo their neighbors. Some scholars believe that the Egyptians built the Great Pyramid to be the biggest sundial ever; Pharaoh Thutmose III built two famous ones at Heliopolis around 1300 B.C. The Egyptians also used obelisks to figure out the summer and winter solstices. They noted that at the summer solstice the shadow was at its shortest, and the winter solstice coincided with the longest shadow. Halfway between those points, at the vernal and autumnal equinoxes, the day and night were of equal length. The obelisks, or *gnomons* (as they were later called by the Greeks), were dedicated to the sun god Ra by the Egyptian priests. Some of the clever ones came up with a portable sundial, or "time stick," in the tenth century B.C. With all of the wars raging through the Mediterranean area at the time, it was probably smart to be mobile.

In 689 B.C. a solar eclipse awed the Middle Easterners. Isaiah, one

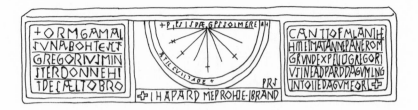

This sundial, in the church-yard of Kirkdale Church in Yorkshire, England, dates from 1064.

of the biblical prophets, was said at the time to have ". . . brought the shadow ten degrees backward, by which it had gone down in the dial of Ahaz," (Ahaz was the king who introduced sundials to the people of Judah). Some scholars have suggested that the two events were related. You can read about it in II Kings: 20.11.

Between the fifth and third centuries B.C. the sundial was improved in many ways. Instruments were constructed that did not require turning at noon, and concave surfaces appeared. A portable sundial, or "hemicycle," was developed by the Babylonian priest-astronomer Berossos.

A few years before the birth of Christ, the Egyptian obelisks at Heliopolis were moved, on the orders of Caesar Augustus, to the Temple of the Caesars at Alexandria. They became known as Cleopatra's Needles, as she was currently the ruler of Egypt. A hemicycle, unearthed at the foot of one of the Needles, is now in the British Museum. In thanks for assistance in constructing the Suez Canal, one of the obelisks was given to the United States in 1880, and may now be seen in New York's Central Park.

The Romans brought their sundials to Europe in the first century B.C., but as late as the Middle Ages, few people knew the time of day or even the year. Their lives were simply geared to sunrise, sunset, and the tides. Those sundials that did exist were marked as their makers elected. One of the oldest that we know of was built on the wall of Kirkdale Church in Yorkshire, England, about 1064 A.D. It was marked to show *tides*, the name of the day-periods at that time. Other churches installed mass dials, which were simply marked with five divisions to let their congregations know when it was time to pray.

As people's lives got busier through the sixteenth and seventeenth centuries, the demand for public sundials increased. One of the first was installed in the new Oxford University Corpus Christi College courtyard in 1581, another was placed on the cathedral wall in Chartres, France, and hundreds followed. For the well-to-do medieval executive, already finding time to be a problem, portable sundials with folding gnomons and built-in compasses became available. In the late seventeenth and early eighteenth century, ivory and silver sundials which opened and closed like a small book were popular. The two covers were connected by a cord which acted as the gnomon when the sundial was in use. An ingenious sundial was created for a church, utilizing a stained glass window on which the dial was drawn. The gnomon, mounted outside on the wall, cast a shadow like a clock hand for the benefit of those suffering under the parson's lengthy sermonizing.

Fortunately, the astronomical observations of the ancients had provided the knowledge required to effectively construct an accurate sundial. To mark the time correctly, the dial must be designed for a particular latitude, the gnomon must point due north, and its angled side must point to the polestar. But they succeeded, and sundials have remained popular over the centuries. The largest one in the world today is found in Jaipur, India. Its dial covers almost an acre, and its polished marble gnomon stands one hundred feet high.

You may like to grace your own garden with a sundial. Be warned that most of those sold in garden stores are inaccurate, but it's relatively easy to correct them, or even to make your own from scratch.

Start by looking up your latitude on any map. Chicago, for example, is 42°. Then call any local airport and ask for the compass deviation in your area. That's the amount by which a compass will be inaccurate due to magnetic interference. They'll give you the information in terms of degrees east or west of north. In the central part of the United States, the deviation will be no more than 10°, but on both coasts it will go as high as 25°. Now you'll need a compass, a protractor, and a spirit level. You can draw your sundial and its markings, or if you have a sunny day at home, you can set it up and mark the shadow points at hourly intervals.

Whether you decide to make your gnomon simple or artistic, the angle of the sloping edge must be the same as your latitude (see dia-

How to make a simple sundial.

Align gnomon with true North.

Mount gnomon one inch from edge of dial.

1"

Mark shadows each hour.

Dial must be level.

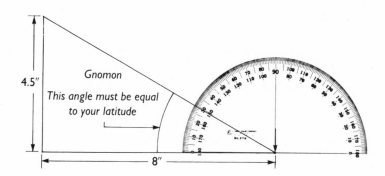

4.5"

Gnomon

This angle must be equal to your latitude

8"

gram). Use the protractor to mark this angle on the gnomon, and then cut it accordingly. Attach it at a right angle to a flat plate or board about ten inches square. Set your sundial up in the garden, in a shade-free location; orient it accurately to the north with the compass (applying the deviation for accuracy), and use the spirit level to insure that it is horizontal.

When the sun causes the gnomon's shadow to point directly north, it will be noon. Depending where you live, and whether daylight saving time is observed in your area, the time by your watch may be anything from 11:30 A.M. to 1:30 P.M., for the sun recognizes no man-made conventions. Mark the dial at noon's true shadow, then at each hour thereafter. If you're making your sundial in June, you can probably mark the shadow points from 5:00 in the morning until 7:00 at night. To design your sundial geometrically, use the procedure shown at the end of the chapter. For the sake of clarity, no decoration has been shown, but if you feel you would like to add an inscription, here are some of the traditional ones:

I MARK THE SUNNY HOURS

TEMPUS FUGIT
Time Flies

TEMPUS AD LUCEM DUCIT VERITATEM
Time Brings Truth to Light

IL EST PLUS TARD QUE VOUS CROYEZ
It Is Later Than You Think

LAYING OUT A SUNDIAL

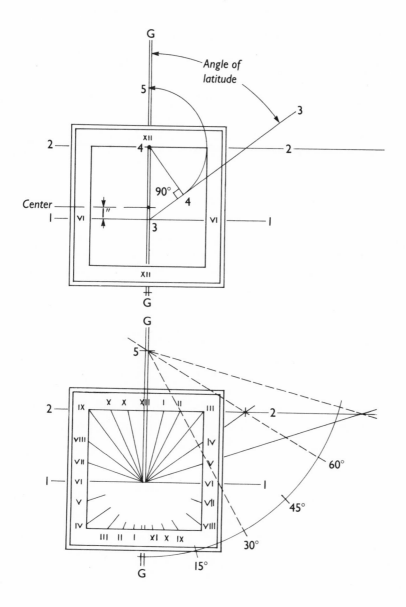

1. Draw the outline of your dial on a sheet of paper, leaving a generous margin. (Your dial can be round or square.) Mark the true center carefully. Draw line 1-1 one inch below the center. Draw line 2-2 at the dial's edge, extending it outward as shown.

2. Draw lines G-G to represent the sides of the gnomon (don't draw one line representing its center). Mark the positions for VI and XII.

3. Use a protractor to draw line 3-3 at an angle equal to your latitude.

4. Draw line 4-4c at 90° to line 3-3, intersecting with the edge of the dial.

5. Placing a compass pivot on 4c and the point on 4, draw an arc to intersect G-G at 5.

6. Use the protractor to mark a series of 15° angles from point 5, and mark each place at which they cross line 2-2. Then draw lines from each mark to point 3 to mark the positions of the other hours. Repeat the procedure for the remaining side of the dial.

TARGETING TIME

*How we spend our lives · Planning ·
Self-development · Body maintenance · Human
relations · Symptoms of poor time targeting ·
Coming to grips with time use ·
Developing time targets*

The purpose of using time is to achieve some desired result. When we succeed, we get a sense of satisfaction or achievement which persuades us to repeat the exercise, using different result targets. We learn this naturally, very early in life. It becomes the basic, essential pattern of our lives. When our time targets are personal, we're looking after our own best (or worst) interests; when our time targets are identified by others, and we agree to put our time at their disposal, we expect to be paid for it or we must be forced or persuaded into it. The conscious direction of our time lies at the core of our being.

Most people, as they get older, wonder where their lifetime has gone. Many studies of the subject have been made, and the average distribution of time for a seventy-year-old man looks like this:

Sleep	23 Years	32.9%
Work	19	27.2%
Leisure	9	12.8%
Religion	1	1.4%
Eating	6	8.6%
Travel	7	10.0%
Illness	3	4.3%
Personal Care	2	2.8%

When our time-directing consciousness is idle, we are bored. When it is blocked or hampered, we become anxious and stressed. Both states are less pleasant than that enjoyed when the time flow is directed to, and achieves, a series of positive result targets. And the further out from that flow we get, the more we are likely to suffer from mental and physical deterioration.

Those whose lives are fulfilled and happy are those who have identified a series of time targets that build, one upon another, to even higher levels of skill, expectancy, and reward. It may begin with time targeted on the attainment of good grades in school, then progress to time targeted to producing an unmet need in the marketplace or to creative and artistic ends, and finally to the creation and nurturing of a new generation who may carry on the building process. The selected targets may not all be beneficial, but our lifetime is long enough to be tolerant of error, and permits us many opportunities. We need only score a hit on a limited number of time targets to succeed in life; the misses are soon forgotten. But if we refuse the selection process or continue to select time targets that experience has shown to be harmful, we begin to slide. If the trend continues, we can become antisocial and unemployable. It's a tough world. There's no way you can get more time; you can only learn to target it more effectively.

Basic target areas include some that may never be fulfilled, but to which conscious attention and energy must be applied throughout our lives.

Planning to determine what you want to do with your future time as targets shift and change.

Brain maintenance by reading, viewing, experiencing, exercising, and memorizing.

Body maintenance by exercise, relaxation, and health care.

Human relations by talking, listening, and other actions that demonstrate feelings.

Unfortunately, these basic targets are usually obscured by those that loom larger, labeled in various ways to demand immediate attention. They are calculated to force you to react, instead of "proacting," and to do things that others want you to do rather than what you want to do.

The advertising that fills the airwaves is aimed at persuading you to pick time targets that will benefit the sponsors, whether it's the time to earn an automobile and drive it around, or the time to earn and use skis or a TV set. All of those around you will, to some extent, encroach upon your right to select your own time targets. You may let this occur willingly when driven by emotion and eager to share yourself with those you love. You may let it occur when demands from the system or from your boss pile up, because that's what they pay you for. But sooner or later, if you are to gain a reasonable level of mental equanimity, it is essential to broaden your sights to include those four basic time targets.

Those who should be scoring better in targeting their time usually exhibit the following symptoms:

- They feel guilty about any form of activity that might imply that they're not working as hard as possible.
- They feel harried, with *expected* activities always pushing *elected* activities aside.
- They procrastinate, inventing very good reasons to put off decisions and actions.
- They don't enjoy their work and/or their home life.
- Their physical and mental health is below par.
- They adopt autocratic, militaristic mannerisms, and tend to withdraw from social contact.
- They attempt to escape from pressure by excessive use of alcohol or drugs.

Better time targeting can bring order back to chaotic lives, increase one's sense of well-being, and improve one's health. If you decide to improve your life through better time allocation and management, there are a number of starting gates to choose from, depending upon your state of affairs.

If there is a discernible part of your workday, or a specific type of activity that you feel is sapping your time, read the appropriate chapter in this book to gain ideas on improving the situation. For example, if meetings are taking much of your time but showing few results, read *MEETING TIME*; if the telephone is bogging you down, read *TELEPHONE TIME*, and so on.

For the individual whose waking hours are so stressful that he or she has lost sight of the basics (time to think and plan, time to maintain the mind and body, and time for human interaction and relationships), time *must* be found somehow. It's there, but it is probably hidden. It rarely becomes evident unless the whole can of worms is opened up for inspection, and that means a short program of self-analysis, using one or more of the techniques discussed under *RECORDING TIME*. Once you have a reasonably accurate picture of your current targets, some rational approaches to ordering them can begin. They will fall into one of three categories:

- Candidates for elimination.
- Spin-offs.

Ye Gods! annihilate but time and space
And make two lovers happy.
Alexander Pope, 1728

- Candidates for productivity improvement.

These categories apply to both personal and business time targets. To develop some ideas for improving the targeting of your personal time, read *HOUSEHOLD TIME* and *LEISURE TIME*.

In the business environment, activities that are candidates for elimination are the first to investigate. Scrutinize your activity record carefully, and test all significant activities with some searching questions.

(Before you start, insure that you correctly understand the requirements of your job. If they are not already spelled out, your first step must be to establish them, as well as the measurement factors, i.e., on what basis your performance will be judged. Distinguish clearly between the job *purpose* and the job *description*, and don't confuse them. Job descriptions are usually out of date before they're printed.)

> Assume you were just hired for your job function. Are there any tasks that you would *not* do, even though you may be doing them now?
>
> Is every time target you use related in some way to your functional goals?
>
> Is every time target you use related in some way to your personal goals?
>
> Is any time wasted because you don't trust the motivation or ability of another person?
>
> Has the need for any report you are producing been reestablished within the last six months?
>
> Are any of your time targets caused by a lack of personnel, services, or information?
>
> Could any of your time targets be addressed by another person *at lower cost?*

Anything that is taking your time but cannot survive the above criteria should be eliminated as a time target, or moved to delegable "spin-off" tasks.

While you are making your analysis, discern between "urgent" and "important" tasks. Identify those that are delegable, short- and long-term. Break complex tasks down. Remember that the objective is to get rid of any time target that is not an absolute "must." If it must be retained, then try and make it a candidate for delegation. Read *DELEGATION TIME* to deal with all these time targets.

Finally, you're down to the third category of time targets—those that you're stuck with—which are the essence of your job function. Tor Dahl, president of the International Management Productivity Council, told me during a visit last year that he has yet to encounter a managerial group whose productivity cannot be raised *at least 35 percent* by the application of sound time management practices. Why not set that as your own goal?

The time targets that have been reduced by your analysis work may now be relabeled in accordance with your priorities. But take care, particularly if you are a senior manager. I agree with Peter Drucker, who says that no more than 50 percent of a senior manager's time should be planned in detail. They must keep enough flexible time to deal with unexpected matters and be able to step back from the fray to think. The answer, for effective managers, is to put those activities among their prime time targets.

Once some elective time has been created, a proactive time and objectives program can begin.

> Use the *TIME PAYOFF ANALYSIS* chart in Appendix G to document your plan, and measure your success in following it through with periodic rescoring.

> List and number your time targets on a single sheet of paper and keep it close at hand. Use your desk agenda or the Time Target Scorepad in Appendix F to track your daily success in directing your time to your important targets, and note anything that deflects it. Work on corrective action to improve your aim every day.

> Aim at higher payoff targets first. As targets are demolished or switched, update your target list. If appropriate, make separate long-term and short-term lists.

TELEPHONE TIME

*Calling and answering habits ·
Caller analysis · Building response skills ·
Using the right equipment · Voice messaging ·
Electronic mail · Call preparation*

Although it's one of the twentieth century's major inventions, most business executives agree (see *EXECUTIVE TIME*) that the telephone can be one of management's top time-wasters. The problem is very similar to that of our expressways. They did cut travel time when first constructed, but as traffic volume increased their efficiency dropped. Our telephone system is operating at 20 percent efficiency today for the same reason. On the average, a caller will connect with the person he or she wants in only one out of five calls placed. Telephone tag ensues, sometimes for days, with the telephone company the only beneficiary.

Timing of telephone calls is usually random. That means that, statistically, as many are made at an inconvenient time, interrupting somebody, as are made at a good time for both parties. Perhaps nothing is more frustrating than to have a long-winded caller interrupt an urgent task. It's the classic situation of being asked to talk about draining the swamp when you're up to your armpits in crocodiles.

Conversely, the telephone can be an enormous time-saver when used effectively. So what can be done to improve the odds and make it serve you better? Communications experts offer these time-saving suggestions:

Check Your Calling Habits

Place as many calls as possible early in the morning. Telephone traffic is lightest then, and people are more available.

If you can have an assistant or secretary set up outgoing calls, continue to do so, in spite of any advice to the contrary. But recognize that this task needs intelligence, and the ability to cope with unexpected situations. Don't delegate it unless your support person has these qualities.

First thing in the morning, plan your telephone day, allowing for time zone differences and the habits of those with whom you want to connect. Build a time preference file, based on call experience. Whenever possible, give the call schedule to your secretary, and have him or her make the connection at the listed times.

Try to make all of your outgoing calls in concentrated blocks of time. The momentum that is built as one call follows another will help to keep them short and to the point.

Telephone effectiveness also improves when the boss sets a good example, and does not force subordinates to take calls from him or her except in an urgent situation. It should be made clear that a call back can be made at the convenience of the called party, *unless you say otherwise*. Secretaries should be firmly instructed on this routine—particularly the ones who enjoy basking in the light of their boss's rank, and the associated power to pull people out of meetings with the magic name. "Are you busy?" is not a good question to ask of a subordinate. What's a person supposed to say to the boss? Ask a direct question, such as "Do you have someone with you?" so that a straightforward response can be made.

Check Your Answering Habits

Who should answer your phone? Frankly, there's no pat answer. It's necessary to collect some facts before deciding. Keep a call record for a few days. Include the caller's name, the time and purpose of the call, and what action resulted. Then figure out the percentage of calls your secretary could have handled, compared to those you *had* to take. If more than 70 percent of the calls fall into the latter category, it's a waste of time to have anyone else pick up the phone. If your secretary could have taken 70 percent of the calls, he or she should take them all, and pass them over to you when necessary.

In training someone to screen incoming calls, whenever possible have them advise the caller (before asking their name) of your unavailability, but promise a call back. Some selected callers and urgent calls should go through immediately of course, according to a preset list. Don't expect your secretary to guess at the priority. The president of a farming products company with whom I worked years ago told me, "My list has only two names, the President's and my wife's. I doubt that he will ever call, and she knows better!"

Help your secretary by categorizing a list of your usual callers by

The average person spends two years of his or her life returning telephone calls.

priority. Then you can set screening levels according to the type of work you may be doing. Level 1 calls should be the only ones to interrupt a meeting, for example. Tell your secretary what level you are working at, so that the screening helps instead of hinders.

It's wise to be alert to opportunities for answering standard telephone queries as efficiently as possible. For example, how does your company's receptionist answer an individual seeking directions to your office? Try calling up yourself and see. You'll probably find it simpler to get to Timbuktu. Make it easier on everybody by providing the receptionist with a written sheet of carefully prepared, accurate instructions for each of the local major roads. Then, having asked which direction the caller will be coming from, he or she can read off the appropriate directions.

Sharpen your own response skills. When a caller says:

"Do you have a minute?"

Always ask what the call is about before agreeing to talk. Then, if you don't want to take the call immediately, say "No. Do you mind if I call you back?"

"Do you have any information on . . ."

Say "Can I look it up and let you know?"

To signal that you wish to cut the call short, practice using conversation stoppers like:

"Well, we must hang up . . ."
"Well, thanks for calling. I have something I must get back to . . ."
"I know you've got lots to do, so I must let you go . . ."

To cut off a long-winded caller, say:

"I know you're busy, and I have a meeting coming up, so I'd better hang up."

Never give a telephone caller preference over a visitor. If the phone won't stop ringing, pick it up and tell the caller that you have a visitor and you'll call back. Put a cutoff switch on your phone, if all else fails to divert or hold calls.

Lack of success in controlling the telephone is often the fault of users who regard it as an instrument for breaking the routine, rather than a communications tool. They enjoy the "surprise package" syndrome every time they pick it up. The telephone can be a tangible display of their presence, while much of their work may be intangible. It brings people seeking their help, with the attendant feelings of satisfaction and worth. If these factors are important to you, you can continue the game. But if you also want to accomplish more with your time, some rebalancing of priorities will be necessary.

Designate one or two hours each day during which everyone within the organization (and, to the extent possible, those outside too) makes a serious attempt to stay off the telephone. Tell your suppliers about the arrangement, and ask their cooperation. These "no call" hours can be used for the tasks that demand more than a few minutes of concentration.

Use the Right Equipment

The many new telephone instruments with time-saving features that have appeared since the industry was deregulated make it possible to custom design the basic hardware to specific needs. The communications survey services available from reputable companies which sell telephones are well worth using, and usually free.

Touch-tone instruments should replace any rotary telephones that are still around. They save about eight seconds in dialing every manual call, and permit the use of other time-saving features.

Call timers and recorders may be simple desktop reminders of passing time, or full-scale automatic recorders that list called numbers and call duration. The latter are valuable for professional offices which normally bill their clients for telephone expenses. They must usually be installed by a commercial telephone service organization.

Speed dialing is invaluable for those who make frequent long-distance calls to the same group of numbers. It may be accomplished by a limited memory bank within the telephone, or by the automatic access of a computer index file and modem dialing. Its advantages include faster and more accurate hands-free dialing than when using a card file or directory; its disadvantage is that telephone numbers change more frequently than most people expect, and maintaining the electronic file can take more time than a desk file. Before investing in this feature, a thorough analysis of your calling patterns is recommended.

Call waiting provides a single-line user with an audible signal that another caller is trying to get through when the telephone is in use. If the warning helps to curtail the present call, it may be useful, but the habit of putting the first party on hold while the second call is investigated is unmannerly and wastes time. If your telephone is so busy that people can't get through, it's much better to add another line.

Call forwarding permits the automatic transfer of a call to any telephone number you designate. While this feature may be useful for physicians and others who must be on call, electronic answering devices and/or message services are more practical for many needs.

Hands-free operation is made possible by a built-in voice-actuated microphone and speaker, or new microdevices that are carried in the ear, and offer wireless transmission within a fifty-foot range (more information on this technology is available from Plantronics Inc., of Santa Cruz, CA 408-426-6060). The time- and money-saving value of these features is entirely dependent on the number of calls made, and the necessity to perform concurrent tasks, but their convenience for those who need to work with their hands while talking is outstanding.

Voice messaging, using a new breed of sophisticated answering devices, avoids time-wasting telephone tag by permitting the caller to dictate a message immediately if the callee is absent, or to transfer to another extension. Messages can be recovered *and answers dictated* from any telephone; the replies are then placed in the first person's "call box." Automatic call-routing, under the control of the caller, is supported by electronic voice guidance. A message can be sent to an entire group of people simultaneously, at times when transmission rates are lowest, or sent to suit the convenience of recipients in different time zones.

Friday is the only day named for a female—the Norse goddess, Frigga. Above, a Nordic goddess dating from about 700 B.C.

British Airways, one of the first airlines to install a voice messaging system, claims that they save half a million dollars annually in improved handling of calls, using equipment manufactured by the industry's technical leader, Octel Communications Corp. (Milpitas, CA 408-942-6500). Voice messaging systems work because, on the average, 60 percent of telephone calls do not need two-way conversation and, therefore, messages are more succinct, with attendant time and cost savings.

Electronic mail can substitute for telephone communication, if a network of computer terminals with printers is available. While providing some of the benefits of voice messaging, it suffers from lack of mobility, and duplicates telephone equipment rather than improving its innate capability.

Many businesspeople need to use the telephone to set up meetings with hard-to-see executives. These calls work best when a prior letter of introduction has been sent to arrive on a Monday or Tuesday morning, seven to ten days before the call. The letter should be brief and include the following, in order: (1) An opening paragraph, stating the subject. (2) A rationale of the recipient's need for the communication. (3) An attention-getting description of the idea or product that you want to present. (4) A brief list of benefits. (5) Evidence that the idea or product works. (6) A meeting proposal and promise of a confirming telephone call.

Prepare for the call by writing down all possible objections to your suggestions and valid counter-arguments. If you expect to be making numerous similar calls, it may be worthwhile to organize your answers on file cards.

Make the call before 10 A.M., and refer to your letter. Don't waste time trying to sell your idea or product. If there is a negative attitude, refer only to the evidential part of your letter. Limit your objective to arranging a meeting. Give a specific date and time, about two weeks ahead, and have a second date and time ready if the first doesn't work. Follow up the call with a letter of confirmation.

The telephone can be a valuable time-saver or an expensive time-waster, depending upon how it is used. Establishing an intelligent use protocol is the only way to ensure effective control. That means educating and involving all of the key people in your organization, and working out a combined telephone communications plan that reflects the needs of each individual, instead of taking it for granted that everybody will work out their own salvation. Take advantage of appropriate new telephone hardware and upgrade your telephone habits and skills, and your time payoff can easily double.

See also COMMUNICATION TIME.

TIME AND AGE

The five critical life periods ·
The aging body · The aging brain ·
Aging and the environment

Primitive societies often used the age of a man as a rough measure of the passage of time. In some remote areas, the practice continues. For example, in Australian aborigine society, children too young to work are considered to be the "first age," persons able to work make up the second age, and old people (called "once-men" or "once-women") are the third. Mankind has tried to slow the aging process since the dawn of recorded history—at least as long ago as 300 B.C., according to Sumerian and Egyptian writings. Bacon wrote *The Cure of Old Age and Preservation of Youth* in the Middle Ages. Benjamin Rush published his observations on aging of the body in 1793. But it was not until the early twentieth century that gerontology became a full-fledged science, incorporating psychology, medicine, and physical therapy.

For the first time, scientists are beginning to unwrap the mysteries of the aging process, and to learn how we must adapt, physically and mentally, to the body's changing needs as the years roll along.

There's some urgency, because the over-fifty-five group will increase four times faster than the general population over the next fifty years. By the year 2050, one in three Americans will be part of it.

There are five critical periods in our lives that significantly affect how we feel and act. They are: our childhood, high school years, the first years of marriage, middle age, and preretirement.

The normal adult impression of time—past, present, and future—is called *noetic time*. A living organism must have a brain containing about 10^{10} neurons before it can handle *noetemporal* concepts. Our brains have that capacity, as do other primates. But evolution has dealt us an extra ace. We have retained some of the neural structures of our reptilian and mammalian ancestors too. P. D.

MacLean, writing in the *Journal of Nervous Mental Disorders* in 1967, first described how they each interact and contribute to our sense of being.

Our reptilian brain component deals only with basics like hunger, sex, and aggression. It operates only in the present. So does the older mammalian part of the human brain, which handles self-preservation on a broader scale. The newest, or *neomammalian*, brain area first developed about 200,000 years ago. This is where our unique ability to remember the distant past and dream about the far-off future resides, together with our sensing and communication neurons.

The more primitive brain areas are normally dominated by the newer sections. But when lack of sleep, danger, or emotional factors interfere, that dominance is lost, releasing the unreason of nightmares, blind aggression, and antisocial activity linked with the primordial swamps. Hopefully, that legacy will continue to fade as future generations evolve. In the meantime, the best we can do is follow the advice of our religious leaders to suppress the vestiges of animalism that we still retain, and glory in our noetic advantage.

For a human baby, time sense develops only after it leaves the womb. Prior to birth the embryo and then fetus are totally subject to the mother's circadian rhythms. Not so for monkeys and rats. Their day/night synchronization is developed in utero, sparing their parents the sleepless nights that human mothers and fathers endure before their offspring get its or their act together. It usually takes about twenty-six weeks before a human baby's feeding and sleeping cycles adapt to our normal living rhythms, and its internal body clock synchronizes with the sun, as described in *BODY TIME*. It takes longer for their mental time sense to develop.

> Time hath a wallet at his back, wherein he puts alms for oblivion.
> *William Shakespeare,*
> *Troilus and Cressida,*
> *Act III*

Childhood

Young children sense time differently than adults. Until they are about eight years old, they exist in an extended time sense, and their hours pass more slowly than those experienced by grown-ups. It is believed that this is due to the child's faster mental response.

High School Years

High school boys are, in general, not happy with themselves; somewhat fearful of their future and socially clumsy, they find it difficult to stick to most tasks. They have difficulty in selecting specific career directions, and engage in much fantasy. "Making it big" and "really living" are frequently expressed goals, probably influenced by the wealth of consumer-oriented advertising to which they are exposed.

Constrained by societal influences, high school girls in the 1940s were frequently considered to be lazy, manipulative, restless, and suspicious, while feeling dependent and ambivalent in terms of their life goals. Most were concerned with future marriage and family ideals, and considered school and employment but a bridge to that end. Their emotional drives tended to focus on other girls, horses, and entertainers.

Today's female high school students, some critical of their mothers' unrealized potential, are a different breed. Many want to seize the opportunities that are opening up and achieve independence, rather than settle for life as a dependent spouse. The transition is not without trauma. Aiming for intellectual career achievement, they find they are often expected to settle for the life of a decorative secondary citizen.

Marriage

Newlywed young men become more impulsive, restless, and unkind than at other times in their life. They still lack poise and are inclined to be unconventional, sarcastic, and hostile, while their restlessness causes them to experiment with a wide variety of activities and social contacts. Their satisfaction with life is lower at twenty than at any other age. They will daydream forward in time, as opposed to daydreaming backwards, as older men do. Both men and women develop more friendships at this time in their lives than at any other. Many people of both sexes lose interest in religious activities, although quite a few regain it in their later years. They become more aware of the value of well-directed education, nonmaterial job values, and the time that will be required to achieve high earnings. Men's contact with their brothers and sisters usually drops significantly after marriage.

New brides' warmth and possessiveness increases through their early married years, but their energy level stays low for some time. More than 80 percent of young married women in the United States retain full-time employment after their marriage.

Middle Age

The middle-aged man becomes cautious and more honest in relationships, and develops an interest in masculine pursuits. He may think his work is more important than it really is, and frequently questions the success of his career. Some of his expenditures may be triggered by a need to prove that he has "made it." Twice as many men as women in this stage will develop drinking problems.

As they enter middle age, many women find that unhappiness with their lives deepens around the age of forty. This decreases as they reach retirement age, when many of their negative feelings are supplanted by growing assertiveness and interest in intellectual or creative pursuits. Socializing becomes important to most middle-aged women, as their activities and roles become simplified.

Preretirement

As men approach retirement, they usually become more socially amenable; hostility wanes, as well as the range of their interests and ambitions. Marital relationships often improve as a result. There is an attraction to "play" pursuits, often with an athletic orientation. Clocks impose a pressure that was not felt in earlier years.

A modern trend toward avoiding the negative role of "retiree" is apparent, and is probably one of the best things that could happen for those who want to keep their clock ticking longer.

THE AGING BODY

As time works on our bodies, the effects of gravity, diet, and cell reproduction efficiency bring some major changes. Those described below, with techniques for slowing them, apply to normal, healthy persons. Changes that may come from infection or genetic causes are not within the scope of this book.

Bones are primarily affected by gravity, especially those in our backs which suffer most from the thousands of hours which most of us spend sitting in poorly designed chairs. Regular exercise, weight control, and better seating are the only known deterrents. Consider a high work surface at which you can stand as an alternative to sitting.

Everyone's bones become porous and subject to disease and fractures as aging slows bone cell reproduction; most of us lose 10–25 percent of our bone mass by the time we are eighty. Those that lose more—about fifteen million in the United States—are said to be affected by osteoporosis.

Current thinking is that everybody should "bank" at least one gram of calcium daily until they are thirty years old, to guard against the eventual loss. That requires six glasses of milk—much more than most people want to drink—so alternative sources should be used, such as almonds, cheese, yogurt, and dark green vegetables. Contrary to Popeye's belief, spinach, chard, and beet greens, which contain oxalic acid, don't contribute much calcium because the acid blocks its absorption. They are, nonetheless, good sources of iron.

After thirty, the body can't absorb as much calcium, so instead of eating it switch to saving it. That means avoiding excessive nicotine, caffeine, alcohol, soda waters, and protein foods, all of which promote rapid calcium excretion. Get regular exercise that puts some pressure on the bones. Man developed as an active creature, and exercise is very important. Swimming is rated most highly for older persons' continued health.

Teeth and gums suffer from insufficient saliva production as we get older, so it is important to increase mouth hygiene, especially daily flossing and brushing, and get regular professional care.

Body tissue, skin, and muscles deteriorate through changes in metabolism and the immune system's efficiency, reduced assimilation of nutrients, and difficulty in eliminating wastes. Increasing zinc and iron in the diet can counter the process. A hormone called thymosium has shown positive results in revitalizing the immune system. And avoiding exposure to the sun's ultraviolet rays will do wonders for the skin, plus help you avoid cancer. Moisturizing creams are helpful, and can be expensive if you want them with a fancy label; if not, sitting in a hot bath for twenty minutes and then smoothing on petroleum jelly will achieve exactly the same effect.

Heart and blood problems stem from hardening and blocking of the arteries, reducing blood circulation, and increasing blood pressure. Circulatory problems can also affect the brain, for as oxygen flow is reduced, portions of the brain are killed, producing strokes or problems with the nervous system and sensory functions.

After decades of research, *excess* cholesterol (particularly low-density lipoprotein)* is clearly identified as the villain. Some is necessary for health, but most of us eat three times too much of it. Egg yolks, liver and other organ meats, marbled red meats, lobster, sardines, and shrimp are loaded with it. Put more white meat and less solid fat in your diet and you can extend your life significantly. Re-

As we advance in life, we acquire a keener sense of the value of time.

William Hazlitt

---

* Low-density lipoprotein (LDL) is concentrated in fats that are solid at room temperature (butter and meat fat), palm oil and coconut oil, chicken skin, fried foods, sausages, cookies, and cakes.

duce your cholesterol input by 1 percent and your chance of a heart attack drops 2 percent. It's that dramatic.

Brain aging was once thought to be caused by the daily loss of about 100,000 cells that all adults undergo. But as we start out life with billions of brain cells, many of which we never use, the daily loss seems insignificant. Other theories have surfaced recently. They focus on the chemical neurotransmitters which link the neurons (see *MEMORY*). As time passes, the level of neurotransmitters drops, or they become clogged with fatty waste that slows them down. Loss of brain power in the aged may also be linked to REM sleep loss caused by an unnatural slippage in the body clock (see *BODY TIME* and *SLEEP TIME*).

Old people may become physically ill from emotional stress. They may also fall into senility because people seem to expect it. A thirty-year-old has merely mislaid a key; the same loss by an older person signals senility to many families.

Treat an old person as an idiot and they may become one. Men over seventy are quite prone to senile psychosis, or deterioration of the intellect, often induced by those around them. They may also succumb to affective psychosis, brought about by physical and emotional stress. Paraphrenia (which resembles schizophrenia) can follow. Each of these disorders will change the living habits of the aged person, and can affect their social attitudes to such an extent that geriatric counseling may be advisable.

In spite of these degenerative factors, it is believed that mental attitude may prolong healthy living, because of the brain's ability to control bodily functions, and slow or eliminate the effects of time. Older people should not live alone, and should interact socially as much as possible. They should fight the tendency to adopt fixed habits and sedentary days by exploring new things and changing their activity patterns. A mind that is put to work every day will stay alert.

The *senses* begin to decay at age sixteen. The eyes and the ears are the first to lose acuity, but for most of us they retain enough efficiency, even if we have to use eyeglasses or hearing aids. Help is available for those whose sight and hearing is severely affected. Permanent plastic lenses can now be attached to the cornea for those forced to undergo cataract removal, and ultrasound treatment has been very successful in dealing with glaucoma.

Taste and smell are reduced as the clock ticks on, but the former may be preserved by insuring there is enough zinc in one's diet, and the latter by simply sniffing more often.

> To be seventy years young is far more cheerful and hopeful than to be forty years old.
>
> *Oliver Wendell Holmes*

Aging and Diet

Scientists point out that, in terms of the adaptation time line, we have only recently graduated from being hunters and gatherers. Our bodies still demand the basic sustenances of our cave-dwelling forebears. A high intake of unnatural foods and substances can kill human beings long before their natural time. Fresh fruit and vegetables, yogurt, honey, nuts, fish, and white meat are recommended by gerontologists, together with adequate quantities of calcium, zinc, and iron.

The time of day at which we eat various foods, or take any medication is important (see *BODY TIME*), and it seems that if we want to live longer, we must eat less too. We seriously overload our digestive systems with our present eating habits.

Aging and Environment

Even for the most healthy human being, there are molecular and environmental factors that control his or her life expectancy. As late as 1951, it was believed that cells would reproduce eternally, given the right sustenance, so that, theoretically, man might achieve immortality. Then Leonard Hayflick, perhaps simply using tighter research controls than his predecessors, showed that cells in bisexual organisms do stop reproducing after a certain time. But there is evidence that they may be revitalized by certain hormones, and this is an active area of research today.

It is not by the gray of the hair that one knows the age of the heart.
E. R. Bulwer-Lytton

Marauding cells called *free radicals** can devastate living microorganisms and, unfortunately, oxygen is one of the primary sources. After we inhale, many of the oxygen cells that enter the bloodstream are free radicals. Fortunately, the body has some natural scavengers like glutathione that combat them. And recently, scientists have shown that vitamins C and E, and the food preservative BHT can stop them too. Using these substances as diet supplements can help to slow the clock, particularly after any exercise. Lester Packer, director of the Membrane Bioenergetics Group at Lawrence Berkeley Laboratory in California, has reported success in reducing post-exercise radical levels by taking a potion of 400 International Units of vitamin E, 1000 mg. of vitamin C, and 10 mg. of beta carotene.

---

* A free radical molecule has an extra electron, which causes it to ferociously attach itself to any other molecule it can find. The result is often cell mutation, damage, or "suicide." Oxygen, petrochemicals, and body fat breed free radicals, and their growth rate may be accelerated by ultraviolet sunlight.

The Nobel Prize was given to Snell, Benacerraf, and Dausset in 1980 for identifying a group of genes in the DNA string that control our immune system. Current thinking is that they may also control our life clock, for as long as they are active we can fight off free radicals and other cell-destroying agents. But as they atrophy, our body cells' natural enemies take over. As work continues to map the DNA helixes in their entirety, gerontologists hope that they may find the answers they need to prolong life by slowing the aging process. In the meantime, the best we can do is to study our family genetic history and develop a lifestyle and eating habits that may counter the prevalent causes of death, using what knowledge we have. It won't stop your body clock from stopping one day, but it can keep it going many years longer.

TIME
ETYMOLOGY

*The origins of words associated with
time and its measurement*

T he origins of time words, some going back more than three thousand years, lie deep in the roots of many cultures. Those that follow illustrate a few of the contributions made over the centuries as the science of timekeeping developed.

Age   Derived from the Latin *aevum*, which also gave us "eon," meaning a lifetime or age. The Medieval English was *ai* and *awa*, the latter becoming "always."

Circadian   A compound word from the Latin *circa* (about) and *dies* (day) used to describe the rhythm of life that takes place in one day.

Clepsydra   This name for a water clock is derived from the Greek words *klept* (to steal) and *hydor* (water).

Clock   The first mechanical clocks were built by monasteries to sound their prayer bells regularly. The Latin word for bell was *clocca*; the French is *cloche*, hence clock. After the invention of the pendulum, the French word for clock became *pendule*.

Day   Originated in the ancient Norse *dagning* or daybreak; the Germanic *dag*, meaning the hot period of a twenty-four-hour cycle; and the Sanskrit *nidagha*, also meaning heat. In Old English, the word became *daeg*, and later *dei*.

Gnomon   The name originally given by the Greeks to the obelisk or vertical column whose shadow marked the passage of the sun, meaning "one who knows."

Horoscope   The Greek compound word *horoskopos*—literally, "hour-surveyor"—meant that part of a zodiacal sign that breached the horizon at a given moment, and together with a diagram that showed twelve signs in position, gave ancient astrologers their basis for casting nativities, or predicting a person's life.

Minute   From the past participle *minutus* of the Latin verb "to lessen." An interesting derivative, during the American Revolution, was the name "minuteman," given to a member of the militia who held himself ready for action at a minute's notice.

Month   Compounded from the Greek *mene* or moon; the Indo-European root word for measure, *me*; and the Old English *maeth*, "measurement by the moon."

Second   A direct descendent of the Latin *secundus*.

Time, Tide   Both originated in medieval Britain in the fourteenth century. The basic sense of the word "tide" was in fact "time," because daily life was linked to tidal changes. The Old German and Armenian root is *ti*. The well-known saying "Time and tide wait for no man" dates from the sixteenth century.

Watch   The Old English name given to night watchmen was *waecce*. It was adapted to portable clocks, or watches, in the sixteenth century.

Year   "Year," "hour," and "yore" are all closely linked, and stem from the Greek and Roman *hora*, meaning a period of the day. In Greek mythology the three Horae—Dice, Eunomia, and Irene—were jointly responsible for the passage of time, in addition to their respective control of justice, order, and peace. In medieval England, following the Roman occupation, *hora* became *hore*, a root word with variations of *ure* and *our* and later "hour." The same root gave us the word for extended time—at first *gear*, then *yer*, and finally "year."

TIME MUSEUMS

*Where to find interesting clock
and watch collections*

The many ways in which timekeepers have influenced the course of history, science, art, and fashion can often best be appreciated by a visit to one or more of the fascinating time exhibits that exist in this country and in Europe. Many people have found that a glimpse of horology, the art of measuring time, will open doors to related subjects, providing a fascinating learning experience.

Priceless collections of mechanical and electronic marvels, illustrating man's struggle to understand his universe, may be explored in the major museums—the Smithsonian Institution has a representative collection, for example—but more interesting exhibits are often found in smaller museums that focus exclusively on horology. Those described below are well worth visiting:

In America

American Clock and Watch Museum
100 Maple Street
Bristol, Connecticut 06010

Telephone 203-583-6070
Open 11 A.M. to 5 P.M. every day, April through October.

An extensive collection of about two thousand American clocks and watches dating from 1860 are to be found in this interesting museum, which emphasizes Connecticut-made items.

In the Barnes wing of the museum, the Ingraham Library holds an extensive collection of research materials on the American clock and watch industry. Access, for research only, may be arranged by appointment with the curator.

Bily Clock Exhibit
Main Street
Spillville, Iowa 52165

Telephone 319-562-3627
Open 10 A.M. to 4 P.M. daily in April, 8 A.M. to 5:30 P.M. daily
May through October, and by appointment only December
through March.

Picturesque Spillville began as a Czech village surrounding a
lumber mill established on the Turkey River by Joseph Spielman in
1849.

The two Bily brothers, expert Czech woodcarvers, began building clocks in 1915, using exotic native and imported woods. Their first masterpiece, the Apostle clock, brings out the twelve apostles in an hourly parade, and was later expanded to include a cathedral. Their Pioneer clock, completed in 1927, depicts historial events. The Parade of Nations clock was finished in 1934. These and many more intriguing timepieces, most with moving figures and musical chimes, are housed in the building occupied by the composer Anton Dvořák in 1893.

National Watch and Clock Museum
514 Poplar Street
Columbia, Pennsylvania 17512

Telephone 717-684-8261
Open 9 A.M. to 4 P.M. Tuesday through Saturday.
Closed Sundays, Mondays, and all public holidays.

Housing the largest collection of clocks and watches in the United States, this museum is owned and operated by the National Association of Watch and Clock Collectors, Inc. (NAWCC). Covering four centuries of timekeeping, the galleries include German musical clocks, nineteenth-century French clocks and watches, American timepieces dating from 1780, European, and tower clocks.

A magnificent statue clock, in onyx and silvered bronze, originally in the Smithsonian Institute, is a particularly fine example of French period timepieces.

The museum library contains more than 2,500 volumes devoted to horology, plus 21,000 U.S. Patents and nineteenth-century trade publications, supported with a computer-based index. Call to arrange group tours.

Time Museum
Clock Tower Inn
7801 East State Street
Rockford, Illinois 61125

Telephone 815-398-6000 Ext. 2941
Open 10 A.M. to 5 P.M. Tuesday through Sunday.
Closed Mondays.

This broad and educational private collection of timekeeping devices from those used by early man to the atomic clock was established from the horological collection of Seth Atwood, its founder and director, and is now one of the most interesting in the

This magnificent German astronomical and automaton clock was designed and constructed by Christian Gebhard and his two sons between 1865 and 1895. Various figures appear at each quarter hour, and at noon there is a procession of the disciples of Christ. Photograph courtesy of the Time Museum, Rockford, Illinois.

United States. On view are more than 3,000 rare clocks, watches, sundials, astrolabes, incense clocks, water clocks, sandglasses, chronometers, automata, electronic clocks, and navigational instruments.

Some of the gems in the beautifully displayed collection include a reconstruction of the 1088 A.D. Su Sung waterwheel mechanism which preceded the invention of mechanical clocks; a working Swiss tower clock movement dated 1541; rare examples of sixteenth and seventeenth century European clocks and watches designed by masters such as Huygens, Tompion, and Harrison; French decorative clocks from the Louis XV and Louis XVI periods; English longcase clocks and precision timekeepers; early American clocks and watches by Eli Terry and his contemporaries; a remarkable group of precision timekeeping instruments developed over the last hundred years; and examples of the latest atomic age and electronic devices with incredible timekeeping precision.

Among other marvels, the Time Museum houses the most complex clock ever made, requiring four years of effort by the Norwegian horologist Rasmus Sornes after a lifetime of study and preparation. Standing over six feet high, the clock's dials, globes, and hands display an incredible range of calendrical, astronomical, and planetary information, accurate to one tenth of a degree for solar time over 1,000 years, and encompassing the 26,000-year period of the earth's axis precession. Crafted in gold and silver-plated brass, this remarkable instrument is unique, from its illuminated sun to the intricate motions of all of the planets in the solar system, including Pluto which has an orbit of 248 years.

The museum includes an intimate theater, presenting a program of timekeeping development, and an attractive store where one may find a treasure trove of time literature, models, and merchandise. Dorothy A. Mastricola, public relations director, should be contacted for group visits.

When traveling in Europe, you might explore these fine museums:

In Switzerland

Museum of Horology
Route de Malagnou 15
CH-1200 Geneva
Switzerland

Open 10 A.M. to noon and 2–6 P.M. daily except Mondays. Admission is free.

Housed in an attractive eighteenth-century house, this fine collection is presented in a series of chronologically-ordered rooms, illustrating clockmaking from sundials to modern chronometers.

Some of the interesting pieces to be seen here are an astronomical table clock (Millenet, 1712); early clocks from France, England, Germany, and Switzerland; a small silver rabbit watch, with the movement contained within the body; clocks with automata; and a reconstructed workshop with tools.

International Museum of Horology
CH-2300 La Chaux-de-Fonds
Switzerland

Open 10 A.M. to noon and 2–5 P.M. every day except Monday.

Founded in 1902, this comprehensive world-class museum covers the entire history of timekeeping, with special attention to Swiss watchmaking.

In addition to the priceless exhibits, the museum presents audio-visual programs and educational workshops, expert antique clock restoration, horological conferences, and displays of watchmaking machinery.

Detailed information on the collection is available in the visitors' lobby on arrival. One then proceeds across a bridge, surrounded by turret clock movements, to the main exhibition galleries, where the story of timekeeping unfolds, supported by continuous audio-visual commentary and a watchmaking demonstration.

Modern horology is represented by scientific exhibits and demonstration of the development of power sources, clock and watch manufacturing, and world timekeeping.

Beyer Museum of Time Measurement
Bahnhofstrasse 31
CH-8000 Zürich
Switzerland

Telephone 01 221 10 80
Open weekdays only. Free admission.

The Beyers have been watchmakers for six generations, and have gradually assembled a watch and clock collection on their premises in Zurich, regarded as one of the most important in Switzerland. It includes time-measuring instruments from 1400 B.C. to modern atomic clocks.

The exhibit features a magnificent seven-tier pagoda clock with bell chimes, revolving figures, and four dials, constructed for the Chinese Imperial Court in 1780 by the English clockmaker, James Cox; a magical clock, created in 1836 by J. F. Houdin of Paris, which causes objects to vanish and reappear; a wonderful series of Black Forest clocks demonstrating the folk art of the region and important pendulum clocks; English clocks; table clocks; Nuremberg clocks and watches; automata; and pocket masterpieces by Berthoud, LeRoy, Earnshaw, and Arnold. Scientific evolution in timekeeping is exhibited by a group of quartz master clocks, with accuracies up to one millionth of a second per day.

Kellenberger Clock Collection
Stadthausstrasse Town Hall
CH-8400 Winterthur
Switzerland

Open 2–5 P.M. daily except Monday, and additionally from 10 A.M. to noon on Sundays.

A charming exhibit of Renaissance turret clocks and table clocks, and primitive clocks made of iron and wood (some with moving figures), from the Konrad Kellenberger collection. Many are in operation.

Le Château des Monts Museum of Clockmaking
CH-2000 Le Locle, Neuchâtel
Switzerland

Open 10 A.M. to 5 P.M. Tuesday through Friday and Sunday 2–5 P.M., April through October.
Admission free.

This museum houses both the Le Locle city and Sandoz collections, the latter devoted primarily to clocks and watches that include some function other than timekeeping. Mechanical singing birds, moving human figures, and animals may be seen, together with an explanatory film shown on the first Sunday of each month at 3 and 4 P.M.

The museum's general collection covers mechanical timekeeping from the sixteenth century to the early twentieth century, and is augmented by a remarkably detailed miniature model of a clock-maker's workshop and several old turret clocks.

In England

History of Science Museum
Oxford, England

Open 10:30 A.M. to 1:00 P.M. and 2:30–4:00 P.M. weekdays;
10:30 A.M. to 2:00 P.M. Saturdays. Admission free.

A major and rich collection of horological interest is to be found in the museum in this lovely city. It includes the first English orrery, made by Tompion and Graham in 1710, Geoffrey Chaucer's notes on astrolabe construction, early turret clocks, lantern clocks, long-case clocks by Fromanteel and others, a large display of watches and scientific instruments, and representative examples of important antique clock and watch designs.

City of Liverpool Museum
Liverpool, England

Open 10 A.M. to 5 P.M. weekdays, and Sundays 2–5 P.M.
Admission free.

Another of the major collections outside London, the exhibits here illustrate European watch- and clockmaking from the sixteenth century, including workshop methods and tools, a working replica of the eleventh-century Su Sung water clock, sandglasses, lantern clocks, skeleton clocks, long-case clocks, watches, and marine chronometers.

Kirkstall Abbey
Leeds, England

Open daily 10 A.M. to 6 P.M. in summer, 10 A.M. to 5 P.M. in winter, and Sundays 2–5 P.M.

Not your usual museum, a clockmaker's shop is included in the reconstruction of two old streets of shops, illustrating nineteenth-century life in the city. The collection contains no masterpieces, but comprises an interesting cross section of working domestic Victorian clocks and clockmaker's tools.

Willis Museum
Basingstoke, England

Open 2:30–5:30 P.M. Mondays, and Tuesdays through Saturdays 10 A.M. to 12:30 P.M. and 1:30–5:30 P.M. Admission free.

A small collection, but containing some unusual turret clocks and tool exhibits. The watch collection focuses on those made locally.

Other collections outside the London museums may be seen at:

Usher Collection, Lincoln
Bridewell Museum, Norwich
Parkington Collection, Bury Saint Edmonds
Tiverton Castle, Tiverton, Devon
Royal Albert Memorial Museum, Exeter
Prescot Museum, Prescot, Lancashire
Isle of Wight Clock Museum, Alum Bay

In Austria

Vienna Clock Museum, Vienna

Open 10 A.M. to 6 P.M. Tuesday through Friday; Saturday 2–6 P.M.; and Sunday 9 A.M. to 1 P.M. Admission free.

This principal Austrian collection was unfortunately subjected to wartime looting, but still contains a valuable collection covering five hundred years of European clock- and watchmaking. Included are early spring-driven timepieces, mantle and long-case clocks, two magnificent astronomical clocks (1769 and 1815), enamelled watches, Japanese clocks, Austrian clocks, and many fine examples of repeating and musical watches.

Unusual items include clocks with automata, organ clocks, cuckoo clocks, and clocks with unique mechanical power trains, one of which will run for five years without winding.

In Germany

Abeler Museum, Wuppertal-Eberfeld
Clock Museum, Furtwangen

Bavarian National Museum, Deutsches Museum, Museum Insel, all in Munich

Wuppertal Clock Museum, Wuppertal

In France

Museum of Clocks and Watches, Besançon

TIME PAYOFF ANALYSIS

*Matching activities to goals
effectively · Using the Time Payoff Analysis
worksheet · Analyzing the results*

Effective time management requires more than a knowledge of how the time is spent. If one's life is to be lived to the fullest, it is equally important to identify better alternative uses of time. "Better" means what *you* think is better. No matter what that is, learning to control your time will put you in control of your life.

Time management plans that do not relate the use of time to personal goals are incomplete. Simply recording how one's time was spent over a set period shows only part of the picture. Known (or estimated) time allocation must also be assessed to determine:

- if tasks or activities are matched to real goals;
- if present activities should be changed or eliminated;
- how improved time payoff can be realized.

Time payoff analysis (TPA) allows you to most effectively audit your time utilization. It will show you how well you are targeting your time to meet your chosen goals—whether it's business time, leisure time, or all of your time—and highlight areas which need improvement. It will show you which of your activities give you the best return, or payoff, on your time. Finally, as you rearrange your activities for better personal productivity, it will provide a yardstick to measure your improvement.

For those who have never before completed a time payoff analysis, it is perhaps advisable to adopt a "broad brush" approach at the outset. Learn what is happening to the major blocks of your time, and then focus upon smaller elements.

Beware, too, of the natural tendency to overestimate the time spent on unpleasant tasks, and to underestimate the time spent on interesting and absorbing activities.

THE TIME PAYOFF ANALYSIS WORKSHEET

Manual Time Payoff Analysis

On the following pages, you will find instructions for the worksheet that is designed for your personal time payoff analysis. Full-size sheets and detailed instruction for their use will be found in Appendix G.

The TPA worksheet provides space for the entry of current goals, and a ranking of their relative importance.

Space is also provided for entering your activities. If you're not sure what they are, or how much time they take, read *RECORDING TIME*. Then use one of the methods described there to get a good fix on them and how much time each takes.

The Impact Rating Scale is used to assess the impact of each activity upon each goal, using the impact rating chart in the top left corner of the worksheet. The assessments, or ratings, are entered in the matrix grid. When the grid is completed, the ratings are totaled for each line and column.

Assessment score percentages are established by dividing each line and column total by the grand total (458 in the example).

Finally, the assessment scores are measured against the goal values. Their differences are entered in the Applied Time line and the Activity Rating column.

The Applied Time line will show the goals that need more of your time, if you are really going to achieve them, and those that consume too much of your time. Goals 4 and 10 in the example have a score of zero, meaning that the appropriate amount of time is devoted to them. If too much time is being given to any goal, the total will be a positive number; if insufficient time is being given, it will be a negative (bracketed) number. Larger numbers indicate greater mismatch of goals and the time devoted to them.

The numbers in the Activity Rating column will indicate the effectiveness of each of your activities, where you're getting the best payoff on your time.

Higher numbers show those activities that are being performed more effectively; lower numbers indicate those performed less effectively. An attempt should be made to escape from the least effective activities, by eliminating or delegating them (see *DELEGATION TIME* and *EXECUTIVE TIME*). The time created by so doing may then be allocated to more effective activities. Subtract the lowest figure in the Activity Rating column from the highest to get an overall score. This figure which results will grow smaller as your activities become better related to your goals. An ongoing measure of your success in allocating time more effectively is thus available.

Analyzing the Results

The completed sample worksheet provides some interesting insight into the activities of this marketing executive. The analysis shows, for instance, that he would do well to reduce the time he spends in distributor meetings and on internal correspondence, as their effect on his goals is minimal. Those activities in which he is more effective are indicated by the higher numbers in Column R. He should try and increase the amount of time devoted to them, switching time from less-effective activities. More time devoted to planning and reading, for example, would pay off handsomely for him.

The amount of time being spent in investigating the purchase of a computer is too low (M23). Either the goal's value must be downgraded or he must commit more time to the project. This type of time juggling is the essence of goal achievement and personal productivity, and underscores the value of the time payoff analysis approach.

The highest positive figure along line 23 (L23) indicates that the executive's election efforts are extensive. He may be guilty of overkill, spending more time on the goal than he should.

The practical value of time payoff analysis is that it pinpoints the

It is those who make the worst use of their time who most complain of its shortness.
Jean de la Bruyère,
Les Caractères

weak links between goals and activities, and permits a reassessment of the situation at any time.

Correcting the worst areas will probably require some change in direction or habits, some form of self-improvement, or some re-examination of goals. Assistance in tackling these tasks will be found in the relevant sections elsewhere in this book.

TIME SAMPLING

Statistical sampling methods to save time
in human resource management

What may be done at
any time will be done
at no time.

Old Scottish proverb

Statistical time-sampling procedures may be used to solve problems in human resource management and develop an accurate knowledge of work loads and activity patterns. Called *sampling procedures*, they save time by eliminating the need to continuously check activity detail in clerical and other complex job functions. A system of "control-through-sampling" will show where time is going without the necessity of constant checks, every minute of every hour. Work sampling can be used to maintain an ongoing record of productivity and changes in complex work functions. Sampling checks may be used for personal time recording, too, substituting for detailed time logs. (See *TIME RECORDING*.)

Sampling procedures were first developed as a fact-finding tool by a British statistician, L. C. H. Tippett. They are based upon the laws of probability, and require the periodic recording of a person's activity on a random basis. The checks must never follow a schedule or pattern. Only truly random checks will give accurate results. Achieving true randomness is not easy; therefore, a table for random time sampling is necessary, as shown.

RANDOM SAMPLING TIMES

This table of random sampling times is based on computer-generated random numbers. It provides 25 check times each day for a period of 7 days. If fewer than 25 daily checks are required, drop out those times adjacent to the higher bracketed numbers first. In column 1, for example, the first number to be dropped would be 3:15, the second 1:35, etc. The figures show the hours and minutes from the start of the check period at which observations should be made. The times should be rigidly observed throughout the measurement period. If more than 25 checks are required, columns may be combined and duplications dropped out.

1	2	3	4	5	6	7
(19)0:05	0:20	0:10	0:15	(18)0:05	(23)0:10	0:15
0:20	(18)0:50	(16)0:35	0:25	0:25	0:25	(21)0:20
0:55	(24)1:20	0:55	(16)1:20	0:45	(21)0:30	(16)0:35
(22)1:10	(21)1:45	(24)1:00	1:40	1:05	0:40	(15)0:50
(20)1:20	1:55	1:10	1:55	(21)1:50	1:10	1:00
(24)1:35	2:00	1:45	2:00	(20)2:10	1:20	1:25
2:30	2:30	(19)2:00	2:30	2:20	1:30	(23)1:40
3:05	2:40	2:05	(15)2:50	2:30	2:25	(22)1:50
(16)3:10	3:10	(21)2:45	3:10	(19)2:35	2:35	1:55
(25)3:15	(23)3:30	2:50	(18)3:30	(17)2:50	2:40	2:45
3:25	(22)3:40	(22)3:00	3:45	(23)3:00	(24)2:55	(25)3:05
(21)3:45	3:50	3:20	3:50	(16)3:10	(19)3:05	3:50
4:00	4:05	3:30	4:30	3:40	3:15	(19)4:00
4:10	(16)4:15	(20)4:40	(20)4:40	(24)3:45	(17)3:25	4:25
(18)4:35	(17)4:20	4:45	5:10	(15)4:30	(15)3:30	(18)4:45
4:55	(19)4:25	4:55	5:20	5:00	3:40	(20)5:00
5:00	4:30	5:00	(17)5:30	5:45	(16)3:50	5:10
(15)5:05	(15)4:35	(18)5:55	(25)5:45	(22)5:50	4:00	(24)5:15
(17)5:35	5:20	(25)6:00	(19)5:50	5:55	4:15	6:20
5:55	5:35	6:05	(21)6:15	6:00	4:25	6:25
(23)6:20	6:15	(23)6:35	6:20	6:35	(18)4:35	6:50
6:45	(20)6:40	(15)6:40	(24)6:25	6:45	(22)5:40	6:55
6:50	(25)6:45	7:10	6:50	(25)7:00	(25)6:45	7:15
7:10	7:10	7:35	7:30	7:45	6:55	7:40
7:25	7:35	(17)7:50	7:55	7:55	(20)7:35	(17)7:45

8	9	10	11	12	13	14
(17)0:05	0:25	0:05	(25)0:05	(22)0:10	(25)0:10	0:10
(18)0:20	0:30	0:15	(18)0:15	0:20	0:15	(17)0:15
(15)1:05	0:40	0:40	0:20	0:30	1:10	0:20
1:25	(24)0:45	1:30	0:25	1:30	1:25	(22)0:25
1:30	1:00	1:45	0:55	(19)1:45	(21)1:30	(24)0:50
2:05	(18)1:10	(21)2:20	1:20	1:50	1:40	(18)1:25
2:25	(17)1:25	2:25	1:35	2:25	1:45	1:35
(24)2:40	1:40	(22)3:10	1:55	(25)2:35	(16)2:05	(23)2:10
(16)3:00	2:15	(20)3:40	(17)2:10	(17)3:05	2:40	(20)2:15
3:20	2:20	(15)3:50	2:30	3:10	(19)2:45	2:40
4:25	2:30	4:15	2:45	3:50	2:55	2:55
4:45	(15)2:40	(24)4:20	(21)2:50	3:55	(22)3:40	3:35
4:50	2:45	4:30	(22)2:55	4:05	3:45	(21)3:40
(25)4:55	(21)3:05	(25)4:40	(15)3:00	4:10	(18)3:50	4:35
5:05	(16)3:30	4:55	(16)3:30	(21)5:10	(24)4:05	(16)4:45
5:15	3:35	5:00	3:35	(16)5:25	(20)4:25	(19)5:05
5:50	4:00	5:15	(23)3:45	(15)5:30	4:55	5:10
5:55	4:15	(19)5:20	4:05	(24)6:00	5:15	5:50
(22)6:00	(23)4:50	5:25	5:00	6:05	5:45	6:05
(20)6:10	(20)5:45	(23)6:05	(19)5:40	6:15	(15)6:20	6:20
(19)6:20	(22)5:50	(18)7:15	(24)5:50	6:30	6:25	7:05
6:35	6:25	7:25	6:25	(18)6:50	(17)6:30	7:10
(23)7:10	(19)6:50	7:35	7:20	(23)6:55	6:35	7:20
7:15	(25)7:05	(16)7:55	7:40	(20)7:25	(23)7:35	(25)7:50
(21)7:30	7:30		(20)7:50		7:50	(15)7:55

The procedure for making a sampling check study begins with the determination of how many checks will be made, and what level of accuracy is desired. For full-scale audits, an accuracy of 5 percent is standard, at a confidence level of 95 percent. Less stringent measurement standards can often give adequate data for decision making, however. The number of required checks and accuracy of a sampling audit may be calculated with this formula:

$$S.p = \sqrt[2]{\frac{p(1-p)}{N}}$$

where S is the relative accuracy of the sample audit, p is the percentage occurrence of an activity, and N is the number of random observations.

Initially, the percentage occurrence of an activity may be estimated, in order to calculate the other factors.

Sampling techniques may be used to measure all work functions and waiting time that, due to their complexity or length of cycle, do not lend themselves to normal work-study procedures. Observations or checks may be made over a period of days or weeks, without the need for trained analysts. A study may be interrupted at any time without affecting the results.

In conducting any audit procedure, it is important to list all available control information such as cost accounting and budgetary data, periodic statistical analyses, profit accountability, and physical inspection procedures. Unless the controls have been scrutinized within the last year, they probably need revision. The story is told of a recent British Army study of procedures used by gun crews in the field. The analyst noted, after observing their activities, that one man appeared to do nothing except stand to attention as the gun was fired. A detailed check of the regulations provided the reason. He was there to hold the horses. You probably have some horse holders in your organization. They may be assiduously preparing reports whose usefulness has expired, or completing forms that are unnecessary. Paperwork systems tend to be self-perpetuating, and should all be periodically reviewed for possible elimination or improvement.

Businesses that have extensive clerical operations find that sampling techniques provide valuable management information, at low cost. Record the controls that you want to keep, but look for their shortcomings. Is a control subject to human error? Is it based on subjective data? Does it encourage people to try and beat the system? Is the informational feedback too slow? Most managers are surprised how many of their controls fail these tests. More time savings will come by replacing ineffective controls with more accurate ones. Then:

- Eliminate every activity that appears unnecessary, and simplify those that remain, as much as possible.
- Standardize products, parts, forms, and procedures.
- Check the life span of all products and services.
- Get rid of marginal activities.
- Question pet projects carefully.

With accurate task knowledge gained through sampling studies and simplification of controls, it is usually possible to delegate more of the "system-oriented" tasks to subordinates who can perform them. Only abnormal results need then be communicated, for managerial follow-up. This is putting "management by exception" to work.

Use all the help you can get in random sampling audits—company auditors, questionnaires, specially assigned assistants, and consultants. Auditing a business with the right sampling tools will focus managerial time more effectively and help to move the human resource team into a strong success-oriented mode.

TRAVEL TIME

Travel experts' tips for saving time on trips ·
Trip preparation · Protecting your body
and your wallet while you're away

Whenever you leave your home base, it's very likely that you will suffer the frustration of wasted time as soon as you put yourself in the hands of airlines and other carriers. We all have our horror stories. Some of the problems are caused by weather or accidents; most are caused by human error.

Protect yourself from the mistakes made by carriers' personnel, and improve your travel time by using some of these tips from travel experts:

Make your luggage distinctive by tying a colored ribbon on the handle, as well as labeling it with your name and address. It will be easier for you or luggage handlers to spot. If you travel by sea, you'll probably be given alphabet stickers to put on your luggage as an aid to sorting in the customs shed. Stick a Z label on your baggage, no matter what your name is. That will usually insure that it is put closest to the exit and checked first, speeding you on your way through customs.

Seal *anything* containing liquid, such as toiletries or medicine, in a plastic overwrap. Baggage compartments in planes are not pressurized, so leaks are likely. A fountain pen left in a suit pocket can be a disaster. Take a few ziplock plastic bags with you.

Use shoes to protect small objects like travel alarms. Wrap the item in a sock and tuck it in a shoe.

Put a list of packed items in your carryon luggage. Lost luggage claims are rising steeply.

Consider adding to your travel kit:

- A comfortable hat that you can stuff in a pocket.
- A 100-watt electric bulb, for reading in bed. Hotels are notorious for the dim bulbs in bedside lamps.
- A flat rubber universal stopper for washbasins.

- Soft toilet paper.
- A lightproof changing bag, if you're taking photographs. Cameras can always jam; with a bag, you can often fix the problem without losing exposed film.

Write to Samsonite Traveler Service, P.O. Box 38300, Dept. 20, Denver, CO 80238 for a free booklet on luggage and packing.

There are many mistakes made at flight check-in counters, especially when you arrive late. Make sure the airline clerk puts the correct destination tag(s) on your luggage *before your bags go on the conveyor*. Ask what your destination code is, if you don't know it. Insure that the tickets for subsequent flight segments are returned. Many trips are ruined by human error at the check-in point.

Take the time to write down the location of your car if you park in an airport garage. Don't just stuff the claim check in your pocket without thinking; put it away deliberately, and tell yourself where you are putting it. Claim checks are easy to lose.

Always assume that your flight will be delayed, and have something to do—reading or writing materials, or suchlike. Airline personnel frequently give poor delay information, and their "twenty-minute" delay can often stretch to hours. If the problem is a delayed incoming flight, and timing is crucial, a call to the airline at the flight's point of origin can frequently get you more accurate status information than the screen at the point of arrival.

Make sure you have more information in your wallet than normal: addresses of people to whom you may want to send cards; your eyeglass prescription or other essential health data; a duplicate list of your passport and credit card numbers, bank account and traveler's check numbers, and so on. Leave one copy in your hotel room, keep the other with you.

While You're Away

Carry only the cash you can afford to lose, watch your credit cards, and use American Express traveler's checks as much as possible. *Don't* leave anything valuable in your room; use the hotel's security safe. Recently, my room in an upscale New York hotel was burglarized while I was having breakfast. Dealing with the security people and filing the necessary police report cost the whole morning, apart from the monetary loss. The risk is worse in foreign countries.

Your stomach's sensitivity to changes in water is high. Even in areas with sanitary water supplies, you can have a problem. One

TEMPUS FUGIT
Time Flies

drink of the wrong stuff can put you out of action for days. In foreign countries, follow the wise; drink *no* water unless it's bottled, boiled for at least twenty minutes, or disinfected. Use bottled water to clean your teeth, don't let them put ice cubes in your drinks, and don't take the restaurant's word for it that their water is safe. Let your stomach ease into its new environment.

If you do get caught by traveler's diarrhea, keep away from solid food and milk, drink plenty of hot tea (caffeinated only; the tannin helps) and fruit juices, and eat honey to replace your lost glucose. If your problem doesn't go away in within four days, or you detect further unhealthy symptoms like blood in the stools, get to a doctor.

Protect Yourself

Keep a low profile when you're in a foreign land. Don't argue, be patient in lines, and don't show off jewelry and expensive watches. If you're walking, keep well out on the sidewalk, and move purposefully. Stay aware of what's going on around you, and don't become isolated. If you become "casually" surrounded by strangers (including children), forget manners and quickly push yourself free. Crime is becoming more frequent in most countries and the risk should not be underestimated. Last year more than 50,000 U.S. passports were reported stolen, costing their owners, in some cases, their entire vacation. From the moment you get off your plane, keep the following tips in mind:

Don't take your eyes off your luggage at the airport, particularly the smaller cases. Thieves may work with a large case with its bottom removed. If they can drop it over a piece of your luggage, it vanishes instantly. All it takes is for you to swing around when some stranger points down the room and asks, "Is that yours?"

Don't leave luggage visible in rental cars. Hatchbacks are cheaper to rent, but easily broken into. The trunk is safer, but not much. If your luggage is in the car, you should stay within sight of it. Cameras and purses on the backseat are taboo. Motorcycle-riding thieves use a hammer to break car windows, and will grab your belongings when you're stopped in traffic—sometimes by their accomplices.

Spin around immediately if you're jostled or shoved—it makes it tough on a pickpocket; so does wrapping an elastic band around your wallet, which should *never* be in your back pocket.

Don't carry purses. Use cross-straps with front clips for cameras. Shoulder straps invite thievery.

Dost thou love life? Then do not squander time, for that's the stuff life is made of.
    Benjamin Franklin

chologists say that your stressed or depressed state will likely ruin the trip, and you won't resolve any of the underlying causes of your trauma. The best way to cope with this situation is to think through your problem(s) in familiar surroundings with people you know and trust. A weekend away may be useful in doing this, but then it is important to deal with the issue, confront the problem, and get it out of your system. Only then, when life seems to be worthwhile once more, will a vacation become a pleasurable part of the renewal process.

Vacation time planning should also include consideration of how you want to divide the time while you're away. If you want some time alone, or with friends, family, or a traveling companion, plan it out on a calendar. A time-saving advantage of renting your vacation accommodations is that you can invite local family or friends to come and visit with *you*, which cuts your own travel time and expense. It may also give parents the opportunity, if family or friends will baby-sit, to do some sight-seeing or shopping without the children.

As you plan your vacation, you may be thinking, "I just want time to relax and do nothing." Don't bet on your ability to do it for very long. The pressure of doing nothing can quickly become heavy, without practice. Hedge your bet with a flexible plan that will give you the option of something to do, if you want. That in itself will help you to relax, because your inactivity isn't enforced. Our normal busy lives make us forget how to relax. We feel guilty if we're still in a bathrobe after 9 A.M. Learning how to relax again takes some practice. Remember, though, that doing nothing is an essential part of self-renewal, and brings the reward of a rare opportunity to hear the voice of your inner self. Give yourself a little time to strip away, layer by layer, your impulses to be *doing something*. Slow down, stop feeling guilty, and realize instead that you're entitled to *play*. You've earned it.

Use the facilities of national or local promotional services to get advance information on events in the area you plan to visit and those en route. If you're driving, break up the journey with planned, day-long stops at fairs, exhibitions, rodeos, and similar events. If you're flying, you can often make stopovers without additional fare cost. A day or two in Paris or London can be added to a trip to Rome, for example. A telephone request to the nearest consulate or embassy of any foreign country will usually bring you the information you want. A call to the chamber of commerce or visitors bureau of any place in America or Canada will do the same.

Making Arrangements

With your vacation plan settled, you can use a travel agent, make arrangements yourself, or a combination of both. Learning about the place you're going to visit should be part of the fun. Call 800-242-4634 for AT&T's *Consumer Directory*. It's a good buy at $9.95, and contains many good travel resources. Browse in your library or travel bookstore, get a good map and guidebook of the area, and start getting excited about the trip.

Get a recommendation on a travel agency (known in the trade as a TA) before you do business with them. Ask around. Talk to the person who handles your company's travel arrangements. The world is so big that good TAs must specialize. Don't expect to get knowledgeable advice on a European trip from a TA who handles primarily domestic travel. They'll waste your time and money. Learn how to work with a TA by getting the American Society of Travel Agents' (ASTA) free publication *You and Your Travel Agent* by writing to:

> American Society of Travel Agents
> Fulfillment Department
> 4400 MacArthur Boulevard, N.W.
> Washington, D.C. 20007

If you're planning on a package tour (a good idea for first-timers in foreign countries), send a quarter to the Better Business Bureau for their *Tips on Travel Packages*, at:

> Council of Better Business Bureaus, Inc.
> 1515 Wilson Boulevard
> Arlington, VA 22209

Travel agents often apply some trade skills when asked by a client to suggest a vacation. They will ask questions to ascertain whether you seem to be a psychocentric, midcentric, or allocentric person, because they know that these general population groups prefer certain types of vacations.

The total waste of time (and high cost) of becoming sick in a foreign country should be avoided by insuring that your biological protection is up to par. Don't expect your M.D. to know what shots or vaccinations are in order for a trip to New Guinea. Call the U.S. Department of State's Citizen's Emergency Center (202-647-5225), or a foreign traveler's health insurance service such as Travel International Inc. (202-347-2025). They, and other organizations, sell health care insurance starting at about $40 per person per week. *Do* check your existing health insurance policy for coverage before you spend more money. Never leave the country without laxatives and medication for diarrhea.

Setting Off

As your departure date nears, avoid last minute time problems in packing. Make a checklist of the items you want to take, or you'll overpack. Figure out how to make items do double duty, such as a bathrobe/swimming cover-up combination, and mix-and-match separates. You'll probably be doing more walking than usual; don't pack new or plastic shoes. Put in some extra dress shields.

Read *TRAVEL TIME* and *JET LAG* for ways to make your trip more pleasant, and to reduce time-wasting delays en route.

When you get back home, especially if you've been to a foreign country, you can be a useful resource to others interested in making the best use of their vacation time. Make a few notes on your experience, give a copy to your travel agent, and share them with friends. They'll appreciate your helping to make *their* voyage bon.

WATCHES

*The history and development of watches ·
The early European inventors · The craft guilds ·
The birth of the manufacturing industries ·
The improvement in accuracy ·
The watch industry today*

As a fashionable Parisienne stepped from her coach to the cobbled streets of Paris in 1500, a keen observer would have been intrigued by the pillbox-shaped device at her waist. It was one of the newest portable clocks to arrive from the French and German goldsmiths. They had begun to employ Peter Heinlein's new mainspring, created in his workshop in Nuremberg, to construct the small timepieces. They were not expected to be in vogue for long because they were not as accurate as pocket sundials, but anybody who was anybody had to have one.

Unexpectedly, their popularity continued, and artisans throughout the Continent and in England began to produce more of them. The Dutch astronomer Frisius wrote in 1558, "People are beginning to use small clocks, called watches . . ." Protestant Huguenot goldsmiths, who were having a hard time in Catholic France, took their skills to Switzerland, where records show that watches were soon being made in the town of Calvin. They had no hairspring, and because they were only accurate within an hour a day, they had but one hand. Their spring was connected to the escapement by a fusee and catgut string until 1660, when the catgut was replaced by a thin chain. A separate key was needed for their daily rewinding. The skill of the early *orlogeur* was remarkable, as screws had not yet been developed, and construction depended upon finely made pins and wedges, and hand-cut toothed wheels.

The oldest existing watch, now in the Geneva Museum, was made in France for Bishop Pierre de la Baume and is dated about 1530. The inconvenience of having to open a cover to see the time was solved later in the century by the use of hand-cut rock crystals, and a beautiful specimen watch of this type is in New York's Metropolitan Museum.

More than any other form of timepiece, the watch has always reflected artistic fashion and been closely related to the jewelry industry. So it was as the sixteenth century wore on. Watches were produced in a variety of styles that included hollow animals, skulls, and birds, with the mechanism cleverly built into them. The British Museum has a silver watch of this era in the shape of a dog, made by Jaques Joly in Geneva.

But as the new century dawned, miniature enamel paintings became the rage and soon found their way onto the watches of the day, whose cases reverted to round shapes to accommodate them. Frequently, the subjects were lady friends of the watch owners, and the Swiss miniaturists were perhaps the world's first pin-up artists, decorating their watches with nude figures in classical settings.

While all this frivolous exterior decoration was in vogue, Swiss craftsmen began to produce incredibly complicated "astronomical watch" mechanisms. Jean-Baptiste Duboule (1615–1694) produced a watch that showed the age and phase of the moon, the day of the week, the month, the season of the year, the current zodiacal sign *and* had a built-in alarm. His skill, and that of his contemporaries, was undoubtedly sharpened by the practice, begun in 1601 in Switzerland, of requiring journeymen watchmakers to construct a "masterpiece" alarm watch of their own design before achieving the status of "master" in their trade guild. To insure that enterprising young men might still have enough youthful vigor to be of use to the industry, they began their training as apprentices at the tender age of twelve.

Charles I of England granted a charter, in 1631, to the Guild of Worshipful Clockmakers, which promptly prohibited the import of clocks and watches into the country. Thus protected, the English watchmaking industry developed quickly, and became the watchmaking center of the world over the next fifty years. In 1660, the industry was helped by Robert Hooke and Thomas Tompion, who invented the first balance spring, and Nicholas Facio, who figured out how to make jewel bearings.

Another English clockmaker, Daniel Quare, using the new balance spring's ability to improve the accuracy of the watch movement, designed the first watch with a minute hand in 1680. Quare was a well-connected Quaker, and in keeping with Puritan principles, designed pocket watches, as displaying one's watch was con-

Telling the time from a hand-dial:

You can always tell the time outdoors, provided you know your latitude. Hold your hand horizontally, using the left hand pointed west for before-noon time, the right hand pointed east in the afternoon. Hold a stick with your thumb, tilted over the palm at roughly the angle of latitude. (Any map will tell you this. For instance, Denver falls on latitude 39.45. A 40° angle would suffice.)

Here, the shadow indicates: 7 A.M.—the top joint of the third finger of the left hand.

10 A.M.—the bottom joint of the little finger.

sidered ostentatious. He gave them a built-in striking mechanism that sounded the closest quarter hour when a lever was discreetly pressed, using some ideas of his friend, Edward Barlow. Their watches were christened "repeaters."

What was originally a novelty for the amusement of the rich had now become interesting to a broader public, whose awareness of time was newly sharpened by the proliferation of clocks in church towers and public buildings.

Demand for watches began to rise, and the watchmakers were hard put to keep up with it. But in the Swiss mountains, near Neuchâtel, lived a talented youngster named Daniel Jean-Richard who was destined to become the father of the enormous Swiss watch industry that exists today. There is much Swiss folklore surrounding young Daniel, but evidence exists that he was an established master watchmaker by 1692. He became the Henry Ford of Le-Mont-sur-Le-Locle and began to manufacture watches from parts and subassemblies supplied by others. He encouraged the local cottage industry to start making the parts he had been forced to buy elsewhere, and by 1756 the little Le Locle valley produced more than *fifteen thousand* watches. Today, it boasts many of the major factories in the watchmaking industry. They put up a statue of Daniel in the town square.

But in spite of the Swiss industriousness, England was still the major watch and clock supplier to the world, and guarded its markets jealously. Immediately before the American Revolution, in fact, the only way the Swiss could sell watches in the New World was to stamp "London" on them. Which they did, of course, thoroughly confusing historians who have since tried to figure out which watch came from where. But England deserved its reputation. John Harrison developed the first reasonably accurate ship's chronometer there in 1735 (see *CLOCKS*) and Thomas Mudge, clockmaker to George III, introduced the first detached lever escapement in 1760. Glass crystals and jewel bearings were used in 1764, and further improved the eighteenth-century English dominance of the watch trade.

Meanwhile, the French and Swiss craftsmen were not idle, although the turbulent political times in Europe made trade difficult for them. Abram-Louis Perrelet invented a self-winding mechanism for watches, and in 1776 Pouzet developed a method of driving an independent second hand. They did not know of Mudge's new escapement, however, and continued to use the cylinder escapement until about 1880. They revived the popular Renaissance-style decoration and added tiny moving figures, called *automata*, to the dials. Then the Parisian master craftsman Breguet began making his watches thinner and, in 1790, Jaquet-Droz designed the first *watch bracelet*, to be worn on the wrist. With their new slim form and convenience, the French regained the fashion spotlight, and the bulky English timepieces fell into disfavor.

The new empress, Josephine of France, gave the watch bracelet design a boost in 1806, when she commissioned two gold bracelets for her daughter-in-law from the Paris jeweler Nitot. One held a watch and the other a calendar, to suit the current First Empire fashion of a bracelet on each wrist, and both were encrusted with pearls and emeralds. As watch mechanisms became smaller, the engravers and enamel miniaturists who meticulously decorated the watch cases were given new challenges. Their skills were impressive; one expert, Charles-Frédéric Racine, demonstrated his remarkable skill in 1812 by painting the Lord's Prayer in a 1/24th segment of a 14-millimeter dial.

4 P.M.—*the top joint of the little finger on the right hand.*

By 1826, thin, flat watches were being produced with new cylinder escapements and separate bridges forming the backplate, as conceived by Lepine in 1744. One Genevese watchmaker, Meylan, managed to astound everyone by installing a complete watch movement inside a twenty-franc gold piece. He was also responsible for inventing musical watches and an "alarm watch-ring," which pricked its wearer painfully to wake him from his slumber. It did not enjoy commercial success.

The first stem-wound watches, which did away with the need for a separate winding key, were made by Audemars in 1838. Another version was presented by Adrien Philippe, for which he won a medal at the 1844 Paris Exhibition. The event brought him to the attention of the Comte de Patek, and a few years later they formed Patek-Philippe & Cie.

6 P.M.—*the top joint of the second finger.*

In the United States, Aaron Dennison and Edward Howard, noting Eli Whitney's success in producing precision parts by machine, decided to apply the technique to watchmaking. After some initial false starts, the American Watch Company was established in Waltham, Massachusetts, in 1860. Their ability to turn out good quality watches at low cost began to threaten the European imports, and mechanization became the "watchword" throughout the industry. Elgin National Watch Company and the Hamilton Watch Company led a surge of new operations, and by 1869 there were no fewer than thirty-seven competing pocket watch manufacturers in the country. In Switzerland, Georges Roskopf developed the cheap pin-lever escapement that was later used by Ingersoll, which became the U.S. Time Corporation.

The skill of the nineteenth-century watchmakers seemed to have no limit. A tiny watch only 4.5 millimeters in diameter was made for Czar Alexander II. Ball watches appeared, wound by turning one half against the other; then came watch stems that both wound and adjusted the watch, which became the standard. In 1880, German naval officers first began to use plain gold wristwatches made in Switzerland by Girard-Perregaux, who later expanded the idea to the general market. But although the Swiss had gained direct entry to the United States following the American War of Independence, they were unable to interest Americans in wristwatches. Our Yankee forefathers preferred their silver pocket watches with engine-turned cases, or the reliable domestic "railroad" watch.

In 1893, middle-class America was shown a $1.50 pocket watch by Samuel Ingersoll at Chicago's World Columbian Exposition. Heavily advertised, its sales skyrocketed, and the price was reduced to $1. Ingersoll sold more than fifty million of them. Meanwhile, in England, the wristwatch was finally accepted as here to stay. Its convenience made it a military necessity as World War I began. But American watch manufacturers, determined that the style was but a fad, stuck doggedly to producing pocket watches. Most of them went out of business as a result.

A major step forward was made in 1920, when Charles Guillaume, at Sèvres, France, received the Nobel Prize for creating *invar*, a nickel-steel alloy that was not affected much by temperature changes. Watches at that time were already accurate to less than three-quarters of a second per day, but balance wheels made from invar were so much better that a completely new rating system was introduced in Geneva, which calculated daily accuracy to .01 second. In 1925, self-winding wristwatches reappeared, with mechanisms much better than those of the previous century.

The first company to produce a hermetically sealed watch was Rolex, in 1926. With the advent of precision manufacturing, wristwatches were now accurate to about two seconds per day. In the U.S., the movements were usually supplied to jewelry firms, who designed and made the cases. To compete with the cheap pin-lever watches, credit selling for more expensive watches was begun in the thirties. The U.S. public rushed to buy quality watches for a dollar down and twenty-five cents per week, and the industry grew like mad. New firms like Bulova and Benrus were born who knew little about watches, but a whole lot about merchandising. Bulova, in July 1941, produced the first television commercial in the United States.

Nineteen-forty-seven saw the first alarm wristwatch, made by the Swiss Vulcain company.

However well constructed, a mechanical watch has a basic problem in that the step ratio from the spring to the balance wheel is about 1:4,000. To cram that mechanism into the size demanded by today's market means incredible accuracy in gear concentricity and accuracy, with resulting cost. The answer was to use electric battery power and simplify the gearing. A galvanometer drive gave way to an induction drive and that, in turn, was superseded in 1953 by the resonance drive. The electronic watch was born. It used a miniature tuning fork, actuating a tiny ratchet to move the hands for analog movements. With very little friction, and fewer mechanical parts, it could maintain accuracy for about twelve months, powered by miniature batteries.

The United States presently imports 191.7 million watches annually, with a value of $1.3 billion. This includes 64.3 million with quartz analog movements, 113.6 million with digital movements, and 13.8 million with mechanical movements. The primary exporting countries are:

Casio's CGW-50-1. This digital alarm chronograph pictures planet rotation on the display of the watch.

Hong Kong	117.2 million units
Japan	30.9 million units
Mainland China	12.0 million units
Switzerland	9.9 million units

The output of digital watches from mainland China jumped from 1.2 million units in 1987, with major market loss by the Swiss over the same period. The average unit value for Chinese watches is eighty-four cents.

Recommended books for further reading:

Baille, G. H. *Clocks and Watches, 1344 to 1800.* West Orange, NJ: Saifer, 1981.

de Carle, D. *Watch & Clock Encyclopedia.* New York: State Mutual Books, 1985. Covers entire history of antique clocks and watches in Europe and the United States, with line illustrations.

Kahlert, H., et al. *Wristwatches: History of a Century's Development.* (Illustrated) West Chester, PA: Schiffer, 1987.

Landes, D. S. *Revolution in Time: Clocks and the Modern World.* Cambridge: Harvard University Press, 1985.

WORD-PROCESSING TIME

*Insuring that WP saves time, instead
of wasting time · Top-rated WP software ·
Getting started · Building skills
and knowledge*

The vast range of choice in word-processing methods that technology has put in our hands carries a dangerous lure: the latest turbo do-it-all PC word processor and software may become a time sinkhole. The time and drudgery that you *can* save with a computer may easily be eaten up by fiddling with complicated software gimmicks and overproduced text output, unless you plan your relationship with your word processor carefully. Basically, the new breed of electronic word-processing products offers the ability to edit and revise text without retyping, or resorting to scissors and paste. And that remarkable benefit comes with the lowest-cost word processor. As you spend more money on hardware and software, you can certainly improve the look of your printed word, but it is impossible to learn all of the features of the advanced word-processing programs without spending between forty and a hundred hours on learning. If you think this time investment is worthwhile, go ahead. But avoid the trap of laboring over meticulously produced documents that are, in effect, simple memos, likely to be quickly scanned and discarded by the reader.

How does one keep word-processing time to a minimum? Get your answer by making a step-by-step analysis of the most frequent WP tasks that you are called upon to do and then matching them carefully to the right hardware and software. Pick the features that appear to fit your needs, then visit a software store and ask to see a demonstration. Three top-quality programs are *Word 4.0* (Microsoft Inc.), *WordPerfect 5.0* (WordPerfect Corp.), and *Wordstar 2000 3.0* (Micropro Inc.). Two other good programs are *Alexander* (Design Enterprises) and *Easy Word II* (DAC Software).

The WP software that incorporates spelling checkers, dictionaries, and synonym finders or thesauruses are valuable time-savers, since they are simple to use and significantly reduce time spent looking up words. Give preference to those programs that incorporate them when making a purchasing decision.

When you've made your purchase and have your new software installed, start using it right away, but in the simplest way possible. Balance hands-on learning with *results*. This way, you'll become familiar with the program quickly, and avoid wallowing in a morass of formatting commands before you produce something useful. When I first began to use *Microsoft Word*, I ignored style sheets, glossaries, galleries, and windows and focused on producing some simple text paragraphs, and moving them around the page with the basic formatting instructions. At that point, that was complicated enough. When you feel that you've got the basics under control, move forward and tackle more sophisticated features. It's a good idea to copy some text that you've produced into a test file that you can experiment with as you learn. Keep at it, and change your work patterns to take advantage of the more sophisticated techniques as you absorb them.

Don't hesitate to browse for instruction books in your bookstore since most manufacturers should be ashamed of the manuals they issue with their software. Save your time by getting some well-written help. Look for manuals that give actual step-by-step examples of command procedures, rather than a lot of descriptive text. They'll get you going faster.

There are three primary steps in word processing—text creation, text formatting, and text printing. The first two steps can be combined; in other words, you can format as you go if you wish. This method should only be used with regular, previously used, and well-known WP tasks, copy-typing, or working from somebody else's draft. If there's any creative effort involved, leave all of the formatting until the text is complete, or you'll find time is slipping past as you tinker with margins, tabs, headers and footers when you should be writing. Get your thoughts down, then print a draft and mark it with all of the changes you want. *Then* do your formatting all at once, in half the time.

To save time formatting individual documents, invest a few minutes in creating a "template" file that contains only formatting commands and nonvariable text. Bring the template to the screen when needed, add your text, and refile under a new name. In a business environment, format-template, read-only disks may be distrib-

uted throughout a department, with significant time savings for everybody—especially newcomers.

The better WP software programs, such as *Microsoft Word*, recognize the value of templating with a "style sheet" capability, which permits fast selection from a library of preformatted styles for any desired document. These are big time-savers, particularly when complex formats with multiple columns, inserts, and merged data are employed.

Macros go one step further. Macro is the name for a short keystroke sequence that automatically executes a long string of commands. If your equipment supports these shortcut aids, it's worth the effort to learn how to manage them. They're powerful time-savers because they allow you to incorporate *any* keystrokes—not just format commands. With a little imagination, macros can cut many minutes from word-processing chores.

One of the best sources for support as you build WP skills will be your local user group. Contact them and go to their meetings or use their bulletin board if you have a modem. Personal computer word processing today is a powerful tool. Taking the time to become skillful is essential if one is to derive its benefits; otherwise, it can be an expensive investment.

the right individual for your purpose? What sort of writing style will get his attention? How serious or urgent is the subject? *What results do you want?* Write with the answers to these questions in mind.

4. For anything but the simplest memo, *outline first.* The few minutes you take to do this will result in significantly less rework and editing. Use file cards for long reports and text, so you can shuffle them. If you use a word-processing program like *Word* (Microsoft Inc.), take full advantage of the outlining features.

5. Don't write when you're annoyed—or if you do, don't mail it for twenty-four hours. Then read it over and throw it out. You'll see why.

6. Insure that all possible reference information is included. Overdo it rather than underdoing it.

7. Don't decry longhand drafts. They can be very helpful in organizing the mind. Triple space rough drafts with minimum $1\frac{1}{2}$- inch margins to give adequate space for corrective notes. If you don't, you're likely to avoid some needed correction simply because there isn't room to write.

8. Insure that you, and everyone in your organization who writes, has a good dictionary and thesaurus at hand. Use them to avoid trite phrases, but keep your vocabulary within the bounds of familiarity.

9. For reports and proposals, use this format:

Saturday was named for the Roman god Saturnus. The above drawing shows a sixteenth-century woodcut of the god devouring his children.

Introduction A one- or two-page description of the circumstances that initiated the proposal or report.

Objectives Start with a terse, one-paragraph statement of the basic overall objective. Then list subobjectives, and describe each one.

Work Statement (Proposals) Describe all of the tasks that will be undertaken in chronological order.

Discussion (Reports) Provide the facts and conclusions. Put all supporting data in referenced appendices unless essential for understanding.

Time, Cost, and Administration Cover all details of project scheduling, fees and expenses, and program administration.

Conclusion Use this section to "sell" the project, and sign off with "Respectfully submitted," etc.

Appendices Keep all supportive documentation in this section. For proposals, include biographies of the task force, client references, and marketing literature.

10. For meeting minutes, use a terse, telegraphic style. Use a right side "action" column to record who is responsible for performing each task discussed.

11. Wherever possible, use Speedletters, form letters, and referral slips attached to original correspondence.

12. Dictate correspondence with an electronic system—it's at least one-third faster. In buying a system, easy backspacing is the key feature to look for. Voice-actuation is useful, but not essential. You should use a battery-operated pocket cassette dictation unit, as well as a 110 v. desk unit. Use the pocket unit when driving for notes to yourself, as well as for dictation. It can also be used to record and play back addresses and route directions as you travel.

A pocket recorder can save time in many other ways. Here are some:

If you live in a vacation area which brings many visitors to your home, escape from the repetitive "tour guide" task. Make the definitive tour once by yourself, describing the route and the sights to look for as you go. Note where to stop for refreshments, views, and shopping. If necessary, key your remarks to a map. When visitors arrive, give them the cassette and the map and let them guide themselves around, even if you have to loan them your car.

Walk through your home and make a voice inventory of your possessions to back up insurance claims in case of loss. When you buy new items, dig out the cassette and add them to the list, with a note of the date and cost. The cassette can be transcribed if and when required.

Make a "home instruction" cassette. Include directions on turning off utilities, fuse locations, emergency phone numbers, where to find things, etc. Leave it with house- and baby-sitters when you're away.

Dictate notes on sales calls as you drive away, while your memory is fresh.

If you're involved in an auto collision, dictate all the information you may require to process a claim, or for legal purposes. If you have your recorder in your top pocket, you can probably capture others' statements, too.

Use your imagination, and you will find the pocket recorder a valuable time-saving tool.

When you're dictating correspondence, it's important to keep the transcriber's needs in mind. The dictation checklist shown

I saw Eternity the
   other night
Like a great ring of
   pure and endless light.
All calm, as it was
   bright;
And round beneath it,
   Time in hours, days,
   years,
Driv'n by the spheres
Like a vast shadow
   mov'd; in which the
   world
And all her train were
   hurled.

Henry Vaughan

below reflects the information most often forgotten, according to professional transcribers. You may wish to keep a similar card where you can see it as you dictate.

DICTATION CHECKLIST:

IDENTIFICATION, DATE, TIME
WHAT IT IS/WHEN IT'S NEEDED
WHAT PAPER SHOULD BE USED
CIRCULATION
WHAT ENCLOSURES/WHERE THEY ARE
ANY SPECIAL MAIL HANDLING
APPROXIMATE LENGTH
DRAFT OR FINAL QUALITY
MARK THE END

Train yourself to give this information whenever you dictate, and save everyone's time. Dictate punctuation, line spacing, paragraph indents, and always spell any name when you first use it. Use the following standard phonetics:

Alpha	Hotel	Oscar	Victor
Bravo	India	Papa	Whisky
Charlie	Juliet	Quebec	X-ray
Delta	Kilo	Romeo	Yankee
Echo	Lima	Sierra	Zulu
Foxtrot	Mike	Tango	
Golf	November	Uniform	

WRITING OUTPUT

In the last decade, the options for producing written text have multiplied enormously. Typewriters have become electrified and computerized, and word-processing programs form the core of most personal computer systems. The problem with this plethora of page-makers is in selecting the right equipment for the job. Most first-time users seriously underestimate the time it will take to learn how to use their new machines, and spend hours struggling with PC file management and database systems which are rarely used.

The important question facing many harried businesspeople is whether they should adopt new writing-production methods to capitalize on the features offered by the electronics industry, or stay with their traditional work patterns. Which approach will be cost and time effective for them? Is an electric correcting typewriter still their best bet, or will additional investment in an electronic memory typewriter or a word-processing computer pay off?

Memory typewriters have an electronic memory that will hold about two hundred pages of double-spaced text. Most have video screens on which the text appears as typed; it can be edited and stored electronically, and printed out with the same unit. Automatic spelling checkers and mail-merge features are included with top-end machines. Mail-merge permits reproduction of form letters with automatic insertion of different addressees. Less expensive than a microcomputer, memory typewriters are limited to text production. They do that very efficiently, though, and as a writing tool they deliver the sophisticated capabilities of a word-processing computer with the simplicity of a typewriter.

Personal computers have the great advantage that they can handle any level of word processing, plus a wide range of additional tasks. In the business office, a complete analysis of all required administrative tasks should be made as part of the equipment selection process. The hardware components that complete a computer system are usually specified separately, so that file storage capacity, working memory, printout quality and speed, intercommunication capability, and other features are customized to requirements.

For the business manager, the key factor in selecting electronic writing equipment is whether they personally will learn keyboarding skills and the rudiments of computer program commands. That decision is basic. For those who will, there are many time-saving benefits (see WORD-PROCESSING TIME). For those who, for whatever reason, elect to keep their hands off keyboards, handwritten notes and dictation must suffice. Whatever writing procedure is followed, remember you're judged by results—not words—so keep them to a minimum.

YEAR

Ancient attempts to define a year ·
The Egyptian and Assyrian methods ·
Modern definition

The year is a unit of time equal to one 584-million-mile revolution of the earth around the sun. Unfortunately, it does not occur in a convenient number of complete days, and the 365.24-day period gave the ancients conniptions as they tried to fit it into a sane calendar. They were never entirely successful.

The Egyptians, in fact, did not use the sun when they began to devise a calendar around 4000 B.C. They picked on Sirius, the brightest star they could see, and set the length of a year at 365 days, when Sirius seemed to repeat its passage in the sky. They arbitrarily split their year into twelve nameless thirty-day months and then tacked on five holidays.

Although their priest-astronomers must have soon realized that they hadn't figured correctly, because Sirius would rise later and later as the years passed, they did nothing about it. Historians have trouble dating the Egyptians' activities, because they were uninterested in numbering their centuries, but we do know that the Sirius year was used for many centuries, and was still in use as late as 139 A.D.

Other Mediterranean civilizations tried different systems. The Babylonians used the moon as their marker, and established a six-month year. Moonrises were easier to tally than sunrises. They quickly realized, though, that the moon was not repeating its performance in that short a period, so they doubled their year to twelve months. Wrong again. The resulting 354-day year very quickly got out of whack. Their answer was to throw in an extra month when it seemed to be needed.

Meanwhile, by about 2000 B.C., the Assyrians had created a 360-day year. They, too, realized it didn't fit the pattern of the heaven's cycle, so they added fifteen corrective days every third year for a while, experimented with other systems, and finally, in 1100 B.C., threw up their hands and adopted the Babylonian approach.

The Greeks came up with a more complex but workable system using both lunar and solar cycles, called the Metonic calendar. It required the addition of seven extra months irregularly inserted into a span of nineteen years. The Jews adopted it too, about 400 A.D., and the Hebrew calendar is still based upon it.

Numbering the years has always been a problem for historians, because there was no universal Year One. The time of the last disaster provided as good a starting point as any for the early tribes, most of whose members had a hard enough time remembering days, let alone years.

The highlight of the Greeks' calendar was the Olympic Games every four years, and so this event was used to date their years, such as the "third year of the XII Olympiad."

Both the French and American revolutionary leaders toyed with schemes to reestablish Year One as that in which they seized power, but fortunately this came to naught. The British Parliament, however, continues to date its acts on a regnal year basis, like "The tenth year of the reign of Queen Elizabeth II."

The year-numbering system created by Dionysius Exiguus in 500 A.D. is still used today. He calculated the birth of Christ (incorrectly) as the twenty-eighth year of the reign of Augustus Caesar, which he then designated as 1 A.D.

For the last 1000 years, the *tropical, solar,* or *equinoctial* year was defined as that between two vernal equinoxes of the sun, i.e. 365.24220 mean solar days, or 365 days, 5 hours, 48 minutes, and 46 seconds.

During the last century, however, our ability to measure time improved so much that it became evident that the earth's rotation, and thus the year, is far from constant. The tropical year* is decreasing, and the sidereal year is increasing. The 1956 International Committee on Weights and Measures therefore established, using the remarkably accurate cesium atomic clock, a new standard for the year. (See *MEASUREMENT OF TIME.*) It is 31,556,925.9747 seconds, as of January 1, 1900, at 12 hours ephemeris time.

The sidereal year is 365.25636 mean solar days in length.

The light-year is the distance light travels in one sidereal year, 5.879×10^{12} miles.

You take care of every day . . . and let the calendar take care of the years!

Ed Wynn

---

*The tropical year is measured by the sun; the sidereal year is measured by distant fixed stars.

APPENDICES

DELEGATION EXERCISE
Part I

Assignment: To determine how best to increase the store's area by 25 percent.

Possible Assignees: John Segal, a newly-hired industrial engineer.
Mary Beckerman, the store's supervisor.
Dave Jackson, an experienced materials-handling engineer.

FIRST CHOICE: _____

REASON: _____

Assignment: To determine the causes of a recent increase in absenteeism.

Possible Assignees: Bill Davis, the employee relations manager.
John Billings, the shop foreman whose section is the worst hit.
Lisa Jordan, a statistical specialist in the data-processing department.

FIRST CHOICE: _____

REASON: _____

Assignment: To determine the number of company cars that should be purchased next year.

Possible Assignees: George Dale, the vehicle maintenance supervisor.
Bill Murphy, the assistant comptroller.
Amy Dawson, the purchasing agent.
Dennis Kahn, a new employee who previously worked in a car rental and leasing firm.

FIRST CHOICE: _____

REASON: _____

Assignment: Organize the company's summer picnic.

Possible Assignees: Jean Simpson, the president's secretary.
Bill Andrews, the union president.
John Baker, the cafeteria manager.
Wayne Smith, the plant manager's assistant.

FIRST CHOICE: _____

REASON: _____

DELEGATION EXERCISE
Part 2

The activities listed below are those performed by James Rock, a manager in a small manufacturing firm. He has competent employees working for him. Which should he continue to do himself, and which could he delegate?

ACTIVITIES	DELEGATE	DON'T DELEGATE
1. Assembling information for a report.	_____	_____
2. Ordering supplies.	_____	_____
3. Firing an employee.	_____	_____
4. Copying confidential material.	_____	_____
5. Preparing draft of an important letter.	_____	_____
6. Logging visitors and telephone calls.	_____	_____
7. Approving the annual budget.	_____	_____
8. Keeping the files up to date.	_____	_____
9. Approving file procedures.	_____	_____
10. Routing mail.	_____	_____
11. Making travel reservations.	_____	_____
12. Preparing expense reports.	_____	_____
13. Devising alternative solutions to a serious problem.	_____	_____
14. Preparing the annual budget.	_____	_____
15. Accepting a speaking engagement.	_____	_____
16. Screening telephone calls.	_____	_____
17. Tracking an important project schedule.	_____	_____
18. Determining which road carrier is best.	_____	_____
19. Planning emergency procedures.	_____	_____
20. Honoring a twenty-five-year employee.	_____	_____

DELEGATION EXERCISE ANSWERS
Part 1

1. John Segal, the industrial engineer. That's what he's trained to do. The store's supervisor may want to approve the plan. The materials-handling engineer may provide input.

2. Bill Davis, the employee relations manager. During his investigation, which is a staff function, he might seek input from the shop foreman, and he might use the statistical specialist to tabulate his findings.

3. Nobody. This determination should not be delegated.

4. John Baker, the cafeteria manager. He has most knowledge of mass feeding.

Part 2

The following numbered activities may be delegated downward:

1, 2, 5, 6, 8, 10, 11, 12, 13, 14, 16, 17, 18, 19.

These activities should not be delegated: 3, 4, 7, 9, 15.

Activity 20 may be delegated upward.

DELEGATION PLAN WORKSHEET

ACTIVITIES	NOT TO BE DELEGATED	TO BE DELEGATED	TO BE ELIMINATED
1.			
2.			
3.			
4.			
5.			
6.			
7.			
8.			
9.			
10.			
11.			
12.			

FUNCTION ANALYSIS WORKSHEET

FUNCTION GOAL OR RESPONSIBILITY	D	W	M	A	VALUE	LIKE/ DISLIKE	D
TOTALS							

DATE _____ FUNCTION _____   ESTIMATED TIME

D RATING: DO = DO IT MYSELF   DEL = DELEGATE   DUMP = ELIMINATE
VALUE RATING: 1-5   5 = ESSENTIAL 1 = USEFUL

INFORMATION LOCATOR

MORE INFORMATION ON THIS
SUBJECT MAY BE FOUND IN:

FILE NAME: _____

FILE NUMBER: _____

SOURCE NAME	VOL.	DATE	PAGE	TITLE OF ARTICLE, ETC.

MEETING EVALUATION

Give your assessment of meeting climate and process, using the following scale:

Happens all the time	5	Sometimes	2
Most of the time	4	Rarely	1
Usually	3	Never	0

The group members:

	A	B	C	D
Level with me	☐			
Accept me as I am				☐
Understand what I mean		☐		
Interrupt or ignore my comments			☐	
Will tell me when I "bug" them		☐		
Are interested in me				☐
Understand the real "me"		☐		
Act judgmental			☐	
Respect me as a person, apart from rank				☐
Leave me out of the discussion			☐	
Recognize my needs		☐		
Let me feel I can "be myself"				☐
Know when something bothers me		☐		
Try to ridicule me			☐	
Tolerate my mistakes	☐			
Misconstrue what I'm trying to say			☐	
Try to spare my feelings	☐			

MEETING CLIMATE RATING SCORES:
(*Add vertical columns*)   ___ ___ ___ ___

The meeting(s):
Start late	___
Include too many people	___
Give me little valuable information	___
Run too long	___
Lack an agenda	___
Have poor temperature/ventilation	___
Are scheduled too frequently	___
Are not directed or chaired effectively	___
Disclose poor participant readiness	___
Waste my time	___
Are in an inappropriate setting	___
Include the wrong people	___
Are scheduled with inadequate notice	___
Are called for negative reasons	___
Solve few, or no problems	___

Reduce confidence in management	—
Are scheduled at an inappropriate time	—
Produce no teamwork	—
Have little or no follow-up	—
Don't use A/V equipment properly	—

MEETING PROCESS RATING SCORE:
(*Add column*)   —

MEETING EVALUATION SCORING KEY

Meeting Climate

Column A scores reflect the level of openness or honesty that was sensed in the meeting. Scores of 15–20 are reflected by cohesive and effective groups in development stages 4 and 5. Expression of honest feelings and opinions is unrestricted and unpunished. Scores of 8–14 indicate healthy progress beyond the discovery stage, but with some residual secretiveness or shyness present. Scores below 8 are found in new groups, still in the polite stage, or in groups which have not achieved interactive honesty and are thus probably ineffective.

Column B scores indicate the level of interpersonal sensitivity present in the group. Scores above 15 are generated by groups whose members actively strive to build a working team climate. Scores from 10–14 reflect a group in transition, but with some self-centeredness blocking progress. Scores below 10 are found in groups where members are uncomfortable with one another, and suspicious of one another's motives or goals.

Column C scores reflect the group's team-blocking or disruptive tactics. Scores in this column should be *subtracted* from the overall total. Individuals should be encouraged to speak out when they feel put down or ignored, so that those causing the problem may examine their attitudes and delivery.

Column D scores indicate the level of team-building effort present in the group. Scores above 15 show groups functioning well, with much group loyalty among its members. Midrange scores between 8 and 14 may be lacking, as individuals tend to feel either strongly positive or negative in this area. If midrange scores are found, one or two members of the group may be causing concern, while others are providing adequate support. Scores below 8 will come from groups in formative stages, unlikely to be truly effective.

An overall score may be derived by adding A, B, and D scores,

NAME _____ DATE _____

1:00		1:30		2:00		2:30		3:00		3:30		4:00		4:30		5:00		5:30		6:00		TOTAL TIME (Mins.)
	1:15		1:45		2:15		2:45		3:15		3:45		4:15		4:45		5:15		5:45			

DAILY TOTAL TIME

TIME ANALYSIS CHART: BUSINESS CONTRACTOR

TASK LIST	7:30	7:45	8:00	8:15	8:30	8:45	9:00	9:15	9:30	9:45	10:00	10:15	10:30	10:45	11:00	11:15	11:30	11:45	12:00	12:15	12:30	12:45
PLANNED BREAK PERIOD																						
UNPLANNED WAITING																						
TRAVEL																						
RECORD KEEPING																						
BUSINESS MEETINGS																						
BUSINESS PAPERWORK																						
OFFICE ADMINISTRATION																						
INVENTORY MANAGEMENT																						
TELEPHONE CALLS IN																						
TELEPHONE CALLS OUT																						
SALES CALLS																						
SITE ANALYSIS																						
JOB DESIGN																						
SALES PAPERWORK																						
FACILITIES MAINTENANCE																						
PERSONAL DEVELOPMENT																						
PUBLIC RELATIONS																						
METHODS TESTING																						
OTHER (DESCRIBE)																						

Now, using the Impact Rating Scale in the top left corner of the worksheet, assess the impact of each activity upon each goal. Fill in each cell of the grid D4–O20 with your assessments.

When the grid is complete, total your ratings for each line in Column P. Then total Columns D–O along Line 21.

To calculate your Time Payoff Ratings in Column Q, divide each figure in Column P by the figure in P21 and multiply by 100. (P4 divided by P21 × 100, etc.)

Your Activity Ratings in Column R are the difference between the figures in Column Q from those corresponding in Column C. (C4 – Q4, etc.) Write the answers in Activity Rating Column R with + or – signs, or brackets, to show positive or negative results. Then total, ignoring the positive or negative signs, 4 ÷ 20 and write the answer in R21.

Along Line 22D–O, calculate the Assessment Score percentage for each goal. (D21 divided by P21 × 100, etc.)

Along Line 23D–O, enter the difference for each figure on Line 22 from the corresponding figure in Line 2. (D22 – D2, etc.) Enter the line total (D–O) in P23, ignoring the positive or negative signs.

ANALYZING THE RESULTS

Time Payoff Rating

Those activities in which you are more effective are indicated by higher numbers in Column Q. You should try and increase the amount of time you devote to them, by switching time from less effective activities.

Activity Rating

In Column R, those activities on which you should spend more time will have negative values, and those that are consuming too much of your time will have positive values. As the number increases in either direction, so does the severity of the problem. An ideal level of activity will show as a zero.

Goal Score

The figures along Line 23 indicate how successfully you are allocating time to your goals. A zero is ideal. If the figure is positive, you may be guilty of "overkill," and spending more time on a goal than you should. If it is negative, you are giving insufficient time to the goal. It is particularly important to match the higher-rated goals with an appropriate level of applied activity.

TIME PAYOFF ANALYSIS WORKSHEET EXAMPLE

	IMPACT RATING SCALE		GOAL 1 INCREASE MIDWEST SALES BY 8%	GOAL 2 REDUCE INVENTORY BY $500,000	GOAL 3 TAKE COMPUTER TRAINING COURSE	GOAL 4 DEVELOP NEW SALES BONUS PLAN	GOAL 5 RECRUIT NEW SECRETARY
1	ESSENTIAL 10 SIGNIFICANT + 5 MAJOR + 9 SIGNIFICANT - 4 MAJOR - 8 SOME VALUE 3 IMPORTANT + 7 LITTLE VALUE 2 IMPORTANT - 6 MARGINAL USE 1 NO EFFECT 0						
2	GOAL VALUE DISTRIBUTION (100 PTS):		10	5	8	8	3
3	WEEKLY ACTIVITIES	HRS	%	RATE THE IMPACT OF EACH ACTIVITY ON EACH GOAL IN THE TABLE BELOW				
4	TELEPHONE	5.3	9.0	8	2	0	2	3
5	INTERNAL MEETINGS	3.5	6.0	7	7	0	6	1
6	DISTRIBUTOR MEETINGS	6.0	10.4	10	3	0	1	0
7	FIGURE WORK	2.3	5.9	5	8	0	10	0
8	SELF-DEVELOPMENT	6.0	10.4	0	0	10	0	0
9	TRAVEL	5.0	8.7	6	0	3	0	0
10	SALES CALLS	1.0	1.7	9	6	0	0	0
11	HANDLING CUSTOMER COMPLAINTS	1.5	2.6	6	2	0	0	0
12	INTERNAL MAIL	5.0	8.7	3	3	0	3	1
13	EXTERNAL MAIL	8.0	13.8	5	1	0	0	3
14	TRADE COUNCIL WORK	3.0	5.2	0	0	0	0	0
15	SHOPPING	1.0	1.7	0	0	0	0	0
16	GOLF	4.0	6.9	0	0	0	0	0
17	PRODUCTION LIAISON	.5	.9	0	3	0	0	0
18	WORK WITH AD AGENCY	3.0	5.2	7	0	0	0	3
19	BUSINESS READING	2.0	3.5	2	0	9	4	7
20	PLANNING	.8	1.4	8	9	3	9	4
21	TOTALS	57.9	100	76	39	25	35	22
22	ASSESSMENT SCORE %			17	9	5	8	5
23	APPLIED TIME OK = 0 TOO MUCH: + NOT ENOUGH: -			7	4	⟨3⟩	0	2

Brackets indicate negative values   A   B   C   D   E   F   G   H

GOAL 6 MAKE UP SLIDE PROGRAM FOR REGIONAL SALES MEETING	GOAL 7 REDUCE ADMIN. EXPENSE BY 10%	GOAL 8 RUN FOR ELECTION TO INDUSTRY COUNCIL	GOAL 9 INVESTIGATE AND PURCHASE PERSONAL COMPUTER	GOAL 10 LOSE 12 POUNDS (EXERCISE)	GOAL 11 LOCATE COLLEGE FOR JOHN	GOAL 12 WRITE ARTICLE FOR JOURNAL	TOTAL MUST BE 100	TIME PAYOFF RATING	ACTIVITY RATING
12	15	4	18	10	10	7			
RATE THE IMPACT OF EACH ACTIVITY ON EACH GOAL IN THE TABLE BELOW									
1	3	8	0	0	6	0	33	7.2	1.8
4	10	0	0	0	0	0	35	7.6	⟨1.6⟩
1	1	0	0	0	0	0	16	3.5	6.9
0	3	0	0	0	4	3	28	6.1	⟨2.2⟩
0	0	3	0	4	0	4	21	4.6	5.8
0	0	4	0	0	10	0	23	5.0	3.7
0	0	0	0	0	0	0	15	3.3	⟨1.6⟩
0	5	0	0	0	0	0	13	2.8	⟨.2⟩
3	5	0	0	0	0	0	18	3.9	4.8
4	1	9	0	0	6	3	32	7.0	6.8
0	0	10	0	0	0	10	20	4.4	.8
0	0	0	10	0	0	0	10	2.2	⟨5⟩
0	0	9	0	10	3	0	22	4.8	2.1
0	9	0	0	0	0	0	12	2.6	⟨1.7⟩
10	0	4	0	0	0	3	27	5.9	⟨.7⟩
8	4	7	3	0	9	9	62	13.5	⟨10.0⟩
7	8	4	3	2	10	4	71	15.5	⟨14.1⟩
38	49	58	16	16	48	36	458		65.3
8	10	13	3	3	10	8			
4	⟨5⟩	8	⟨14⟩	⟨7⟩	0	1	55		
I	J	K	L	M	N	O	P	Q	R

is there an
action required:
or
do it t vit

informaition

B L u r r y

if you have to snul inform
I don't need you for in
so much you see to a
there is a minimum
rock too much inform